THAILAND

Hanoi

RED RIVER
DELTA

MEKONG

VIETNAM

Siem Reap
+ Angkor Wat

Bangkok

CAMBODIA

Tonle Sap Lake

Hua Hin

Phnom Penh

Chau Doc

Ho Chi Minh City

Kampot

Can Tho

MEKONG
DELTA

Phuket

MALAYSIA

Langkawi

Singapore

Penang

EQUATOR

Kuala Lumpur

Melaka

D1465804

BALI

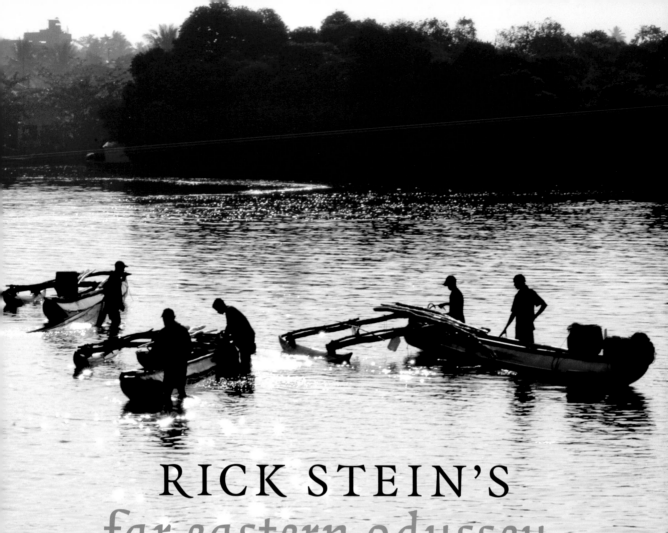

RICK STEIN'S
far eastern odyssey

BOOKS

This book is dedicated to Edward, Jack and Charles and Sarah, Zach and Olivia

10 9 8 7 6 5 4 3 2 1

This book is published to accompany the television series entitled
Rick Stein's Far Eastern Odyssey, first broadcast on BBC2 in 2009

The series was produced for BBC Television by Denham Productions
Producer and director: David Pritchard
Assistant producer: Arezoo Farahzad
Executive producers for the BBC: Tom Archer and Jo Ball

The Random House Group Limited Reg. No. 954009

Addresses for companies within the Random House Group can be found at
www.randomhouse.co.uk

A CIP catalogue record for this book is available from the British Library

ISBN 978 1 849 903370

The Random House Group Limited supports the Forest Stewardship Council® (FSC®), the leading
international forest certification organisation. All our titles that are printed on Greenpeace
approved FSC® certified paper carry the FSC® logo. Our paper procurement policy can be found
at www.randomhouse.co.uk/environment

Commissioning editor: Shirley Patton
Project editor: Mari Roberts
Assistant editor: Laura Higginson
Home economist: Debbie Major
Design and art direction: Smith & Gilmour
Prop stylist: Penny Markham
Map illustration: David Dean
Calligraphy: Peter Horridge
Production: Bridget Fish

Colour origination by Altaimage, London
Printed in China

CONTENTS

Do you know those cheap plastic chairs in Southeast Asia whose legs are apt to collapse under a Westerner's weight? They come in pastel shades of pale green and blue, or faded red and scruffy white. I particularly remember them at the Ta Ouv restaurant in Kampot, Cambodia, because in addition to the worry about the legs giving way, there were also the gaps between the wooden planks, under which flowed the Kampot river. The planks were spaced just wide enough apart to fit the spindly legs and pitch you over anyway. Our table had been painted pale green but was now more wood than paint. We ordered Angkor beer while we waited for our food, loc lac and stir-fried chilli crab with green peppercorns.

We had just been filming in the kitchen where I had noticed, with some amusement, the number of dogs wandering through. It had been very busy in there. By one set of windows were three giant terracotta pots on wood burners, one containing stock for the soups the Cambodians adore, the others rice. In the centre were two large tables, on one of which was a considerable number of ingredients: a bottle of fish sauce, a bunch of long lemongrass stalks, sliced shallots and garlic, a pile of snake beans, various battered aluminium bowls containing chillies, chopped peanuts, prahoc – the pungent fermented fish paste from the Tonle Sap lake in the centre of the country near Siem Reap – various saucers of what looked like salt and sugar, and others the chefs described as 'seasoning' and 'soup powder': MSG, in other words. At the other table a couple of chefs were chopping up a pile of rather sinewy-looking beef, presumably for making the loc lac, about which I had heard so much. In one corner opposite the pots some ladies were doing the washing up, squatting on the floor using two big bowls. The dogs were mostly around them so presumably they were pets.

We had asked one of the chefs to allow us to film the making of loc lac and he let us know that now was the time, in between cooking dishes for the busy restaurant. He turned a massive gas burner up to full, planted a large black wok on it and threw in a ladleful of oil followed by a scoop of garlic and ginger. Straight in went the beef, followed by chilli paste, fish sauce, prahoc and, amazingly, a dollop of tomato ketchup. He stirred it, added a spoonful of salt, a big pinch of MSG and turned it out onto a pale blue melamine plate, on which were sliced tomato, onions and lettuce. It was done. He went straight on to cooking the crabs. These had already been chopped into four or five pieces each, claws and legs still moving. Taking the same wok he poured in more oil, added the crabs and stir-fried them over a high heat for no more than two minutes. Then he threw in sliced garlic, a couple of sprigs of green peppercorns, a generous slurp of soy sauce, a similar amount of fish sauce, some sugar, a pinch of MSG and a little water, put on a lid and left the crabs to cook for a couple of minutes, then they were done too. While we were filming, a girl had made a salad of translucent rice noodles with pink shallots, cooked prawns, pork and squid, chopped red bird's eye chillies, roasted peanuts, lime juice, fish sauce, mint, coriander and palm sugar. I spoke rather enthusiastically to the camera about the swagger of these 'young gun' chefs, the speed but also the economy of effort, the heat, the aromas of lemongrass and lime, pungent fish sauce and fish paste, then we all sat down for one of those never-to-be-forgotten lunches. I remember saying that in future all cookery filming was to be like this. We turn up at a fabulously atmospheric kitchen complete with wandering dogs, spend only half an hour filming the chefs because everything is so quick, then sit down to a lovely lunch. I talk about the joy of alfresco eating on a pier out in the Kampot river, then we stop filming and have a few beers. Return to the art deco hotel in Kep for a siesta, then maybe catch the sun setting over the Gulf of Thailand. Yes indeed, filming would always be like that.

But I'm not remembering this just because it was so special. It is also because it seems to me to sum up what we all so like about Southeast Asian cooking: the robust simplicity of the food, the immediacy of it. It takes no time to produce. It's a glorious assault on the senses. It also seems to us to be healthy: vegetables are raw or hardly cooked; there's a lot of seafood; freshwater fish everywhere; meat is used sparingly and rice is mostly simply steamed. It's almost as if we've stumbled on something so obvious we can't believe we've missed it all this time: the combination of hot, sour, salty and sweet, the occasional bitter notes, the enthusiasm for colour and texture that seems lacking in our own cuisines. Take the Thai green papaya salad, for example: the crispness of unripe papaya, the

crunchiness of green beans, the brittleness of roasted peanuts, the chewiness of dried shrimps and the softness of tomato, all given a light bruising in a mortar and pestle. It's food of considerable sophistication, delivered in seconds.

This book, like so many of mine, is an account of a journey I made to what I've rather cheekily called the Far East. Some people's eyebrows were raised at the expression, thinking it suggested that here in the UK we're still at the centre of the world; others thought the Australians, who often are a bit sensitive about living on the other side of the globe, might regard it as an affront. But as my Australian fiancée, Sarah, might say, 'It's a joke, Joyce.' In fact, over in Europe we might as well be called the Far West since it's all happening over there now. Events are unfolding in Asia not necessarily tranquilly, though. Before setting out on the journey, I was warned about bombs in Indonesia and the worsening political situation in Thailand. In Cambodia I was shattered by the still obvious legacy of the Khmer Rouge. In Vietnam, we were escorted everywhere by a slightly sinister government official and there are still political exhortations from loudspeakers in the streets of Hanoi every afternoon. Many thought we were mad going to Bangladesh, sure to be drowned in a cyclone, and there was shooting in the streets of Dhaka soon after we left. In Sri Lanka, we watched the bombing of Colombo by a couple of tiny Tamil Tiger planes and thought it was a fireworks display, and though the civil war is officially over I can only hope the peace won't be short-lived. But if you listened to people at home, you'd never go to most of the marvellous countries I travelled through, and you'd miss the lovely food and friendly people. That to me is the real point of food: it brings the best out in us all.

But there is no such place as the Far East. I could have called it my Southeast Asian Odyssey, but I wanted to go to the Indian subcontinent as well – anywhere where outrageously spicy food was the norm. I chose to go to Bangladesh rather

than India for two reasons. I was intrigued by the fact that the majority of Indian restaurants in the UK are actually Bangladeshi, and I wanted to see whether the food they cook in Bangladesh is different from what you get in Britain. Secondly, and the same reason I didn't go to China, is that India is too big a subject, a book of its own. The other country I visited in the subcontinent was Sri Lanka.

It was a wonderful trip. Memories of a train journey through the night and being awakened at dawn in Thailand with a thick glass of absurdly sweet milky tea, or casting off from the jetty in Phnom Penh into the Mekong river and the current that would take us down to the delta. Of endless hops in the little planes of airlines such as Dragon Air, Nok Air and Firefly. Of fabulous old hotels where people like Somerset Maugham and Graham Greene stayed. Sunrise and the spectacular strangeness of Angkor Wat, equal in its impact to the Taj Mahal, or sunset out at Halong Bay in North Vietnam, on a boat cruising through countless vertical-sided limestone islands topped with jungle and past floating fishing villages where even the primary school was on a pontoon.

The recipes in the book are those I found on my travels and a few I had to include because they're classic dishes, such as the aromatic chicken pilau with cinnamon, tomato and nutmeg from Bangladesh, which I had at lunch in Dhaka but whose recipe I didn't collect at the time. The recipes are as close as I can get to the real thing using ingredients available outside Asia. The only serious change I have made is to remove the MSG. I don't have any worries myself about the side effects of it. Indeed in his book *On Food and Cooking*, one of my food heroes, food scientist Harold McGee, says that 'toxicologists have concluded that MSG is a harmless ingredient for most people, even in large amounts'. My reason for leaving it out is that it adds, I think, too much savouriness to food. The same effect can be achieved more subtly by fish and soya sauces.

I have to make a confession. While I have celebrated in words the speed and simplicity of these recipes, it's not a 'meals in minutes' sort of book. The cooking is quick but the preparation takes time. There is no substitute for the aromatic pastes, spice mixes and masalas. If you want to taste an authentic Cambodian dish, you have to make fragrant yellowy-green kroeung by pounding sliced lemongrass, fresh turmeric, galangal, garlic and ginger. Similarly the seafood stew on page 190 will not taste anything like the real thing unless you make basa gede, the basic paste of Indonesia, combining turmeric, ginger, galangal and lesser galangal. You won't understand the dark aromatic warmth of a Sri Lankan curry unless you roast coriander, cumin, fennel, cinnamon, cloves and chilli and grind them yourself. There are a few spice pastes and powders you can buy ready-made, which are good, but in the end it is down to pounding or processing if you want the real excitement. I've made some suggestions about the sort of equipment you're going to need on page 315. The reality is you're going to have to enlarge your store cupboard too. In both my houses, in Padstow and Sydney, I have a large plastic box containing things like rice vinegar, black cardamoms, eight different types and sizes of rice and egg noodles, fenugreek seeds, tamarind paste, star anise and cinnamon, fish and shrimp paste, sticky rice, Vietnamese pickled cabbage, dried fish and lots of palm sugar. The pleasure comes when you open the lid, and the smell makes you want to cook.

A very dear friend of mine, Australian winemaker Len Evans, who sadly died a couple of years ago, used to refer to the invisible ties that bind food and wine lovers all over the world as the 'raffia', like the traditional protection round a bottle of Chianti. In Asia the raffia would be a universal love of rice. It is impossible to overestimate its importance. In every country the view is the same. Without rice, a meal is not a meal. In the West we think of rice as the filling component, like mashed potatoes, say. To the Asians, the curry, the stir-fry, the sambal, even a splash of fish sauce – they are there to highlight the glory of rice. In many parts, but particularly Bangladesh and Sri Lanka, it's normal to eat with your fingers. The tendency of Westerners is to add too much curry to the rice, then find you can't mould the food into a ball to put into your mouth with any degree of elegance. As soon as you serve more rice and less sauce, it works. The other major point about the Asian meal is that it doesn't generally follow the starters, mains and sweets progression, as ours does – everything is served at the same time. Desserts don't exist much beyond a plate of fresh fruit. Their sweet dishes are for serving at other times of the day. The idea is that each person at the table makes their own selection, balances their own meal. In most countries a variety of dishes will be served, maybe a couple of wet, curry-like dishes, say a meat and a fish, then there will be some vegetable dishes, perhaps curries, stir-fries or salads, then a variety of accompaniments: sambals, chillies, pickles and chutneys.

Try it at home. If you are cooking an Indian dish, add a dal to a lamb curry, but always include, say, a tomato and onion salad with vinegar, salt and cumin, a raita of yoghurt and cucumber with perhaps a little chopped onion stirred in, and a bowl of chutney. If you're doing something from Thailand or Malaysia, maybe one of the great slow-cooked dishes, such as beef rendang or mussaman curry, add a Thai, Cambodian or Vietnamese salad, that exciting mixture of green papaya or mango or rice noodles with meat or seafood, chilli, lime, fish sauce and onion; maybe add a stir-fry, too, of prawns or pork, and always a little bowl of something hot like a sambal of dried chillies and shrimp paste with tamarind, garlic and fish sauce, nam prik pao, or some sliced chillies with vinegar.

 កម្ពុជា

CHAPTER ONE

CAMBODIA

The defining characteristic of Cambodian cuisine is freshness: basil, coriander and mint, leaves such as morning glory, crunchy vegetables such as snake beans, lightly cooked squashes, slightly bitter gourds, green fruit such as mango, papaya and pineapple used as vegetables, counterpointed by the salty tastes of fish sauce, shrimp and fish paste. Cambodian cuisine is fragrant with lemongrass and lime leaves, hot with bird's eye chilli and, above all, slightly sweet with palm sugar, so important that the sugar palm, a spindly tree with a halo of dark green leaves, is on the national flag.

I'm attracted to the concept of marrying freshness and fragrance with salty pungency. It's almost a tangible statement of the need to balance the yin and the yang, the light and the dark so close to the heart of Buddhism – 95 per cent of Cambodians are Buddhists. Of all the countries I visited on my odyssey, Cambodia was the most disturbing, through the evidence of the terror of the Khmer Rouge's rule in the 1970s, but it was also the most enchanting: beautiful friendly people, a land unspoilt by development and a sense of being somewhere in the world at the beginning of a time when light might well prevail.

It might be a bit far-fetched to say that fish paste is a symbol of the dark forces, but realizing that prahoc is a paste made from fermented river fish, you might have a certain aversion to using it. It certainly has a pungent whiff and it does take some getting used to, but as with shrimp paste and dried shrimps, you quickly see the point – which is the same as salted anchovies in Mediterranean cooking, a savoury note. To the majority of the population of a very poor country it is also a vital source of protein. On my Asian journey, only Bangladesh and Vietnam rival Cambodia for the enormous life-saving importance of river fish. When you consider that the lake right in the centre of Cambodia and close to Angkor Wat, Tonle Sap, increases fivefold during the monsoons, the water rising from one to nine metres so that all the houses are on stilts and the roads run along levees, you realize just how vast the freshwater area of the country is for part of the year. Like the Vietnamese, the Cambodians are resourceful with their fish; not only do they ferment it to make prahoc, but they also smoke it, dry it, salt it, turn it into fish sauce and eat vast quantities of it fresh in dishes like the famous steamed, turmeric-scented amok.

It is often said that Cambodian food is less hot than that of its neighbours Thailand, Laos and Vietnam, though to an outsider it's hard to make that judgement, as everything seems pleasingly hot, especially when almost every dish also comes with sliced fresh chilli. It is true, though, that pepper is often used instead of chilli, the original spice in Asian food before the discovery of the New World. The pepper farms I visited around Kampot produce some of the finest pepper anywhere, and the combination of ground black pepper, salt and lime juice is the essential accompaniment to the marinated beef dish loc lac – it's also very satisfying with a char-grilled steak.

Lucky's stir-fried pork and vegetable soup
Samlor korko

SERVES 4

This is one of Cambodia's national dishes, using an incredible range of ingredients to achieve its complexity of flavour. It was the first dish I saw being cooked in Cambodia, at the Frizz restaurant in Phnom Penh, and it was a good way to start. It demonstrated to me very quickly that Cambodian cuisine is notable for its use of lots of fresh herbs and vegetables, and also the moderate amount of chilli in their food relative to their Thai neighbours – they tend to serve hot chilli as an accompaniment instead. But the most important point the chef Heng, also known as Lucky, made when he showed me this dish was the technique of pounding the paste in a mortar. All the ingredients are thinly sliced first and each is pounded down before the next is added. You may prefer to drop everything into a food processor instead, but leave it to process until the paste is very smooth. Lucky used unripe jackfruit in this soup, but underripe pineapple is almost as good. He also used a leafy herb called kantraub, known in the West as wampi or Clausena lansium, that can be hard to find. I've used coriander – not the same, but keeping faith, I hope, with the dish.

2 tbsp vegetable oil

½ quantity *Cambodian Khmer curry paste* (page 301)

3 kaffir lime leaves, torn

400ml coconut milk

2 tbsp fish sauce

125g piece butternut squash or pumpkin, chopped

100g fresh pineapple chunks, ideally a little underripe

75g snake beans or French beans, in 2.5cm pieces

50g sugar snap peas, trimmed

100g piece aubergine, cut into 1cm chunks

75g pea aubergines (or extra diced aubergine)

125g green papaya, swede or kohlrabi, finely shredded

30g *Roasted rice* (page 299)

200g pork fillet

½ tsp palm sugar

Small handful of coriander leaves, to garnish

Heat the oil in a large saucepan over a medium heat, add the curry paste and fry gently for 2 minutes until it starts to smell aromatic.

Add the kaffir lime leaves and coconut milk, bring to a simmer, then add the fish sauce, butternut squash or pumpkin, pineapple, beans, peas, aubergines, green papaya, roasted rice and 500ml hot water. Bring up to a simmer and leave to cook gently for 3 minutes until the vegetables are almost tender.

Meanwhile, thinly slice the pork fillet across. Then add the pork and sugar to the pan and simmer for a further 2 minutes. Add a little more fish sauce or some salt, to taste, and serve in bowls, scattered with the coriander.

A salad of stir-fried prawns, pork and squid with glass noodles, chilli and mint

SERVES 4

This is quite a meaty Khmer salad. You could almost describe it as a cold stir-fry but that would detract from the wonderfully fresh taste of the lime juice and mint and the crunchy texture of the peanuts against the soft bite of the glass noodles (page 311). I believe these fragrant salads are some of the most exciting dishes in Cambodian cooking, combining as they do four basic flavours – sour, salty, sweet and spicy – in such a dazzling way. It's important to drain the noodles well otherwise the excess water will dilute the dressing and diminish the punch.

Vegetable oil, for frying
100g shallots, thinly sliced
200g dried glass noodles
200g large raw peeled prawns
200g prepared medium-sized
    squid, sliced across into
    5mm-thick rings and
    the tentacles separated
    into pairs
100g minced pork
50g roasted peanuts,
    coarsely chopped
20g mint leaves, finely
    shredded
25g dried shrimp
1 red bird's eye chilli,
    finely chopped
4 tbsp lime juice
1 tbsp palm sugar
3 tbsp fish sauce

Pour 1cm oil into a large deep frying pan. Add the shallots and fry over a medium heat until they are crisp and golden brown. Lift them out with a slotted spoon onto plenty of kitchen paper and leave to drain. Reserve the frying oil.

Bring a large pan of unsalted water to the boil, add the noodles, take the pan off the heat and leave them to soak for 2 minutes. Drain well, roughly cut the noodles into a manageable length with kitchen scissors and set aside to drain even further. If there is a lot of excess water in the noodles, place some folded sheets of kitchen paper into the bottom of a bowl and tip the noodles on top.

Heat 2 tablespoons of the shallot-flavoured oil in a wok or large deep frying pan, add the prawns, season lightly with salt and stir-fry for 2 minutes or until just cooked. Lift onto a plate, add another 1–2 tablespoons oil to the pan and the squid, season lightly with salt and stir-fry for 1–1½ minutes until nicely caramelized. Add to the plate with the prawns. Finally, heat another 1–2 tablespoons oil in the pan, add the minced pork and stir-fry for 1½–2 minutes, breaking it up with a wooden spoon into small pieces as it browns.

Put the noodles into a large bowl and add the pork, prawns, squid, peanuts, mint, dried shrimp and chilli and toss together well. Mix the lime juice, sugar and fish sauce together, toss through the salad and serve at room temperature.

Fried fish in ginger sauce
Chien choon

SERVES 4

This was the second dish that Sophal's aunt (page 27) cooked in her wooden house on stilts. I remembered how unnerving it was seeing the ground so far below through the cracks in the floor. But it is very handy. The Cambodians, and the Vietnamese, are scrupulously clean in their cooking. No matter how poor the householders, they hang their aluminium pans on the outside wall of the kitchen, scrubbed to bright shininess, and they wash everything thoroughly in cold water, leaving it to drain through the slats onto the ground below. This lovely dish of crisp fried fish with ginger, spring onions and coriander couldn't be simpler but it does great justice to the delicate freshwater fish of Cambodia. I recommend you choose farmed bass, gilt-head (sea) bream or silver perch as the best alternatives.

2 × 450g farmed fish, such as sea bass, sea bream or silver perch, scaled and trimmed
Vegetable oil, for shallow frying
20g garlic, thinly sliced
50g peeled ginger, cut into fine matchsticks
1 tbsp palm sugar
2 tbsp fish sauce
½ tsp chicken stock concentrate
3 spring onions, thinly sliced on the diagonal
Small handful of fresh coriander, chopped

Sliced chillies and extra fish sauce, to serve

Cut the heads and tails off the fish. Pour 5mm oil into a large shallow non-stick frying pan big enough to accommodate both fish. Fry them over a medium-high heat for 2 minutes on each side until the skin is nicely coloured but they are not quite cooked through. Lift onto a tray lined with kitchen paper. Pour away all but 1 tablespoon of the oil from the pan and leave it to cool slightly.

Return the pan to a medium heat, add the sliced garlic and ginger to the pan and fry for a few seconds, then add the sugar, fish sauce, concentrated chicken stock and 150ml water. Return the fish to the pan, cover and cook for 4 minutes until done all the way through.

Lift the fish onto a warmed serving platter and spoon over the sauce. Scatter over the spring onions and chopped coriander and serve with sliced chillies and extra fish sauce.

Cambodian marinated beef with a lime and black pepper dipping sauce
Loc lac

SERVES 4 AS A MAIN COURSE OR 8 AS A STARTER

I got this dish from a restaurant in Kampot called Ta Ouv, but I've changed it a little. I have several dishes in the book using Kampot pepper, notably the crab with green peppercorns on page 42. Before the French left Cambodia, and indeed until the Khmer Rouge put paid to any exports from Cambodia, Kampot pepper was the most revered in the world, particularly in France. It has a complex flavour, and is used to great effect in the dipping sauce – just black pepper, lime juice and salt – that accompanies this stir-fry. Sometimes beef loc lac comes on a plate garnished with lettuce, tomato and onion, and it is often topped with a well-fried egg. Wrap the lettuce around the beef, then dip in the hot-sour sauce.

500g rump or sirloin steak

1 iceberg or romaine lettuce heart, broken into leaves

1 beef tomato, halved and thinly sliced

1 small onion, halved and sliced

50g roasted peanuts, chopped

3 tbsp vegetable oil

For the marinade:

1 medium-hot red chilli, roughly chopped

15g garlic, roughly chopped

25g peeled ginger, roughly chopped

Juice of ½ lime

1 tbsp palm sugar

3 tbsp dark soy sauce

2 tbsp oyster sauce

1 tbsp fish sauce

2 tbsp tomato ketchup

1 tsp freshly ground black pepper

For the dipping sauce:

Juice of ½ lime

2 tsp coarsely ground black pepper

Trim the beef of all fat, then cut into 2.5–3cm pieces. Put all the ingredients for the marinade into a mini food processor and blend together until smooth. Transfer to a bowl, stir in the beef and leave to marinate for 20 minutes.

Shortly before serving, arrange the lettuce leaves and sliced tomato and onion on a serving platter. Put the chopped peanuts into a small bowl. For the dipping sauce, mix the lime juice and pepper with ¼ teaspoon salt and divide between 4 small dipping saucers.

Heat 1½ tablespoons of the oil in a wok or large deep frying pan over a high heat. Lift half the beef out of the marinade, add to the pan and stir-fry for 3 minutes until nicely browned on the outside but still rare in the centre (not how they do it in Cambodia, where they prefer it well done, but how I like it). Spoon the beef onto a warmed serving plate and keep warm. Repeat with the remaining oil and beef.

Take the plate of beef to the table with the salad, peanuts and dipping sauce. Instruct your diners to wrap some beef in a lettuce leaf with peanuts, sliced onion and tomato, and dip into the sauce.

Steamed fish curry with coconut, turmeric, lemongrass and kaffir lime leaves
Amok trey

SERVES 4

Fish amok is the most famous dish from Cambodia and it's not hard to see why. Everyone eats fish there. There's so much water around that no one could be unfamiliar with it. So to take catfish and steam it gently with fresh turmeric, lemongrass, galangal, lime leaves and coconut milk, all fragrant local ingredients, inevitably makes the national dish. One of the key points made by Stephàne, who runs the hotel Knai Bang Chatt in the seaside town of Kep, is that Khmer cooking is nothing like as hot as Vietnamese, and this amok is a case in point. At the hotel they steamed the curry in delightful containers made from green banana leaves, but I've used small rice bowls. One other note. When Stephàne made this dish for us he used noni leaves (Morinda citrifolia, also known as great morinda, Indian mulberry, beach mulberry or Tahitian noni). These leaves have a lemony scent, so I've used lemon verbena instead, but use lemon balm or coriander if you can't get hold of this either.

450g white fish, such as haddock, plaice, sand whiting or john dory, skinned
1 tbsp vegetable oil
2 tbsp palm sugar
2 tbsp fish sauce
4 small star anise
2 kaffir lime leaves, shredded
400ml coconut milk
2 eggs, lightly beaten
6 lemon verbena leaves, chopped

For the amok curry paste:
4 fat lemongrass stalks, core roughly chopped
20g garlic, roughly chopped
2 shallots, roughly chopped
25g peeled fresh turmeric or 1 tsp turmeric powder
1 tsp crushed dried chillies
25g peeled galangal or ginger, chopped
2 kaffir lime leaves, shredded
50g roasted peanuts

For the amok curry paste, put the lemongrass, garlic, shallots, turmeric, crushed dried chillies, galangal or ginger, kaffir lime leaves, peanuts and 6 tablespoons of the coconut milk into a mini food processor and blend into a very smooth paste.

Cut the fish across into 2.5cm-wide strips and set aside.

Heat the oil in a wok or frying pan over a medium heat, add the curry paste and fry gently, stirring, for 2 minutes until it starts to smell aromatic. Add the sugar, fish sauce, 1 teaspoon salt, star anise, kaffir lime leaves and the rest of the coconut milk. Remove from the heat and leave to cool and then stir in the beaten eggs, the fish and the herb of your choice.

Spoon the amok into 4 × 350ml heatproof bowls or one shallow heatproof dish that will fit into a steamer, making sure, if using individual dishes, that a piece of star anise goes into each.

Bring 2.5cm water to the boil in a large shallow pan and then place some sort of trivet in the base: a petal steamer, a criss-cross mat of wooden chopsticks or a stackable steamer. Put the dishes into the steamer, cover the pan with a lid and cook over a low heat for 15 minutes until the custard is just set and the fish is cooked. Pierce one piece with a skewer: if you meet no resistance, it's done.

Barbecued pork ribs with star anise
Chheng choum ni chrouk ang

SERVES 3–4

Slow-cooking pork ribs on a barbecue, covered with a lid, is one of the delights of southern American cooking. The idea for this recipe came from the Sala Bai cookery school in Siem Reap, where they do much the same thing with Cambodian flavours. The secret of a really aromatic flavour lies in a long marination with salt and spices, a relatively gentle roasting process of about an hour to achieve meltingly tender pork, followed by a final 30-minute glazing with a sugar-based mixture. If you add the sugar at the beginning of the cooking process, it just burns. Cooking pork on a barbecue gives it a delightful smoky taste.

1 × 1.3kg rack meaty pork ribs
Freshly ground white pepper

For the star anise glaze:
5–6 star anise
4 tbsp palm sugar
25g garlic cloves, crushed
8 tbsp dark soy sauce

For the Asian coleslaw:
175g white cabbage, sliced
50g carrots, finely shredded
1 tsp finely chopped garlic
½ medium-hot red chilli,
    seeded and finely chopped
2 tbsp fish sauce
2 tbsp lime juice
1 tsp caster sugar
2 tsp mixed chopped
    coriander, Thai sweet
    basil and mint leaves

For the ginger dipping sauce:
2 spring onions, thinly sliced
1 slice ginger, finely chopped
3 tbsp dark soy sauce

For the chilli vinegar sauce:
1 red bird's eye chilli, sliced
1 tsp caster sugar
2 tbsp rice vinegar

Grind the star anise to a fine powder in a spice grinder. Mix ½ teaspoon of the powder with 1 teaspoon of the sugar, 1 teaspoon salt and ½ teaspoon freshly ground white pepper, sprinkle over both sides of the ribs and set aside on a tray, covered with clingfilm, for at least 4 hours and up to 24 hours.

If you are using a charcoal barbecue, light it about 30 minutes before you want to cook. If you are using a gas barbecue, light it 10 minutes beforehand. Rearrange the coals or turn off the middle burner for indirect cooking.

Put the ribs onto the rack of the barbecue, bony-side down first, making sure they are not directly over the heat, cover with a lid and barbecue over an indirect medium heat for 30 minutes on each side until the ribs are tender.

Meanwhile, mix another 1 teaspoon star anise powder with the crushed garlic, soy sauce and remaining sugar. Uncover the ribs and brush them generously with the star anise glaze. Continue to cook for another 10 minutes. Turn them over, brush with more glaze, and cook for another 10 minutes. Repeat once more until they are nicely caramelized.

For the coleslaw, mix the cabbage and carrot together in a bowl. Mix the garlic, chilli, fish sauce, lime juice and sugar together and set to one side. For the two dipping sauces, mix the ingredients together in separate small bowls.

Stir the dressing and chopped mixed herbs into the cabbage and carrot. Lift the ribs onto a board, brush once more with any remaining glaze, cover with foil and leave to rest for 5–10 minutes. Cut between the bones with a large sharp knife into separate ribs and serve with the coleslaw and the sauces.

Spicy green mango salad with smoked fish and a sweet and sour dressing

Njham svay trey heu

SERVES 2 AS A MAIN COURSE OR 4 AS A STARTER

I remember rather over-excitedly talking to the camera about the village of Kompong Khleang near Siem Reap being like something out of Raiders of the Lost Ark. The entire village, situated by the Tonle Sap lake, is built on enormously high stilts of solid teak. This is because in the rainy season the lake, swelled with water from Tibet coming down the Mekong river, increases in size by about five times. In such extremes, everyday life is ever-changing. At one time in the year the children are scampering around the stilts, getting in the way of all the masses of smoking trestles where the fish from the lake are salted and dried out in sun and smoke. In the rainy season, you visit your friends by boat and the kids jump out of their front door for a swim. This salad was prepared for me by our guide Sophal's aunt high up in her wooden house, a simple building of bamboo and teak, using dried fish that you could flake with your fingers into the shredded green mango, lime juice and fish sauce mixture, with other texture being given by crunchy roasted peanuts and a little red chilli.

4 smoked mackerel fillets
(about 275g)
Vegetable oil, for deep-frying
1 green mango, weighing
about 450g
1 large carrot, weighing
about 75g
30g shallots, very thinly sliced
1 red bird's eye chilli, finely
chopped
25g roasted peanuts, roughly
chopped
2 tsp palm sugar
1 tbsp fish sauce
About 1 tbsp lime juice,
depending on the tartness
of the mango
15g Thai sweet basil, roughly
chopped

Skin the smoked mackerel fillets and break the meat into small flakes. Pour 2cm oil into a pan and heat to 190°C. Sprinkle the fish into the oil and deep-fry for 1 minute until it is crispy. It will all stick together at this point but don't worry. Lift out onto a tray lined with lots of kitchen paper and leave to cool, then break up into small pieces again.

Peel the green mango and carrot and shred, using a mandolin or shredder (page 315), into 3–4mm wide strips. Put the mango, carrot, shallots, chilli, peanuts and fried fish pieces into a large bowl and toss together. Mix the sugar with the fish sauce and lime juice, add to the salad with the Thai basil and toss together again. Pile into the centre of 2 medium-sized plates, or 4 small plates if serving as a starter, and serve straight away.

Green fish soup with rice noodles, crisp vegetables, herbs, chilli and peanut sauce
Noum bunchjop

SERVES 4

Pradak is a village outside the city of Siem Reap, far and away the most popular tourist destination in Cambodia because of the temples of Angkor Wat. I was driven out there by a French chef, Joannès Rivière. Joannès is the executive chef at the Hotel de la Paix in Siem Reap, and is also tireless in his efforts to get local youngsters into training to become chefs and waiters. This early morning dish of soup with noodles and salad leaves was right up my street, truly local food. I enjoyed the DIY aspect of stirring whatever herbs or salad leaves you like into the soup then adding a palm sugar and peanut sauce with fish sauce and chilli.

250g white fish fillet, such as pollack, whiting or silver perch
4 fat lemongrass stalks, core chopped
40g garlic, roughly chopped
3 green chillies, chopped
25g fresh turmeric or 1 tsp turmeric powder
25g peeled galangal or ginger, chopped
50g shallots, chopped
1 tsp Cambodian fish paste (prahoc) or shrimp paste
400ml coconut milk
2 tsp lime juice

To serve:
400g dried flat rice noodles
Crunchy mixed salad (page 306)
Sweet palm sugar and peanut sauce (page 303)
75g mixed small leaves, such as watercress, ruby chard, spinach, Thai sweet basil
2 green chillies, thinly sliced
Fish sauce

For the curry stock, put 300ml water into a pan with ½ teaspoon salt and the fish. Bring to a simmer and cook gently for 4 minutes or until just cooked.

Meanwhile, put the lemongrass, garlic, green chillies, turmeric, galangal or ginger, shallots, prahoc or shrimp paste and 2–3 tablespoons cold water into a mini food processor and blend into a very smooth paste. Transfer the paste to a medium-sized pan and add the coconut milk and 1 teaspoon salt. Bring to a simmer and leave to cook for 5 minutes.

Remove the fish from the water and, when it is cool enough to handle, break it into flakes, discarding the skin and any bones. Add to the coconut milk mixture, strain in the cooking water from the fish and leave to simmer over a low heat for 2–3 minutes. Then transfer to a liquidizer and blend into a soupy-like stock. Return to a pan, add the lime juice and keep hot over a low heat.

For the noodles, bring a pan of unsalted water to the boil. Add the noodles, turn off the heat and leave them to soak for 2 minutes or until just tender. Drain and divide between 4 shallow soup plates or bowls. Top with the crunchy salad mixture and then ladle over the hot curry stock. Add 1 tablespoon sweet peanut sauce to each bowl with a small handful of the mixed leaves. Serve the sliced chillies and fish sauce separately.

Cured beef salad with lemongrass, peanuts and basil

Pleah saiko

SERVES 4–6

When choosing the recipes for this book, I was worried there would be too many lime juice and fish sauce-based salads, which always contain meat or fish and plenty of crunchy vegetables such as bean sprouts, green mango or papaya, lotus stems and banana flowers, but they are irresistible and all subtly different. This salad, a classic in Cambodia, comes from the Sala Bai cookery school in Siem Reap. I actually made it with the young students there. They were enchanting, so neat and tidy and keen to learn, many of them from the poorest of homes and grateful to have been given a chance.

For the beef:

5 tbsp lime juice

1 tbsp palm sugar

1 stalk lemongrass, core very finely chopped

10g finely chopped garlic

400g piece of sirloin steak, trimmed of all fat

For the dressing:

½ tsp Cambodian fermented fish paste (prahoc) or shrimp paste

2 tbsp fish sauce

2 tbsp palm sugar

3 tbsp lime juice

1 tsp finely chopped garlic

1 red bird's eye chilli, finely chopped

For the salad:

100g shallots, very thinly sliced

100g fresh bean sprouts

15g each fresh mint leaves and Thai sweet basil, shredded, plus a few extra for garnish

50g roasted peanuts, chopped

For the beef, mix the lime juice, sugar, lemongrass and garlic together in a large glass bowl. Very thinly slice the steak across the grain, add to the lime mixture and toss together well. Leave to marinate for 10–15 minutes.

Meanwhile, for the dressing, mix the prahoc or shrimp paste with a little of the fish sauce in a small bowl until it is well combined, then mix in the rest of the fish sauce, the sugar, lime juice, garlic, chilli and 2 tablespoons water.

Pour away the excess marinade from the beef, add the shallots, bean sprouts, mint, basil and half the chopped peanuts and mix together well. Pour over the dressing and toss together once more. Spoon onto a serving platter and sprinkle with the remaining peanuts and a few extra mint and basil leaves. Serve straight away, at room temperature.

Khmer pork, coconut and pineapple curry

SERVES 4

Using pork in stews in the West isn't generally a success. It might be because we think of stews as being rich and dark, and pork is not that sort of meat. But in Southeast Asia, pork curries are a different matter, because the meat suits the fragrant combinations of aromatic ingredients such as lemongrass and kaffir lime, turmeric and ginger. There's a lot of shrimp paste in this as well, which acts a bit like anchovy in our own cooking – you're hardly aware of it but you would know if it wasn't there.

800g lean boneless pork shoulder

1 small pineapple or 200g prepared fresh pineapple cubes

4 small, round green Thai aubergines or 100g purple aubergine

3 tbsp vegetable oil

½ quantity *Cambodian Khmer curry paste* (page 301)

40g fresh coconut, grated

300ml coconut milk

2 tbsp fish sauce

2 tsp palm sugar

1 tbsp *Tamarind water* (page 299)

Leaves from 1 small bunch Thai sweet basil

Cut the pork into 2.5–3cm pieces. If necessary, peel the pineapple, cut it into 4 wedges lengthways, slice away the core and cut the fruit into chunks. Cut the round green aubergines into wedges or the purple aubergine into pieces similar in size to the pineapple.

Heat 2 tablespoons of the oil in a wide-based pan or wok, add half of the pork pieces and brown lightly on all sides. Set aside on a plate and repeat with the remainder.

Add the remaining oil and the curry paste to the pan or wok and fry gently over a medium heat for 2–3 minutes until it starts to smell aromatic. Return the pork to the pan with 300ml water, part-cover and leave to simmer gently for 1 hour.

Uncover, add the grated coconut, pineapple, aubergines and coconut milk and simmer with the lid off for a further 10 minutes. Add the fish sauce, sugar and tamarind water, then stir in the basil. Season to taste with salt and serve.

Phnom Penh noodle soup
Kouy tieuv

SERVES 4

If pho is the most popular noodle dish in Vietnam, k'tieu is the same in Cambodia, and in fact in the Mekong delta of south Vietnam too, where it's called hu tieu nam vang, or noodle soup from Phnom Penh. It occurs in a myriad of subtly different ways but always has chicken or pork stock, sliced and minced pork, bean sprouts and, most importantly, noodles, sometimes made with tapioca, sometimes rice. Like the Hanoi chicken noodle soup on page 68 and the pho on page 58, I think of these dishes as main courses rather than first courses, although of course there is no such distinction in Southeast Asia. To me the best features of this soup are the lashings of tender pork, which make it quite a meaty dish, the flavour of the powdered shrimp and the particularly Cambodian addition of pickled cabbage.

450g piece of belly pork, skin on
1.5 litres *Asian chicken stock* (page 300)
20g dried shrimp
15g garlic, finely chopped
1 tsp palm sugar
200g minced pork
12 large raw peeled prawns
2 tbsp fish sauce
½ tsp freshly ground black pepper
250g dried 5mm-wide flat rice noodles
200g fresh bean sprouts
75g pickled cabbage (optional)
2 spring onions, thinly sliced
Crisp fried shallots (page 299)
Crisp fried garlic (page 299)
3 tbsp fresh coriander, very roughly chopped
4 red or green bird's eye chillies, very thinly sliced
2 limes, cut into 'cheeks', to serve

Put the belly pork, chicken stock, half the dried shrimp, the garlic and sugar into a large pan and bring to the boil, skimming off any scum as it rises to the surface. Lower the heat, cover and leave to simmer for 1 hour. Put the remaining dried shrimp into a spotlessly clean spice grinder, grind to a powder and set aside.

Remove the pork from the stock and thinly slice. Cover and set aside. Add the minced pork to the remaining stock and simmer for 2 minutes, breaking it up with a wooden spoon as it cooks. Then add the prawns with the fish sauce, black pepper and 1½ teaspoons salt, and simmer for 1 minute. Keep hot.

For the noodles, bring a pan of unsalted water to the boil. Add the noodles, turn off the heat and leave them to soak for 3–4 minutes or until just tender.

Drain the noodles well and divide between 4 large bowls. Top with the bean sprouts, sliced pork, pickled cabbage and spring onions and ladle over the hot soup, trying to distribute the prawns equally between each bowl. Garnish each bowl with the fried shallots, fried garlic, coriander, shrimp powder and sliced chillies and serve immediately with the lime cheeks on the side.

Baguette sandwich of char-grilled beef marinated in soy, lemongrass and chilli

SERVES 6 / MAKES ABOUT 24 SMALL KEBABS

One of the most enduring legacies of French colonial rule in Cambodia, Vietnam and Laos is the baguette. It's testimony to the cultural influence of food. I went to a baguette bakery in Siem Reap early one morning eager to verify a story I'd heard that the bakers in this part of the world make almost better bread than the French since they still use the skills from a time when mechanization was unknown. It was very good – if a bit on the sweet side. Each mini baguette was moulded by hand, and each time a batch came from the oven and was dropped into trays still hot, the entire production was sold and gone in three to five minutes. One of the places where they subsequently turned up was on a series of little carts around Angkor Wat, where they were slit open and a skewer of freshly barbecued chilli-hot, soy-glazed beef strips was packed inside together with a delicious fresh salad of shredded mango and cucumber, sharpened with lime juice and fish sauce: a sandwich, in other words.

400g piece of beef topside, trimmed of all fat

1 tsp freshly ground black pepper

2 fat stalks lemongrass, core finely chopped

20g garlic, crushed

100g shallots, finely chopped

4 tbsp dark soy sauce

2 tbsp palm sugar

2 red bird's eye chillies, finely chopped

To serve:

½ cucumber

1 small green mango (weighing about 450g)

12 small par-baked mini baguettes or white rolls

4 tsp fish sauce

4 tsp lime juice

Bottled chilli sauce (hot or sweet)

Thinly slice the beef and then cut into strips, 2.5cm wide. Put the black pepper, lemongrass, garlic, shallots and half the soy sauce into a mini food processor and process into a smooth paste. Transfer to a bowl and stir in the rest of the soy sauce, the sugar, chilli and the beef. Leave to marinate for 1 hour. Cover 24 bamboo skewers, about 18cm long, with cold water and leave them to soak alongside the beef.

For the salad, cut the cucumber in half lengthways, scoop out the seeds with a teaspoon, then, using a potato peeler, cut it lengthways into long thin strips. Peel the green mango and finely shred it. Mix them together in a bowl and leave in the fridge until needed.

Bake the bread according to the packet instructions if necessary.

To cook, weave 2 strips of beef onto each bamboo skewer. Light your barbecue – a disposable foil-tray barbecue would be ideal. When the coals are covered in a layer of thick white ash, grill the beef skewers for 1–1½ minutes on each side until nicely browned on the outside, but still moist and juicy in the centre. Mix the fish sauce and lime juice into the green mango and cucumber salad.

Split open the bread rolls, place 2 skewers of beef inside and slide the meat off into the roll. Add some of the green mango salad and a drizzle of chilli sauce and eat.

Khmer-style rice porridge with chilli, coriander, spicy pork and peanuts

Babah

SERVES 2

This dish is found all over Asia. It is known in China as congee, in Thailand as kao dtom, in Vietnam as chao ga and in Cambodia as babah. The idea of what I call rice porridge might not appeal to you, but all I can say is please try it. Like so many food combinations in the East, the pleasure of this dish is in the contrast of the flavours and textures: the bland, soft, very wet rice, the sharp flavours of chilli, fish sauce, spring onion, garlic pork and coriander, and the crunchy texture of peanuts and bean sprouts. Some recipes call for everything to be stirred in, but I love starting with a bowl of the rice and adding some bits and bobs, and then adding more bits and more bobs as I go along. The next time you're in any part of Southeast Asia having breakfast in a hotel, don't go for bacon and eggs, try the congee pot.

100g minced pork

1 tbsp fish sauce

1 tsp sugar

10g dried shrimp

15g peeled ginger,
    thinly sliced

150g Thai jasmine rice

2 tbsp vegetable oil

30g garlic, finely chopped

To garnish:

4 tbsp fish sauce

1 red bird's eye chilli,
    very thinly sliced

½ quantity Shallot oil
    (page 299)

Large handful of coriander
    leaves

50g bean sprouts

2 spring onions, white part
    only, thinly sliced

50g roasted peanuts,
    coarsely chopped

Put the minced pork, fish sauce and sugar into a small bowl. Mix together well and set aside.

Put 1.5 litres of water in a heavy-based pan over a high heat, add the dried shrimp and ginger and bring to the boil. Cover and simmer for 10 minutes. Sprinkle in the rice and bring back to the boil, stirring. Part-cover and leave to simmer for 30 minutes until the rice is very tender and broken down into a kind of porridge, then turn off the heat.

Mix the fish sauce and chilli together. Put all the garnishes into separate small bowls.

To cook the pork, heat the oil in a small frying pan over a medium heat. Add the garlic and stir-fry for 30 seconds, until just starting to turn golden, then toss in the pork and stir-fry for 2 minutes. Tip into another small bowl.

Spoon the porridge into warmed bowls and top each bowl with the garnishes of your choice.

Stir-fried crab with green Kampot pepper

SERVES 2

The town of Kep on the Gulf of Thailand, about two and a half hours' drive from Phnom Penh, is famous for its crab, and Kampot, about forty minutes' drive from Kep, is famous for its pepper. Not unnaturally, therefore, they have an exquisite dish that combines them both. Small strings of green pepper still on the vine are used. The crab is quickly quartered and wok-fried with garlic, palm sugar, spring onions, fish sauce and plenty of green peppercorns. It's deliciously pepper-hot. We watched the dish being prepared in Kampot and again on Rabbit Island just off the coast, where a fisherman's wife had opened a small beach shack and was cooking the crabs over a wood fire. I'd never seen how to use a wok with wood before. If you want to turn the heat down, you take a couple of twigs away, leave them burning on the side, then add them back when you want it hot again. It is possible to get fresh green peppercorns on the vine in Asian grocery stores, see page 315, but the ones in brine are a good substitute.

1kg raw or cooked whole crabs, such as brown crab, mud crab or blue swimmer
4 Kampot green peppercorn vines or 1½ tbsp green peppercorns in brine, drained and rinsed
2 tbsp dark soy sauce
1½ tsp palm sugar
2 tbsp vegetable oil
20g garlic, finely chopped
1½ tsp fish sauce
6 spring onions, trimmed and thinly sliced on the diagonal

If using live crabs, turn them on their backs with the eyes facing you. First, drive a thick skewer or a thin-bladed knife between the eyes and into the centre of the crab. Then lift up the tail flap and drive the skewer through the underside.

For both uncooked and cooked crabs, break off the tail flaps and discard. Break off the claws, then take a large-bladed knife and cut them in half at the joint and crack the shells of each piece with a hammer or the back of the knife. Chop the body section of each crab in half, then gently tug on the legs to pull the body pieces away from the back shell. Use a knife as an added lever if you need to but the body pieces should come away quite easily with the legs still attached. Turn each piece over and pick off the dead man's fingers (soft gills), then cut in half once more so you have 2 legs attached to each piece. Throw away the back shells or save for stock.

Put the loose green peppercorns, if using, into a mortar or coffee mug and lightly bruise with the pestle or the end of a rolling pin. (Fresh peppercorns on the vine won't need bruising.) Mix the soy sauce with the sugar and set aside.

Heat a large wok over a high heat. Add the oil and the crab pieces and stir-fry for 3 minutes. Add the garlic and green peppercorns and cook for a few seconds, then lower the heat to medium, add the fish sauce and 2–3 tablespoons water, cover and cook for 5 minutes if the crab was raw, 2–3 minutes if it was cooked. Stir in the soy sauce and sugar mixture and spring onions and turn over once or twice. Spoon onto plates and serve.

Stir-fried noodles with beef and spinach in a sweet and sour sauce
Lort char

SERVES 4

If you search the internet for the Russian Market, Phnom Penh, you'll find a lot of people describing it as one of the darkest and dirtiest places they've ever been to. Its name comes from a time during the Vietnam war when Phnom Penh was heaving with Russians, all there to help their allies in the north. It is indeed rambling and scruffy, but for filming it's a dream. I remember seeing shafts of sunlight coming down from holes in the rusty tin roof, cutting through all the smoke and dust in the atmosphere. Yes, it was indeed dirty, smelly and stiflingly hot, but some of the cooking there was fascinating. I recall the turmeric and rice-flour pancakes stuffed with prawns similar to the sizzling Saigon pancakes (Banh xeo) on page 73, and the fragrant orange juice we were served as we waited, where the sweet girl who was pressing them put the skins through the machine a second time to get every last drop of juice out, and then only charged us the equivalent of about 7p per glass. But most of all I remember this fat noodle dish we had for breakfast, a stir-fry of beef and water spinach with some sort of sweet and sour sauce, topped with a fried egg. I have no way of discovering what brand of sauce it was she used but the Thai hot chilli sauce seems to hit the spot. That, and a glass of orange juice consumed while sitting on a beer crate amid shafts of sunlight, and I was happy.

450g fresh thick egg noodles (hokkien mee)
275g slice of rump steak, trimmed of all fat
3 tbsp Thai hot chilli sauce
1½ tbsp fish sauce
1½ tsp palm sugar
1½ tsp cornflour
4 tbsp vegetable oil, for frying
15g garlic, finely chopped
100g fresh bean sprouts
150g leaf spinach, washed and dried in a salad spinner
4 eggs

Bring a pan of unsalted water to the boil. Add the noodles and cook for 1 minute. Drain well and set aside. Slice the steak across the grain as thinly as you can. Mix the chilli sauce with the fish sauce, sugar, cornflour and 1 teaspoon water.

Heat 2 tablespoons of the oil in a large frying pan or wok over a high heat, add the beef and garlic and stir-fry quickly until all the beef changes colour, but don't let it overcook or it will become tough.

Add the noodles and sauce mixture and toss together well, then add the bean sprouts and spinach and stir-fry for a few seconds until everything has heated through. Turn off the heat and keep hot.

Heat the remaining oil in a frying pan over a medium-high heat, crack in the eggs and fry, spooning some of the hot oil over the yolks as they cook, letting them become a little crispy round the edges. Spoon the noodles onto warmed plates and serve topped with the fried eggs.

Steamed mussels with yellow kroeung, coconut milk and kaffir lime leaves

SERVES 4

Because there are so many good recipes in Southeast Asia, I haven't often felt the need to write my own recipes in the regional style, especially of somewhere such as Cambodia. However, I decided I wanted a recipe for shellfish where coconut milk, chilli, fish sauce, lemongrass, lime leaves and lime juice are made into a fragrant sauce with the juices from steamed mussels. This is it. Make sure the mussels are very fresh and tightly closed, so they haven't lost any of their liquor.

2 tbsp vegetable oil

1 quantity *Cambodian Khmer curry paste* (page 301)

400ml coconut milk

1.75kg fresh mussels in their shells, cleaned

4 kaffir lime leaves

2 tbsp fish sauce

2 tsp palm sugar

2 tbsp lime juice

Large handful of fresh coriander, leaves roughly chopped

Heat the oil in a large, deep pan. Add the curry paste and fry for 5 minutes, stirring now and then, until it smells aromatic. Add the coconut milk and simmer for 2 minutes.

Add the mussels and lime leaves to the pan, cover and cook over a high heat for 3–4 minutes until the mussels have just opened.

Add the fish sauce, sugar and lime juice and adjust the seasoning with salt if necessary. Scatter over the coriander and serve in deep, warmed bowls.

CHAPTER TWO 越南

VIETNAM

What an introduction to Vietnam: to board a river boat in Phnom Penh, the capital of Cambodia, and meander down the Mekong to Can Tho in the river delta. The difference between the two countries couldn't be more apparent than what we could see on the river banks. In Cambodia, peaceful village life, children running through the trees and along the banks, clothes being washed in the river, cattle coming down to drink and a sleepy murmur in the late afternoon heat. Later that evening we crossed the border and the personality of the Vietnamese was immediately apparent. Everywhere on the banks was industriousness: boats being mended, cooking on junks, intense cultivation of vegetables and fruit with water irrigation pumps and pipes snaking away up the river banks. Fish farms on either bank: floating pontoons with a couple of wooden huts, each with a barking guard dog or two. A small town where a wide canal joined the Mekong to the Bassac river. Some thumping Vietnamese disco music from a house right on the water. TV masts on high poles like spindly saplings. We picked up the impression of a country really trying to become prosperous and modern. I realized later that what I was seeing was typical of only the Mekong delta and Ho Chi Minh City, and Hanoi and the Red River delta. The rest was mainly still agricultural, and enjoying a hot, steamy, tropical climate where anything grows, as well as really quite cold conditions in the central highlands in winter.

On board the Bassac II, we enjoyed some of the classic dishes of the country: at one stage Vietnamese spring rolls, the fresh ones with limpid rice paper pancakes wrapped round a filling of prawns and pork with mint, Thai sweet basil, bean sprouts, garlic chives and shredded lettuce; on another occasion a pile of crunchy yellow fritters made with shredded potatoes and prawns perfumed with turmeric.

This use of leafy herbs and crunchy items is very common. Many street dishes, like the famous Hanoi char-grilled pork bun cha, are characterized by it. Here a bowl of steaming chicken broth and rice noodles is eaten with crunchy vegetables and salad leaves together with char-grilled minced pork flavoured with garlic and fish sauce. Perhaps this pleasing arrangement is more common in the North: they love the contrast of the crunch with the soft texture of the wide variety of noodles, both rice and flour, that they use, and here their food is very Chinese – not unnaturally, since Vietnam was part of China for a thousand years. This is possibly the most important difference. Vietnamese food is similar to Thai and Cambodian in the sense that the most common flavouring ingredients are lime juice and lime leaves, lemongrass, fish sauce, palm sugar and chilli, but Vietnam's influences are much more Chinese, whereas the other countries have a lot of Indian influence too.

Fried fish with turmeric and dill
Cha ca

SERVES 4

Cha Ca La Vong is a restaurant in Hanoi at 14 Cha Ca Street. Cha Ca means grilled fish, and the street is named after the restaurant. If you go there, you might wonder what all the fuss is about. To call the place rickety would be an understatement. There's only one dish on the menu, and the waiters are abrupt, to put it mildly. The kitchen is rudimentary and the whole place is deeply informal, but in my last book, Coast to Coast, I mentioned that eating some dishes can be a life-changing experience, and this was one for me. The dish consists of cold, silky-soft rice noodles, hot turmeric-scented fish bubbling in oil as it is brought to the table, with herbs and spring onions wilting down in the pan, accompanied by more crisp fresh herbs and leaves and nuoc cham, the traditional hot, sour and spicy dipping sauce. The true recipe is a secret, but I do think my attempt to recreate it allows you to see how satisfying the original is. Interestingly, famous restaurants all over Southeast Asia have that sketchy quality about them, which is so unlike the wildly over-comfortable places of the west.

500g skinned ling fillet, monkfish or john dory
25g peeled fresh turmeric, chopped, or 1 tsp powder
4 fat lemongrass stalks, core finely chopped
2 tbsp fish sauce
1 tsp palm sugar
3 tbsp Tamarind water (page 299)
50g rice flour
½ tsp turmeric powder
4 tbsp vegetable oil, for frying
Large bunch of dill
8 spring onions

For the side dishes:
175g dried rice vermicelli noodles
50g roasted peanuts, chopped
25g small lettuce leaves
25g mixed herbs: Thai sweet basil, mint (Vietnamese, if possible) and coriander
Vietnamese dipping sauce (nuoc cham, see page 303)

Cut the fish into 4cm pieces. Put the turmeric, lemongrass, fish sauce, sugar and 1 tablespoon water into a mini food processor and blend to a very smooth paste. Stir in the tamarind water and pour into a shallow dish. Add the pieces of fish, turn them over to coat well, and leave to marinate for 1 hour.

Just before you are ready to serve, prepare the side dishes. Bring a pan of unsalted water to the boil, drop the noodles in, take off the heat and leave to soak for 2 minutes. Drain, refresh under cold water, drain well and transfer to a serving bowl. Put the peanuts into a small dish, the lettuce leaves and mixed herbs into a bowl, and the nuoc cham into 4 separate dipping saucers.

Sift the rice flour, turmeric and a good pinch of salt into a bowl, add the pieces of marinated fish and toss them around until well coated. Heat the oil in a medium-sized frying pan, add the pieces of fish and shallow-fry for about 5 minutes, turning now and then, until crisp, golden brown and cooked through.

Meanwhile, cut the dill across into 10cm lengths, and trim and finely shred the spring onions lengthways. Add the dill and spring onions to the pan and leave to cook for 1 minute until wilted. Take to the table with all the other bits and pieces.

Ask your guests to put a portion of noodles into their bowl, spoon some fish and herbs on top, then add peanuts and salad leaves, season to taste with the nuoc cham and eat.

Braised catfish in dark caramel sauce
Ca kho

SERVES 2

When I first arrived in Vietnam, after sailing down the Mekong from Cambodia, I was amazed and I have to say slightly concerned by the intensity of the fish farming on both sides of the river. It turns out the Vietnamese are serious exporters of freshwater fish, which turn up in our supermarkets with such unlikely names as Vietnamese Cobbler. I say 'concerned' because I assumed this vast industry turned out an inferior product, but actually a lot of the fish, particularly the catfish, is rather good. And even if some species are a little tasteless, the spiciness and sweet-saltiness of the accompanying flavours make them delectable. Nowhere is this more obvious than braised fish in caramel, traditionally cooked in a clay pot, and eaten during Tet, Vietnamese New Year.

400g catfish or farmed
    salmon, with skin
    and fat left on
25g garlic, crushed
6 spring onions, white
    part only, chopped
100ml fish sauce
1½ tsp freshly ground
    black pepper
4 tbsp vegetable oil
6 tbsp palm sugar
2 medium-hot red chillies,
    cut into 5mm-thick slices

First marinate the fish. Cut the fish into 5cm chunks. Using a pestle and mortar, pound half the crushed garlic with half the chopped spring onion to form a paste. Place the chunks of fish in a bowl and add 50ml of the fish sauce, the crushed garlic and spring onion paste, the black pepper and 1 teaspoon salt. Mix well to coat the fish and refrigerate for 2 hours.

Next make the caramel sauce. This is the most important stage of this dish, because the sauce must not be too sweet, nor too bitter because of overcooking, and have a nice brown-orange colour. Gently heat 2 tablespoons of the oil in a small pan. Add 3 tablespoons of the sugar and stir continuously, increasing the heat slightly if necessary, until all the sugar has melted, caramelized and turned darker brown in colour.

At this stage, cool the bottom of the saucepan by dipping it in a bowl of cold water. Return the pan to the heat and add 150ml water. The sugar will have hardened, so stir gently over a moderate heat until the sugar softens and dissolves again. Add the remaining spring onions to the sauce, stir and set aside.

The fish is traditionally cooked in a large clay pot. However, a large, deep frying pan is ideal. Heat the remaining 2 tablespoons of oil over a high heat. Add the remaining crushed garlic and fry until nearly golden in colour. Add the caramel sauce, another 150ml water, the remaining fish sauce and sugar and bring up to the boil, stirring often.

Add the marinated fish, including any marinating liquid. Once the sauce has returned to the boil, reduce the heat to a moderate simmer. Add the sliced chillies and cook, uncovered, for 20 minutes until the sauce has thickened slightly, then serve.

Stir-fried prawns with mango

Tom sot xoai

SERVES 4

This recipe came from the Bassac II, the boat in which I travelled down the Mekong.
It's not particularly traditional but it's the type of food I like to eat: colourful flavours,
juicy prawns, mangoes, basil, a touch of chilli and some lime juice.

1 firm, underripe (but not
    green) mango
1 tsp cornflour
2 tbsp vegetable oil
10g garlic, finely chopped
100g shallots, finely chopped
1–1½ red bird's eye chillies,
    finely chopped
500g large raw peeled prawns
Juice of 1 lime
1 tbsp fish sauce
Large handful of Thai sweet
    basil leaves
Freshly ground white pepper

Peel the mango and slice the flesh away from either side of the flat stone in the centre. Cut it roughly into 1cm pieces. Mix the cornflour with 1 tablespoon water and set aside.

Heat the oil in a wok or large, deep frying pan over a medium-high heat. Add the garlic, allow to sizzle for a few seconds until just beginning to change colour, then add the shallots and sizzle for another 30 seconds. Add the red chilli and prawns, increase the heat to high and stir-fry for approximately 2 minutes until the prawns turn pink and are just cooked through.

Add 2–3 tablespoons water, lime juice, fish sauce and slaked cornflour and stir-fry for a few seconds to thicken the sauce. Then add the mangoes and cook briefly until they have heated through. Stir in the basil, season with a little white pepper, and spoon onto a warmed serving dish.

Prawn fried rice with pork, pineapple and coriander
Com dua

SERVES 4

I ate this dish at the Tib restaurant in Ho Chi Minh City. If you search the internet for the name of the restaurant, you'll be able to enjoy a virtual tour together with some rather endearing atmospheric music. It's world famous, and it prides itself on what I believe is called Imperial Hué cooking. This dish is very good, though very simple. The aromatic pork and prawns are given a gentle acidity by the fresh pineapple, but the presentation in the 'imperial' style made me laugh, I'm sorry to say. It came in a pineapple cunningly carved to look like a pheasant. Why, I don't know. My presentation simply calls for piling the lovely fried rice on a white plate. It's a home-style dish, after all.

250g long-grain rice
200g *Chinese red roast pork*
    (char siu, see page 300),
    made with pork fillet
2 tbsp vegetable oil
40g garlic, finely chopped
1 medium-hot red chilli,
    halved lengthways, seeded
    and thinly sliced
200g large cooked peeled
    prawns
200g fresh pineapple,
    chopped into small chunks
2 tbsp light soy sauce
4 tbsp *Crisp fried shallots*
    (page 299)
4 tbsp chopped fresh coriander
Freshly ground black pepper

Put the rice into a 20cm heavy-based saucepan and add 430ml water. Quickly bring to the boil, stir once, cover with a tight-fitting lid, then reduce the heat to low and cook for 10 minutes. Uncover, fluff up the grains of rice with a fork and set aside.

Cut the pork across into thin slices and then the slices into slightly smaller pieces.

Heat the oil in a large wok over a high heat. Lower the heat slightly and add the garlic and chilli, quickly followed by the cooked rice, pork, prawns and pineapple and stir-fry for 2 minutes until everything has heated through.

Add the soy sauce, crisp fried shallots, coriander and a little salt and some freshly ground black pepper to taste and toss together well. Pile the mixture onto a warmed serving plate and serve straight away.

Vietnamese beef noodle soup
Pho bo

SERVES 4

Pho is far and away the most famous dish in Vietnam. One of Vietnam's most famous cultural commentators, Nguyen Tuan, wrote 'morning, noon, afternoon, evening, late night, anytime is a good time for a bowl of pho. During the day having an additional bowl of pho is like brewing a second pot of tea when the company is enjoyable … I know our country has high mountains, long rivers, deep seas and heroic people who have built up a glorious history, but I also know our country has pho'. Some think the name pho (pronounced fir) came from the French dish Pot au Feu, others think it's from the Chinese fen meaning rice noodles. It certainly seems to me to have echoes of the French beef and vegetable dish with Chinese noodles, too. I cooked it on the Mekong river boat, the Bassac II, for the TV series that accompanies this book, carefully guided by Angh, the boat-owner's wife. The extra subtlety she introduced to a recipe I've been cooking for years was in the roasting of the spices, ginger and onions before adding them to the broth to darken it and enhance the flavour, and also in slicing the beef as thinly as possible. Normally the Vietnamese would make it with topside, but I've been a bit 'Western' and used the more succulent fillet steak.

1 quantity *Asian beef broth* (page 300)

300g dried 1cm-wide flat rice noodles (banh pho)

200g piece of fillet steak

10g each Thai sweet basil leaves, mint leaves and coriander leaves

5 red bird's eye chillies, thinly sliced

2 limes, cut into wedges

8 spring onions, trimmed and sliced, green and white parts separated

4 tbsp fish sauce

100g bean sprouts

Bring the Asian beef broth to the boil in a pan. Drop the noodles into a pan of unsalted boiling water, turn off the heat and leave to soak for 10 minutes or until just tender.

Meanwhile, finely slice the beef. Put the basil, mint, coriander, red chillies and lime wedges into separate small bowls.

Add the white part of the spring onions and the fish sauce to the broth. Drain the noodles and divide between 4 deep soup bowls. Top with the sliced beef, the green part of the spring onions and the bean sprouts. Ladle over the hot stock and serve with the garnishes, each diner adding them according to taste.

Fresh spring rolls
Nem cuon

SERVES 4/MAKES 8 ROLLS

Vietnamese spring rolls come in two forms; these are made with soft rice papers, wrapped around a filling of fresh herbs, salad, cooked meat and seafood. (See page 62 for the other kind: the crisp fried spring roll.) The object here is to get contrasts of texture and many fresh flavours in the soft-wrapped roll. There are endless combinations, but I find this mixture of prawns and cooked pork, together with bean sprouts, tender vermicelli noodles, mint, Thai sweet basil and garlic chives, to be perfect.

150g piece of *Vietnamese cooked belly pork* (page 300), skin removed

25g dried rice vermicelli noodles

100g soft, hothouse lettuce leaves, washed and dried

50g fresh bean sprouts

Leaves from 2–3 sprigs fresh mint and 2–3 sprigs Thai sweet basil

150g (8) large cooked peeled prawns, halved lengthways

8 ×22cm extra-thin dried Vietnamese rice papers (banh trang)

16 chives (garlic chives if possible)

Vietnamese dipping sauce (nuoc cham, see page 303), to serve

Cut the piece of cooked belly pork across into very thin slices. Cover and set aside. Bring a pan of unsalted water to the boil. Add the vermicelli noodles, remove from the heat and leave to soak for 2 minutes or until just tender. Drain and rinse in cold water to prevent them from cooking any further. Set aside with the pork. Mix the ingredients for the nuoc cham dipping sauce together and divide between 4 small dipping saucers.

To assemble the spring rolls, have all the filling ingredients ready and to hand. Dip one rice paper into a shallow dish of cold water and leave to soften for about 1 minute, then remove and lay on a wet tea towel. In the centre of the paper arrange 2 crossed chives, followed by small amounts of the mint leaves, basil leaves, 2 prawn halves, noodles, bean sprouts, pork and lettuce in layers. Fold the edge of the paper closest to you over the filling, fold in the sides and then roll up away from you to secure everything in a neat parcel. Set the assembled roll aside on one half of another damp tea towel, and cover with the other half, to prevent it drying out.

Repeat this process with the remaining papers, distributing the ingredients equally between them and setting them aside under the folded damp tea towel. When they are all made, arrange them on a serving platter and serve with the nuoc cham for dipping.

Crisp spring rolls with pork, prawns and dried mushrooms

Cha gio

MAKES 14 ROLLS

Crisp spring rolls are possibly the best-known food from Vietnam. They differ from Chinese spring rolls by having a rice-flour wrapper rather than a wheat one. This leads to a much paler-looking roll, which I think is more appetizing. And the crisp spring roll differs from the other spring roll of Vietnam, the soft, fresh version (page 61), by being fried. I overheard a joke recently, where a man was asked whether he preferred food or sex, to which he replied, 'Food. Oh no, wait a minute – sex. No, hang on, food.' Well, that's like me with spring rolls. The crisp, deep-fried ones or the soft, fragrant fresh ones? Either way, the secret to a great Vietnamese spring roll is a mixture of pork and prawns. In my opinion, one cannot be present without the other. Incidentally, the square packages deep frying in the picture opposite are filled with the same mushroom, pork and prawn mixture as the rolls.

15g dried cloud ear (wood ear) mushrooms
25g dried rice vermicelli noodles
300g minced pork
175g large raw peeled prawns, finely chopped
100g shallots, finely chopped
15g garlic, finely chopped
4 spring onions, trimmed and thinly sliced
½ medium-sized carrot (about 50g), coarsely grated
1 tbsp fish sauce
1 tsp palm sugar
1 medium egg, beaten
Freshly ground white pepper
14 × 22cm dried Vietnamese rice papers (banh trang)
Vegetable oil, for deep-frying
Thai sweet basil leaves, mint leaves and lettuce leaves
1 quantity *Vietnamese dipping sauce* (nuoc cham, see page 303)

Put the dried mushrooms into a large bowl, cover with plenty of hot water and leave to soak for 15 minutes. Meanwhile, bring a pan of unsalted water to the boil, drop in the rice vermicelli, remove from the heat and leave to soak for 2 minutes. Drain and refresh under cold water. Drain well, then cut into approximately 3cm pieces with scissors. Drain the mushrooms, cut away and discard any woody parts, then thinly slice.

Put the minced pork and prawns into a large bowl and add the noodles, mushrooms, shallots, garlic, spring onions, carrot, fish sauce, sugar, egg and some white pepper. Mix together.

Place a damp clean tea towel onto the work surface next to a shallow dish of hot water. Place a rice wrapper into the water and leave to soak for about a minute until soft and pliable. Then lift it out and lay it on the damp tea towel. Place 2 generous tablespoons of the pork mixture in a line across the centre of he wrapper, about 3cm up from the bottom edge of the disc. Fold the bottom edge over the filling, give it one roll, then fold in the sides and then continue to roll up. Set aside on a tray, seam-side down, keeping them covered with clingfilm or a damp cloth to prevent them drying out. Repeat to make another 13 rolls. These can be done up to 3 hours in advance.

Heat some oil for deep-frying to 190°C. Deep-fry the rolls a few at a time for 5 minutes, making sure they don't touch each other, until crisp. Drain on kitchen paper and keep warm in a low oven while you cook the others. Serve with the herbs and lettuce leaves, and the nuoc cham for dipping.

Barbecued pork patties with noodles, chicken broth and salad greens
Bun cha

SERVES 4

Bun cha is a lunchtime dish of fine rice noodles served with caramelized barbecued pork patties, in a light fish sauce-based broth, perked up with small slices of lightly pickled mooli and carrot. It is frequently made with strips of marinated pork (photographed opposite) instead of the patties. The meat is cooked quickly so it slightly blackens on the outside while remaining moist inside, perfumed by the smoke created by the juices dripping onto hot coals. It is always accompanied by a basket of fresh herbs and crunchy shredded vegetables with chilli and garlic vinegar.

For the minced pork patties:
250g minced pork
1 tbsp fish sauce
1½ tsp palm sugar
10g garlic, finely chopped
75g shallots, finely chopped
¼ tsp freshly ground
    black pepper

For the broth:
1.5 litres *Asian chicken stock*
    (page 300)
4 tbsp fish sauce
4 tsp palm sugar

To serve:
1 small, crinkle-edged lettuce,
    leaves torn
Large handful of coriander,
    mint and Thai sweet basil
125g fresh bean sprouts
100g finely shredded kohlrabi
    or green papaya
4 tbsp rice vinegar
2 bird's eye chillies, sliced
10g garlic, finely chopped
250g fresh fine rice noodles or
    150g dried rice vermicelli
4 tbsp *Pickled carrot and mooli*
    (page 304)

Mix all the ingredients for the patties in a bowl with ½ teaspoon salt, then shape into about 40 thin patties, each roughly 2.5cm in diameter and weighing about 15g. Set aside for at least 1 hour to firm up and for the flavours to mingle.

Shortly before you are ready to eat, layer the salad greens in a shallow bowl: the lettuce, then the herbs, bean sprouts and kohlrabi or green papaya. Mix the rice vinegar with the chilli and garlic and pour into a small serving bowl. For the broth, bring the stock to the boil in a pan. Stir in the fish sauce and sugar and keep hot. Bring a pan of unsalted water to the boil for the noodles.

Light the barbecue; a disposable foil-tray barbecue would be ideal. Otherwise, heat a ridged cast-iron griddle just before you are ready to cook, then brush lightly with oil. Grill the pork patties in batches over a high heat for 1½ minutes on each side. If you have one, cook the patties in a clamp-style grilling wire, which makes turning them over much quicker and easier. Transfer to a plate and keep warm.

If using fresh noodles, drop them into the boiling water, leave for a few seconds to heat through, separating them into strands with chopsticks, then drain well. Tip into a warmed serving bowl. If using dried noodles, leave them to soak in the boiling water off the heat for 2 minutes, then drain well.

To serve, divide the pork patties between 4 warmed deep soup bowls and add a tablespoon of the pickled carrot and mooli. Ladle over the hot broth and take to the table with the noodles, salad leaves and chilli vinegar for guests to help themselves.

Turmeric-marinated chicken wrapped in lime leaves

SERVES 4

Didier Corlou, a Frenchman, has lived in Hanoi since the mid-1980s. He has a charming restaurant called La Verticale in Ngo Van So street, behind the French Embassy. It's an old colonial house with an airy bar at the top where you can enjoy views of Hanoi, surrounded by paintings and models of fishing boats from his native Brittany. When I talked to him he was a bit grumpy because an unnamed British TV chef had been quizzing him about where he could find even more outlandish Vietnamese food than snake and dog. I sympathized with him; there's a rather regrettable trend these days for finding extreme food in places where you're actually surrounded by some of the best dishes in the world. He cooked this exquisite chicken dish for us. I earnestly recommend you try it on a sunny evening. Marinating the chicken and then wrapping it in kaffir lime leaves gives it a beautiful fragrance.

500g skinned and boneless
    chicken thighs
½ tsp turmeric powder
1 tbsp lime juice
2 tbsp fish sauce
1 red bird's eye chilli,
    finely chopped
1 shallot, very finely chopped
½ tsp freshly ground white
    pepper
Vietnamese dipping sauce
    (*nuoc cham*, see page 303)
About 40 double-lobed
    kaffir lime leaves
Vegetable oil, for brushing

Cut the chicken thighs into roughly 2.5cm chunks. Put the turmeric, lime juice, fish sauce, chilli, shallot, white pepper and 1 teaspoon water into a bowl. Add the chicken, stir well, cover and leave to marinate for 1 hour. Meanwhile, soak 8 long bamboo skewers in cold water.

Preheat your barbecue and leave it to reduce to a medium-high heat. Mix the ingredients for the nuoc cham together and divide between 4 small dipping saucers.

Wrap each piece of chicken in a lime leaf and thread 5 onto each skewer. Brush with a little oil and barbecue for about 2–3 minutes on each side until just cooked through. Arrange on a serving plate and take to the table with the dipping sauce. To eat, slide the chicken off the skewers, discard the lime leaves, then dip into the nuoc cham.

Hanoi chicken noodle soup with bok choi
Bun thang

SERVES 6

*Though this is classed as a soup, to me it is more like a wet main-course noodle dish.
I noticed when filming in China recently that every time we stopped at a restaurant,
all the girls in the crew asked for noodle soup. Like pho (page 58), these bowls, filled
with steaming broth, gleaming noodles and delicate vegetables and herbs like bok choi,
spring onions, coriander and mint, are the best food in the world for those on a diet.
The real pleasure of this is its delicacy, but I always serve a bowl of nuoc cham on
the side for those who like a sharper and hotter taste.*

1 × 1.5kg chicken
25g peeled ginger, coarsely
    chopped
12 spring onions, trimmed
    and halved
20g garlic, sliced
2 star anise
10cm cinnamon stick
20g dried shrimp
½ tsp black peppercorns
450g bok choi
300g dried 1cm-wide flat
    rice noodles (bahn pho)
4 tbsp fish sauce
20g coriander leaves
20g mint leaves
*Vietnamese dipping sauce
    (nuoc cham, see page 303)
    or hot sauce (tuong ot toi),
    to serve*

Put the chicken, ginger, 8 of the halved spring onions, garlic, star anise, cinnamon, dried shrimp, black peppercorns and ½ teaspoon salt into a deep pan in which the chicken fits quite snugly, and cover with 2 litres of water. Bring to the boil, skimming off any scum as it rises to the surface, then lower the heat, cover and leave to simmer very gently for 20 minutes, turn off the heat and leave to cool down for 40 minutes. Cut the bok choi across into 7.5cm pieces and separate the stalks from the green leaves.

Lift the chicken onto a plate and leave until cool enough to handle. Drain the stock into a clean pan and discard all the flavourings except for the shrimp. Skin the chicken, pull the meat from the bones and break it into chunky pieces. Bring a pan of unsalted water to the boil. Add the noodles, turn off the heat, cover and leave to soak for 10 minutes or until tender. Separate the stalks from the leaves of the bok choi and finely shred them lengthways. Cut the leaves across into 3cm wide pieces.

Bring the stock back to the boil, add the bok choi stalks and simmer for 2 minutes. Add the bok choi leaves and cook for a further 2 minutes. Then stir in the fish sauce.

Drain the noodles and divide between 6 large, deep bowls. Top with the cooked chicken, reserved shrimp, remaining spring onions and the coriander and mint leaves. Ladle the steaming hot broth and bok choi over the top and serve with the nuoc cham or Vietnamese hot sauce.

Stir-fried water spinach with garlic and fish sauce

Rau muong xao toi

SERVES 4

You could use young sprouting broccoli stems for this, but there's nothing quite like water spinach – morning glory, as it's also called. As the chef who gave me this recipe explained, it's very important to drop it into boiling salted water briefly first, to set the colour and take some of the crunch out of the stems. If you miss out this stage, it can make the finished dish tough. This is, quite simply, one of the best vegetable dishes to come out of Southeast Asia.

2 tbsp vegetable oil
8 garlic cloves (50g), 6 left whole, 2 finely chopped
450g water spinach (morning glory) or tenderstem broccoli
1 tbsp fish sauce

Heat 1 tablespoon of the oil in a small pan over a medium heat, add the whole garlic cloves and stir-fry until they have taken on a good colour all over. Lower the heat, add 1 tablespoon water, cover and cook for a few minutes until they are sweet and tender. Set aside.

Cut away the root of the water spinach if necessary and then cut the remainder into approximately 7.5–10cm lengths. Drop into a large pan of boiling salted water, bring back to the boil, then drain, reserving some of the cooking water, and refresh under cold water. Drain well.

Heat the remaining oil in a wok over a medium-high heat. Add the chopped garlic and cook until it is just starting to change colour. Add the morning glory and the whole garlic cloves, increase the heat to high and stir-fry for 1 minute. Add the fish sauce, toss together briefly and tip onto a warmed serving dish. Serve straight away.

Prawn and potato fritters
Banh tom

SERVES 4–6/MAKES ABOUT 10 FRITTERS

This is yet another recipe from my voyage down the Mekong river. I was slightly intrigued by this dish because the combination of rösti-like potato and flour batter seems more Western than Asian, but perhaps this is something the Vietnamese adapted from their former colonizers, the French. It's very simple, but the combination of a few prawns, the shredded potato and the turmeric, formed into a fritter, is pretty irresistible as a drinks party nibble.

450–500g small potatoes, such as King Edwards or Maris Piper
16 large raw peeled prawns
Vegetable oil, for shallow frying
90g plain flour
60g rice flour
¾ tsp salt
½ tsp turmeric powder
¾ tsp baking powder

To serve:
1 soft, hothouse lettuce, broken into leaves, washed and dried
Handful of fresh coriander sprigs
Leaves from 1 small bunch mint
2 quantities *Vietnamese dipping sauce (nuoc cham, page 303)*

Peel the potatoes and cut them, on a mandolin or by hand, into thin matchsticks about 5cm long and 5mm thick. You should have 300g matchsticks. Cut each prawn in half lengthways.

Pour a generous 1cm of oil into a large, deep frying pan and leave to heat slowly over a medium heat.

Meanwhile, sift the plain flour, rice flour, salt, turmeric and baking powder into a bowl and gradually mix in 200ml cold water to make a smooth batter. Stir in the potato matchsticks and halved prawns.

Scoop up about 50ml (3 tablespoons) of the batter in a large metal spoon or ladle, trying to make sure you have about 3 pieces of prawn in among the potatoes, and slide the mixture into the hot oil to form a fritter that measures about 9cm across. Drop another 2–3 fritters, well spaced apart, into the oil and leave them to fry slowly for 3 minutes on each side until the potatoes are cooked through and the prawns are golden. Remove with a slotted spoon and leave to drain on plenty of kitchen paper. Keep each batch warm in a low oven.

When all the fritters are cooked, cut each one into 3 or 4 wedges, or leave your guests to do this themselves. Arrange the lettuce leaves, coriander sprigs and mint leaves onto a platter and divide the nuoc cham between 4–6 dipping saucers.

Instruct everyone to put one piece of fritter inside a lettuce leaf with a sprig or two of coriander and a couple of mint leaves, roll up and dip into the nuoc cham to eat.

Sizzling Saigon pancakes
Banh xeo

SERVES 4

These look like crisp stuffed omelettes. Traditionally there is no egg in the mixture;
instead it's made from rice flour, coconut milk, ground yellow mung beans and turmeric,
which gives the pancakes their yellow colour. However, I tried and tried to make them like
this and they broke up every time, so I resorted to adding egg and leaving out the mung
beans. You still get that lovely soft texture from the rice flour but they hold together properly.
The filling is a combination of pork and prawns, and, for crispness, bean sprouts and spring
onions. You serve each pancake cut into four and everyone wraps up a piece in a lettuce leaf
with a few fresh herbs, then dips it into nuoc cham, the classic sauce of lime juice, fish
sauce, sugar, ginger, garlic and chilli.

For the pancakes:
100g rice flour
2 eggs, lightly beaten
175ml coconut milk
½ tsp turmeric powder
½ tsp caster sugar
½ tsp salt
Vegetable oil, for cooking

For the pork and prawn stir-fry:
2 tbsp fish sauce
1 tsp palm sugar
200g pork fillet, thinly sliced
    into strips
150g (8) large raw peeled
    prawns, halved lengthways
2 tbsp vegetable oil
Freshly ground black pepper

For the filling:
225g bean sprouts
6 spring onions, halved and
    shredded lengthways

To serve:
1 soft lettuce, separated into
    leaves, washed and dried
2 large handfuls mixed fresh
    herbs, such as coriander,
    mint and Thai sweet basil
Vietnamese dipping sauce (nuoc
    cham, see page 303)

For the pancake batter, whisk the rice flour, eggs, coconut milk,
175ml water, turmeric, sugar and salt together in a bowl until
smooth. Cover and set aside in the fridge for 30 minutes. For the
stir-fry, mix the fish sauce with the sugar. Put the pork strips and
prawn halves into separate bowls, divide the fish sauce mixture
between them and mix together well. Set aside to marinate,
alongside the batter mixture.

Shortly before you are ready to start making the pancakes,
heat the oil for the stir-fry in a wok or large frying pan over a
medium-high heat. Add the pork and stir-fry for 1 minute. Add
the prawns and cook together for 1 minute, then season well
with black pepper. Set aside on a plate, cover and keep warm.

Remove the batter from the fridge and, if necessary, loosen
with a little water to the consistency of double cream.

Heat a 25cm non-stick frying pan over a medium heat. Add
1 tablespoon of oil, swirl the pan to coat the base and sides, then
pour in about 120ml of the batter mixture and swirl again to coat
the base of the pan. Sprinkle some bean sprouts and spring
onions to one side of the pancake, then a heaped tablespoon of
the pork and prawn stir-fry. Lower the heat to medium and leave
to cook for 2–3 minutes until the underside is crisp and golden,
the edges are brown and the top is pale yellow and set. Fold the
pancake in half over the filling, slide onto a plate, cut into 4
pieces and take it to the table. Repeat the cooking process to
make 3 more, serving each one as it is ready.

Duck braised in spiced orange juice
Vit nau cam

SERVES 6

I first tried this in the Viet Grill, a vibrant restaurant in the Kingsland Road in Shoreditch, East London. Mr Hieu, who owns the restaurant, has enormous enthusiasm for bringing intelligent Vietnamese cooking to London. Interestingly, he doesn't just cook the well-known classics; the menu contains a bit of fusion too, done from a Vietnamese point of view. But this is a classic dish: made aromatic with star anise and sour with lots of freshly squeezed orange. It needs a long slow braise, which was surprising to me at the time because I was then still unfamiliar with Vietnamese cooking in all its many forms.

1 × 2.5kg duck, jointed
    into 6 pieces
50g garlic, crushed
50g peeled ginger, thinly
    sliced
1 litre freshly squeezed
    orange juice
4 tbsp fish sauce
1 tbsp granulated sugar
5 star anise
4 red bird's eye chillies
2 fat lemongrass stalks,
    core finely chopped
Freshly ground black pepper
8 spring onions, white part
    only, plus 1 whole spring
    onion for garnish
½ tsp cornflour

Heat a heavy-based pan over a medium-high heat. Add the duck pieces, skin-side down, and leave to cook for 5–6 minutes until crisp and golden. Turn over and cook for a further 2 minutes until lightly browned. Lift onto a plate and set aside.

Pour all but 2 tablespoons of the oil from the pan into a bowl (save for another dish as it's great for frying). Return the pan to a low heat, add the garlic and ginger and cook gently for a couple of minutes until lightly golden.

Add the orange juice, fish sauce, sugar, star anise, chillies and lemongrass and season with black pepper. Return the duck to the pan, part-cover and leave to simmer for 1½ hours, turning the pieces of duck over from time to time. Cut the white parts of the spring onions in half, add to the duck and cook for a further 30 minutes until the duck is meltingly tender. Trim the remaining spring onion, cut in half and finely shred lengthways.

Lift the pieces of duck into a warmed serving dish and keep warm. Skim the excess fat off the top of the remaining liquid and leave it to simmer vigorously until reduced and concentrated in flavour. Mix the cornflour with 1 teaspoon water, stir in and simmer for 1 minute more. Pour back over the duck, scatter over the shredded spring onion and serve.

Vietnamese hotpot
Bo nhung dam

SERVES 4

I was lucky enough to participate in a Vietnamese hotpot dinner of immense complexity and for a large number of people. As far as I can remember, there was raw beef, prawns, chicken and squid, along with cabbage, quartered tomatoes, slices of pineapple and broccoli stems. You dipped the meat into a simmering broth with chopsticks, then put it on a lettuce leaf, added crunchy vegetables and fresh herbs, rolled it up and dipped it into the most delicious pineapple and chilli sauce. You can also offer everyone rice wrappers, if you have a sense of humour, because after a couple of glasses of wine, softening the wrappers in water and encasing everything in them will be amusingly tricky.

350g (18) large peeled raw
    prawns
350g skinned chicken thighs
    and breasts, cut into strips
3 little gem lettuces, leaves
    separated
10g mixed herbs (mint, Thai
    sweet basil and coriander)
40g cooked rice vermicelli
    noodles (page 312)
125g cucumber, cut into
    5cm long matchsticks
3 red bird's eye chillies, sliced
Pickled carrot and mooli
    (page 304)
20 × 22cm Vietnamese rice
    papers (banh trang),
    optional
Pineapple dipping sauce
    (page 303)

For the hotpot:
2 litres *Asian beef broth*
    (page 300)
1 tbsp rice vinegar
2 tsp palm sugar
15g garlic, crushed
4 lemongrass stalks,
    core thinly sliced
Freshly ground black pepper

Arrange the prawns and chicken on one large or 4 individual plates. Put the lettuce leaves, herbs, rice vermicelli, cucumber, chillies, pickled carrot and mooli in serving dishes, and the pineapple sauce in dipping saucers.

Put all the ingredients for the hotpot together into a wide shallow pan, wok or fondue pot. Bring to the boil and simmer for 5 minutes. Season with 1 teaspoon salt and black pepper to taste. Transfer the pan to some sort of lighted burner in the centre of the table and keep it at a gentle simmer.

Instruct your guests to take a prawn or strip of chicken and, using chopsticks, lower it into the simmering hotpot until cooked to their liking. Then to place this on a lettuce leaf, top it with a few strands of rice vermicelli, some crunchy vegetables or pickles and fresh herbs and roll up. The bundle should be dipped (sparingly) in the pineapple sauce and eaten.

If using rice papers, provide each diner with a plate on which is laid a folded napkin that has been soaked in cold water, and within reach place a shallow dish of hot water (of a suitable size to fit the rice papers). Instruct each guest to submerge a sheet of rice paper in the water until it has softened, about 1 minute, and then lay it out on the opened napkin. Then they should arrange a mixture of the filling ingredients in a line across the centre, fold the side closest to them over the filling, fold in the sides, then roll up away from them to form a neat parcel, which can be dipped into the pineapple sauce before eating.

Although it is not traditional to do so in Vietnam, I like to serve the broth alongside as a soup.

Grilled pork balls with peanut dipping sauce

Thit lon vien nuong co nuoc leo

SERVES 4

If you were very organized, unlike me, you could make a large batch of both the pork balls and the peanut sauce for a party. The pork balls freeze well and the peanut sauce will keep in the fridge for up to a week. If you are having friends around for a meal, I think it's essential to offer everyone something special when they arrive: what I rather irritatingly call a 'nibble', with the odd glass of champers. These are right at the top of my list. They are popular all over Vietnam in restaurants, on street stalls and in home kitchens, as well as all over northeast Asia, particularly Cambodia.

500g minced pork shoulder
100g shallots, finely chopped
20g garlic, finely chopped
2 tbsp fish sauce
1 tsp palm sugar
2 tbsp *Roasted rice powder*
    (page 299)
½ tsp freshly ground black
    pepper

For the peanut dipping sauce
    (nuoc leo):
1 tbsp seedless tamarind pulp
1 tbsp vegetable oil
20g garlic, crushed
100g roasted peanuts,
    finely ground
120ml coconut milk
2 tbsp fish sauce
1½ tbsp hoisin sauce
1 tsp palm sugar
1–2 red bird's eye chillies,
    finely chopped

Crisp lettuce leaves, coriander
    and mint leaves, sliced
    cucumber, and some *Pickled
    carrot and mooli* (page 304),
    to serve

For the meatballs, put all the ingredients together into a bowl with ½ teaspoon salt and mix together well with your hands. Flatten out in the bowl and chill for an hour.

For the peanut dipping sauce, mix the tamarind pulp with 4 tablespoons water and press through a sieve into a bowl. Discard the pulp left in the sieve. Heat the oil in a pan over a low heat, add the garlic and cook until lightly golden. Add the ground peanuts, 200ml water, coconut milk, tamarind water, fish sauce, hoisin sauce, sugar and chillies and simmer for about 30 minutes until reduced and thickened. Set aside. Meanwhile, soak 8 × 20cm bamboo skewers in cold water for at least 30 minutes.

Take a heaped tablespoon of the pork mixture and roll into balls using slightly wet hands. You should make about 24. Thread 3 balls onto each skewer.

Cook them on a barbecue or under the grill for 6–8 minutes, turning now and then, until cooked through. Meanwhile, warm through the peanut sauce, then pour into a small serving bowl. Arrange the skewers on a serving plate with the peanut sauce and serve with a salad plate of crisp lettuce, coriander and mint leaves, cucumber, and some pickled carrot and mooli.

Crab with tamarind sauce
Cua rang voi sot me

SERVES 2

Sometimes when we're filming, my endless quest to find exciting food has to be interrupted by the need to make programmes that reflect the quirkiness of where we are. On this occasion we were in a restaurant in Ho Chi Minh City, where the food was wonderful, particularly this crab and tamarind dish, and the interruption was brought about by an Englishman, Nathan Redfearn, who hires out vintage Italian Vespas and Lambrettas. He explained that skilled Vietnamese mechanics had kept these going for years, making their own spare parts when they couldn't get originals, and thus that you could find much older scooters and in better condition in Vietnam than you could in Europe. And although I didn't mention it on the programme, his wife Ly also happened to be Ho Chi Minh's great-granddaughter, which gave us all a little frisson.

1kg raw or cooked whole
   crabs, such as brown crab,
   mud crab or blue swimmer
Vegetable oil
1 tbsp seedless tamarind pulp
2 tbsp Chinese rice wine
15g garlic, finely chopped
1 small medium-hot red chilli,
   halved lengthways, seeded
   and finely chopped
1½ tsp palm sugar
1½ tbsp fish sauce
½ tsp crushed white pepper
6 spring onions, white part
   only, cut in 2.5cm pieces

To prepare the crabs, follow the instructions on page 42. Heat some oil for deep-frying to 190°C. Deep-fry the pieces of crab for 30 seconds, or until the exposed flesh becomes golden. Lift onto a tray lined with kitchen paper to absorb the excess oil.

Put the tamarind pulp, rice wine and 6 tablespoons water into a small bowl and mix together. Strain through a sieve into a bowl and discard the fibres left in the sieve.

Heat 2 tablespoons oil in a large sauté pan or wok over a medium heat, add the garlic and chilli and stir-fry for 30 seconds. Add the crab pieces, tamarind mixture, sugar, fish sauce and white pepper. Cover and simmer over a medium heat for 4–5 minutes or until the crab is cooked through. Add the spring onions, cover and cook for another minute.

Lift the pieces of crab out of the sauce and arrange on a warmed serving platter. Pour over the tamarind sauce and serve.

Chicken salad with Chinese cabbage, bean sprouts and Vietnamese mint

Ga xe phay

SERVES 4

Spicy, sweet and sour salads such as this appear all over Southeast Asia in one form or another. Here the salad is made with crisp Chinese leaf, although very finely shredded white cabbage could also be used. Universally, a Southeast Asian meal consists of one course only, with perhaps four or six constituent parts: always rice, a curry, a stir-fry, a hot vegetable dish and some pickles, and hopefully a salad like this. I say 'hopefully' because it's the element I always seek out – I love them. The classic herb for this salad is the long-stemmed rau ram, known to us as Vietnamese mint (Polygonum odoratum), which is increasingly easy to get hold of here in Asian grocers. In fact, for a long time I had it growing in my garden, until a harsh winter polished it off, but a combination of Thai sweet basil or coriander and mint works almost as well if you can't find it.

750g chicken thighs and/or breasts on the bone
100g shallots, very thinly sliced
400g Chinese leaf, core removed and the leaves finely shredded
100g bean sprouts
1 large carrot, halved across and finely shredded
15g Vietnamese mint, or a mixture of coriander and mint, or Thai sweet basil leaves, roughly chopped
40g roasted peanuts, coarsely chopped
Freshly ground black pepper

For the dressing:
3 tbsp fish sauce
3 tbsp lime juice
1 tbsp rice vinegar
2 tbsp caster sugar
1 tsp very finely chopped garlic
2 red bird's eye chillies, finely chopped

Put the chicken pieces into a saucepan with 1 teaspoon salt and enough water to just cover. Bring to the boil, lower the heat and leave to simmer gently for 20 minutes. Leave to cool in the cooking liquid. Then remove and discard the skin and bones and break the flesh into long thin strips. Save the stock for another dish.

Put the shallots into a large bowl, toss with ¼ teaspoon salt and leave to soften for 30 minutes.

Mix together the ingredients for the dressing.

Just before serving, add the chicken to the bowl of salted shallots with the Chinese leaf, bean sprouts, shredded carrot, herbs and most of the peanuts. Pour over the dressing, season generously with black pepper and toss together well. Mound the salad decoratively on a plate and serve sprinkled with the remaining peanuts.

Crisp fried sea bass with a tomato, chilli and kaffir lime leaf sauce

Ca chien sot chua ngot

SERVES 4

This is a typical way of cooking fish in the Far East. Fish would be far more popular in the UK if it were cooked like this. It is also very low in calories, in spite of being fried in oil, because the fish doesn't have an oil-absorbing coating of batter or flour. The dish beautifully combines crisp skin and delicate moist flesh with a robust but not searingly hot tomato sauce. I have found that the easiest and most efficient way to cook the fish for this dish is two at a time in a large, deep frying pan. Just take care to monitor the temperature of the oil during cooking, and use the back burner so that you are further away from hot splashes, and should the unthinkable happen and the pan tip over, oil will go over the cooker and not over you.

4 small whole sea bass, sea bream, snapper or sand whiting, each weighing approx. 350g

Vegetable oil, for deep-frying

25g shallots, finely chopped

10g garlic, finely chopped

1 tsp crushed dried chillies, or to taste

2 tbsp fish sauce

2 kaffir lime leaves, finely shredded

Juice of ½ lime

2 tsp palm sugar

200g chopped tomatoes, canned or fresh

1 tsp cornflour

4 spring onions, thinly sliced on the diagonal

Small handful of fresh coriander leaves

Freshly ground black pepper

Trim the fins off each fish, then pat dry inside and out with kitchen paper and season inside and out with salt and pepper.

For the sauce, heat 2 tablespoons of oil in a small, shallow pan. Add the shallots, garlic and chilli and fry for 1 minute. Add the fish sauce, kaffir lime leaves, lime juice, sugar and tomatoes and simmer for 3–4 minutes until the tomatoes are soft and have broken down into a sauce. Mix the cornflour with 1 tablespoon water. Add 60ml water to the pan, bring to a simmer, then stir in the cornflour mixture and simmer until the sauce is just thick enough to coat the back of a spoon. Remove from the heat and set aside.

Heat 1cm oil in a large, deep frying pan until it reaches 190°C. Add the fish, 2 at a time, and fry for 2½–3 minutes on each side until the skin is crisp and golden and the fish is cooked through to the bone. The flesh should lift away easily from the bones at the thickest part, just behind the head. Lift them onto a tray lined with kitchen paper and keep hot in a low oven while you cook the other 2.

Lift the fish onto warmed plates. Bring the sauce back to a simmer and then spoon over the fish. Scatter over the spring onions and coriander and serve.

Steamed rice papers with minced pork and cloud ear mushrooms
Banh cuon

MAKES 16

To me this is a hymn of praise to freshly ground white pepper and cloud ear mushrooms – which might sound a bit odd, so let me explain. White pepper is often nothing more than a tasteless powder found in pepper shakers, but my trip to Kampot revealed the spice to me as having a glorious, almost resinous, turpentine-like aroma, reminiscent of artists' studios. The cloud ear mushrooms, while not having a lot of flavour, have a pleasing cartilaginous texture, almost like pig's ears. And it's the combination of pork, pepper, pig's-ear-type texture and soft rice noodle cushions that makes this such a satisfying dish. These are traditionally made with fresh rice noodle sheets, but for ease I have made them with thin, dried Vietnamese rice papers (banh trang), and they are very successful.

30g dried cloud ear (wood ear) mushrooms
350g minced pork
1 tbsp fish sauce
1 tsp palm sugar
1 tsp freshly ground white pepper
2 tbsp vegetable oil
75g shallots, finely chopped
20 × 22cm Vietnamese rice papers (banh trang)
Crisp fried shallots (page 299)
Vietnamese dipping sauce (nuoc cham, see page 303)

Put the dried mushrooms into a large bowl, cover with plenty of hot water and leave to soak for 15 minutes. Drain well, cut away and discard any woody parts and then finely chop. Put them into a bowl and add the minced pork, fish sauce, sugar and white pepper. Mix together well and set aside for 15 minutes.

Heat the oil in a wok or frying pan over a medium heat, add the shallots and fry for 2 minutes until soft. Add the pork mixture and stir-fry for 1–2 minutes until it has all changed colour and is cooked through. Remove from the heat.

Prepare your steamer: ideally, a stackable one – bamboo or stainless-steel – because there are too many to steam in one layer. If you don't have one, you will have to do them in batches.

Place a clean damp tea towel on the work surface next to a shallow dish of hot water. Place a rice wrapper into the water and leave to soak for about 1 minute until silky, soft and pliable. Carefully lift it out and lay it on the damp tea towel. Place 2 generous tablespoons of the cooked pork mixture in a 10cm line across the centre of the wrapper, about 3cm up from the bottom edge of the disc. Fold the bottom edge over the filling, fold in the sides and then roll up. Place side by side on 2 heatproof plates that will fit inside the racks of your steamer. Repeat the process to make the remaining rolls.

Place each plate of pancakes onto each rack of the steamer, cover and cook for 4 minutes. Uncover, remove from the steamer and scatter with the crisp fried shallots. Serve hot with the nuoc cham.

85

RICK STEIN
VIETNAM

Clams with beer, black beans and ginger

SERVES 4

I kick myself for the fact that while in Hanoi I didn't get around to going to one of the Vietnamese pubs where they sell locally brewed beer called bia hoi. It's in all of the guidebooks as a must-do. This dish is designed to be made with lager-style beer. It is quite an uncompromising northern Vietnamese combination of fermented black beans, garlic, chilli, sesame oil and beer, just the sort of thing for sharing with a couple of friends while propping up the bar somewhere in the smart area of Hanoi.

1.75–2kg carpetshell clams
1 tbsp fermented salted
    Chinese black beans,
    rinsed
1 tsp white sugar
2 tbsp sesame oil
2 tbsp vegetable oil
20g garlic, finely chopped
25g peeled ginger, finely
    shredded
1 medium-hot red chilli,
    halved lengthways,
    seeded if you wish,
    then thinly sliced
120ml lager-style beer
Juice of ½ lime
6 spring onions, thinly sliced
Handful of coriander leaves,
    roughly chopped

Wash the clams well in fresh water. Put the salted black beans, sugar and sesame oil into a small bowl and mash into a coarse paste with a spoon.

Heat the vegetable oil in a large, deep pan over a medium-high heat. Add the garlic, ginger, chilli and black bean paste and stir-fry for about 10 seconds. Then add the clams and beer, turn up the heat to high, cover and cook for about 3 minutes, shaking the pan every now and then, until they have all opened.

Uncover the pan, add the lime juice and spring onions and mix well. Divide between warmed deep bowls, scatter over the coriander and serve straight away.

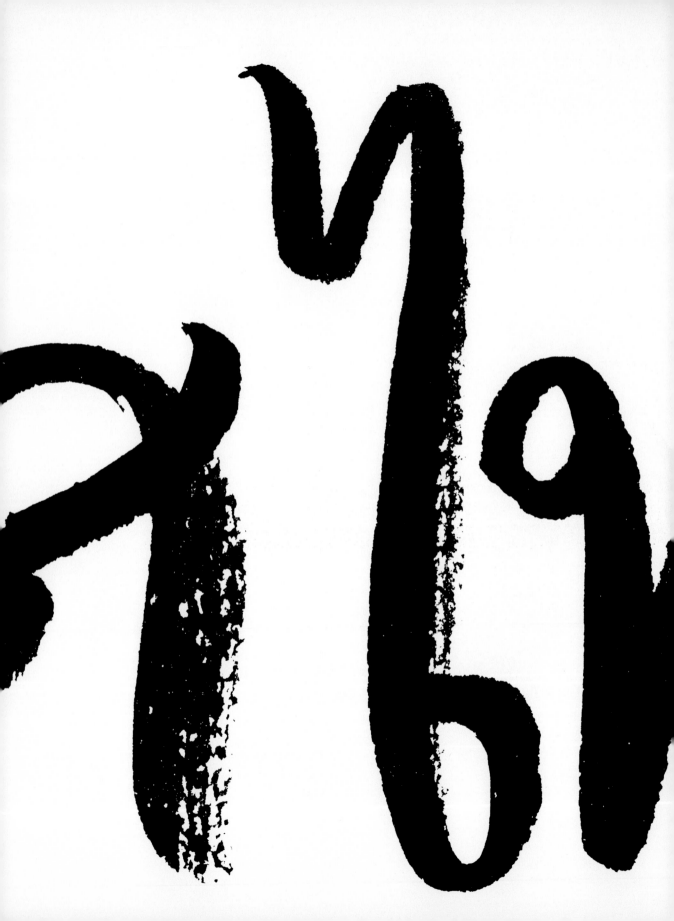

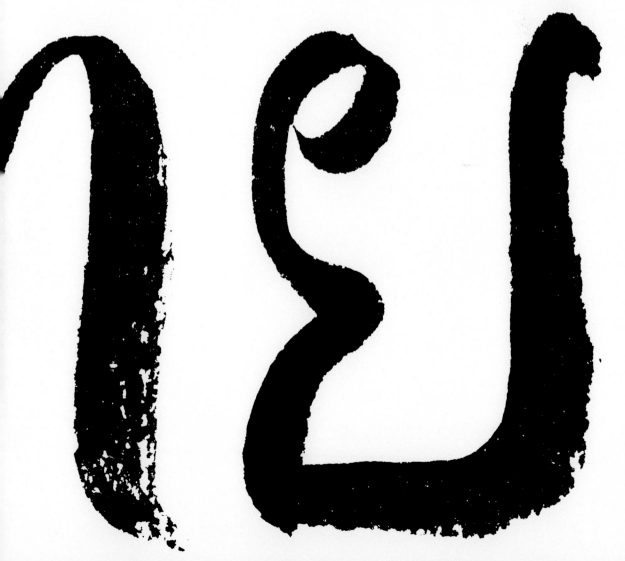

CHAPTER THREE ประเทศไทย

THAILAND

Thai food is where my enthusiasm for Southeast Asian cooking began. The excitement of tasting the flavours of lime, lemongrass, fish sauce, bird's eye chillies, palm sugar and coriander all together, this assault on the taste buds, was a rite of passage for me, like listening to Elvis Presley for the first time in the late 1950s or Led Zeppelin's 'Whole Lotta Love' in the late 1960s – sexy and full of dangerous energy. Thai food seemed just like that: a few chords delivered with great intensity. I was brought up on a cuisine of subtlety and understatement, and here was rock-and-roll food. Since then it's been a total love affair.

My first trip to Thailand seemed to only confirm my first impressions of this energy and excitement: blasting down the Chao Phraya river in a long-tail boat powered by a growling lorry engine on the way to a floating market in Bangkok; or watching in amazement as a train passed right through the centre of Mae Klong market, just outside of the city – all the stall holders quickly shifting their red chillies, green mangoes, boxes, trays, tins and buckets off the track and then straight back after the train had passed through! On either occasion, there would have been Crispy Mussel Pancakes served with sweet chilli sauce, cooked at breakneck speed.

My knowledge of Thai food has improved since then and I've come to realize it's much more sophisticated than those early impressions suggested, but it's still packed with punchy flavour. The most important aspect is, like everywhere in Asia, rice. In Thailand that means jasmine rice in the south and sticky rice in Chang Mai and the north. In no way is that definitive – not much is in cooking – it's just a guide. As with everywhere in the East, too, there's no formality of courses in a Thai meal. Most will consist of plenty of plain rice with a minimum of two or three dishes, which together provide a balance of salty, sweet, sour and spicy tastes. From the recipes in this chapter that might be the stir-fried green chicken curry; oyster omelette from the Sang Thai restaurant; green mango salad with pork, dried anchovies and deep-fried garlic. All the time I would be looking for a balance of flavours, textures and colours. Eating is a communal affair; the more people there are, the more interesting the meal becomes as more dishes are ordered. The same sort of food is served at lunch and dinner. I learnt to order enough dishes for each of us plus one extra. With all this there would be fish sauce (nam pla) and bird's eye chillies, either separately or in the same bowl. If there is any sort of food to be dipped, such as the stir-fried minced beef with lemongrass, chilli and roasted rice rolled in lettuce leaves, there will also be a dipping sauce. Personally I like a bowl of nam prik pao too. I can't get enough of the stiff mixture of grilled dried chillies, shrimp paste, garlic, palm sugar, tamarind and fish sauce.

The most popular way of eating food there is to use a spoon and fork. The spoon is for putting the food into your mouth, the fork just for pushing it onto the spoon. Interestingly, chopsticks are used for noodle dishes, a reminder of the strong Chinese influence in the cuisine.

Crispy mussel pancakes with bean sprouts
Hoi tod

SERVES 2

These are almost like a scrambled pancake, because batter, mussel meats, bean sprouts and egg are cooked very quickly together, and then served with a deliciously hot and sweet sauce. It's a bit like a Thai version of our fried eggs and brown sauce. We ate this at the Or Tor Kor market in Bangkok, which I was pleased to see had all the atmospherics – piles of colourful fruit and vegetables, alluring smells of cooking, interesting people – and was spotlessly clean too. And nowhere was this more important than at the stall selling the crispy mussel pancakes – because the last time we'd filmed such a dish, some years ago, we were all ill after eating it. Despite that, I remained enthusiastic about them because they were so very good.

2 tbsp Thai hot chilli sauce

2 tsp palm sugar

1kg fresh mussels in the
    shell, cleaned

25g rice flour or tapioca flour

15g plain flour

½ tsp baking powder

Vegetable oil, for frying

2 eggs

175g fresh bean sprouts

Freshly ground white or
    black pepper

Small handful of coriander
    sprigs, roughly chopped

Mix the chilli sauce with the sugar and set to one side.

You now need to remove the mussels from their shells by using heat but without cooking them too much. First wash the mussels and remove the beards. Heat a large pan over a high heat for 1 minute. Add the mussels and a splash of water, cover and cook for 1 minute, shaking the pan as they cook, until they have just opened. Immediately tip them into a colander, leave until cool enough to handle, then prise open the shells and remove the meats.

Sift the rice flour, plain flour, baking powder and a large pinch of salt into a bowl and whisk in 5–6 tablespoons water to make a very thin, smooth batter.

For the first pancake, heat 1 tablespoon of oil in a 20cm wide, non-stick frying pan over a high heat. Add half the batter and swirl it around to coat the base of the frying pan in a thin layer. Sprinkle the mussel meats on top, crack over an egg and roughly spread it over the surface of the pancake with the back of a wooden spatula. All this should take no more than about 1 minute, by which time the underside of the pancake will be crisp and golden. Cut the pancake roughly in half with the wooden spatula and flip over the pieces. The idea is not to overcook either the egg or the mussels. Immediately take the pan off the heat and slide the pancake pieces onto a warmed plate.

Return the pan to a high heat, add 1 teaspoon oil, half the bean sprouts and some seasoning and stir-fry for just 30 seconds so they retain their crispness. Tip alongside the pancake, sprinkle everything with some pepper and the coriander and serve with the sweetened chilli sauce. Repeat to make the second pancake.

David Thompson's yellow curry with prawns and lotus shoots

Geng leuong sai gung lai sai bua

SERVES 4

David Thompson probably knows more about Thai cooking than any other 'Westerner'. I remember first tasting his food in the mid-1990s in Sydney and thinking it was quite unlike any Thai food I'd ever tried before. He's spent years researching recipes, often just by talking to cooks, and amassing a wide body of knowledge. He cooked this profoundly aromatic curry for me in Bangkok. It's incredibly easy to do but you will be surprised by its complexity of flavour. David also runs the Thai restaurant at the Halkin Hotel in Belgravia in London, called Nahm.

450g large raw unpeeled prawns (about 16)

4 heaped tablespoons *Thai yellow curry paste* (page 302)

150g lotus shoots, cut into 5cm pieces, or pak choi pieces or fresh pineapple chunks

150ml coconut milk

1 tbsp lime juice

1 tbsp palm sugar

1 tbsp fish sauce

2–3 tbsp *Tamarind water* (page 299)

1 green bird's eye chilli, thinly sliced, to garnish

Peel the prawns, reserving the heads and shells. Put the shells into a pan with 450ml water and ½ teaspoon salt and bring to the boil, skimming off the scum as it rises to the surface. Leave to simmer for 15 minutes.

Strain 300ml of the prawn stock into a clean pan, add the curry paste and simmer for 1 minute. Add the lotus shoots, pak choi or pineapple and the prawns and simmer for another minute or two until the prawns have turned pink and are just cooked. Add the coconut milk, lime juice, sugar, fish sauce and tamarind water.

Spoon the curry into a serving bowl, sprinkle with the sliced green chilli and serve.

Stir-fried minced beef with lemongrass, chilli and roasted rice rolled in lettuce leaves

Laab neua

SERVES 4

The idea of putting finely chopped fish, meat or poultry into a salad leaf with lots of spicy, sour and salty aromatics is common throughout Thailand, Vietnam, Laos and Cambodia. It's a great combination: crisp lettuce with the slightly warm filling, dangerously hot with chilli, perfumed with lemongrass and with a satisfying crunchiness from the coarsely pounded grains of dry-roasted rice. It's worth pointing out that in Thailand these laabs, as they are called, are often made with raw pork, which I regard as a little risky, though I would be quite happy to make this with raw beef.

500g lean minced beef

1 tsp vegetable oil

2 tbsp *Roasted rice* (page 299)

5 fat lemongrass stalks, core very thinly sliced

75g shallots, very thinly sliced

1½ tsp crushed dried chillies

2 red bird's eye chillies, very thinly sliced

4 tbsp lime juice

3 tbsp fish sauce

30g mixed fresh mint and coriander leaves, roughly chopped

1 crisp lettuce, such as iceberg, romaine or little gem, broken into separate leaves

Loosen the minced beef a bit with a fork before you cook it. Then heat the oil in a wok or large, deep frying pan, add the beef and stir-fry it for 4 minutes until it loses its red colour and is only just cooked.

Tip the beef into a bowl and stir in all the other ingredients apart from the lettuce leaves. Spoon the mixture into the leaves, or leave people to do this themselves, and serve straight away.

Tom yam gung from the mushroom farm

SERVES 4–6

There must be more recipes for tom yam than you can shake a stick at, but this one is especially meaningful for me as I watched it being prepared on a farm, during the course of which visit I banged my head quite badly on a low beam in the oyster mushroom shed. We had been on an overnight train from Hua Hin, on our way to Phuket, and none of us had slept because it was a slow train that stopped every 12 minutes in yet another station, or so it seemed. Bleary, we'd had a breakfast of Thai chicken rice and then it was straight on to the farm. The mushroom shed was muddy and I smugly set off walking along a plank while David, the director, went squelching through the mud below. I said, 'Why are you walking in the mud when there's a—' by which time I'd damaged myself so obviously that we had to film the solicitous farmer's wife applying a plaster to my bald head to explain the large gash. The mushrooms were extremely important in the tom yam, as were the farm's own chillies and lemongrass. They might have grown the galangal and kaffir limes as well for all I know, it tasted so special. The main point of the recipe is the generous quantity of everything in it, particularly the coconut milk. This was one of those occasions when I marvelled at the unaffected friendliness of country people.

800ml coconut milk
200g shallots, thinly sliced
20g garlic, thinly sliced
2 red bird's eye chillies, thinly sliced
50g peeled galangal or ginger, thinly sliced
4 fat lemongrass stalks, core finely chopped
2 tsp palm sugar, or to taste
4 tbsp fish sauce
1½ tbsp *Nam prik pao* (page 303)
Juice of 2½ limes
300g large raw peeled prawns
250g oyster mushrooms, thinly sliced
2 plum tomatoes, thinly sliced
4 kaffir lime leaves
4–5 spring onions, trimmed and thinly sliced
Small handful of coriander leaves, to garnish

Put the coconut milk into a large pan with 300ml water and bring to a gentle simmer.

Put the shallots and garlic into a mortar or large mixing bowl (a food processor doesn't really work here) and pound with the pestle or the end of a rolling pin into a rough paste. Add the chillies, galangal and lemongrass and pound a little more until they begin to break up. Add the paste to the pan and simmer for 2 minutes.

Add the sugar, fish sauce, nam prik pao, lime juice and ½ teaspoon salt, followed by the prawns, mushrooms, tomatoes and kaffir lime leaves and simmer for 2 minutes. Stir in the spring onions, ladle into bowls and serve sprinkled with the coriander leaves.

Thai mussaman beef curry
Geng mussaman

SERVES 6–8

I found this curry at the hotel I was staying at during filming, the Royal Orchid Sheraton on the Chao Phraya river in the centre of Bangkok. The Thai restaurant there, called Thara Thong, was unexpectedly good, and I say this because you don't usually expect to find a really good restaurant in a giant hotel catering for international conferences. The chef was very much a home-style cook specializing in royal Thai cuisine, albeit with a no-nonsense head-chef demeanour about her. The mussaman curry is the Thai version of the Muslim curries of northern India, made really special by the use of fish sauce, shrimp paste, lemongrass and palm sugar, but the element I find beguiling is the black cardamom, which gives the curry a delightfully smoky flavour.

1.5kg blade or chuck steak, cut into 5cm chunks
600ml coconut milk
6 black cardamom pods
10cm cinnamon stick
300g waxy new potatoes, such as Charlotte
8 shallots
1 quantity Thai mussaman curry paste (page 302)
2 tbsp fish sauce
1 quantity Tamarind water (page 299)
1 tbsp palm sugar
75g roasted peanuts
Handful of Thai sweet basil leaves (optional)

For the curry, put the beef into a heavy-based pan with 350ml of the coconut milk, an equal amount of water, and the black cardamom pods, cinnamon stick and 1 teaspoon salt. Bring slowly to simmering point, part-cover leaving just a small 1cm gap for the steam to escape, and leave to cook gently for 2 hours, stirring now and then at the beginning of cooking, until the beef is almost tender.

Meanwhile, peel the potatoes and cut into 2.5 × 2.5 × 1cm pieces (using a crinkle-edged chip cutter if you wish). Peel the shallots and split them in half.

Uncover the curry and remove and discard the black cardamom pods and cinnamon stick. Stir in the rest of the coconut milk, the potatoes, shallots, curry paste, fish sauce, tamarind water and sugar and simmer gently, uncovered, for a further 25–30 minutes or until the potatoes, shallots and beef are tender. Stir in the peanuts, scatter over the basil if using and serve.

Stir-fried green chicken curry

Pat kiowan gai

SERVES 4 AS PART OF A THAI MEAL

The Poj Spa Kar restaurant is one of the oldest in Bangkok. It's the sort of place I love to discover in some far-flung part of the world where you get a slight sense that time has passed by the front door. It was there that I had this curry, and it is a different take on the more typical Thai green chicken curry in that the chicken is stir-fried and the curry sauce is much more concentrated and coats the chicken rather pleasingly.

100g small round green Thai aubergines or 100g piece of purple aubergine

1 tbsp vegetable oil

1 quantity *Thai green curry paste* (page 302)

100ml coconut milk

350g skinned chicken thigh fillets, cut across into 2cm-wide strips

1 tbsp fish sauce

2 tsp palm sugar

3 kaffir lime leaves

1 medium-hot red chilli, thinly sliced

45g pea aubergines (optional)

2 tsp lime juice

Large handful of Thai holy basil leaves

Slice each small green aubergine into 6 wedges or the purple aubergines into 2cm pieces. Heat the oil in a wok or large, deep frying pan over a medium heat. Add the curry paste and fry gently for 2 minutes until it starts to smell fragrant. Add 3 tablespoons of the coconut milk and the chicken pieces and stir-fry for 3–4 minutes. Add the rest of the coconut milk, the fish sauce and sugar and bring to a simmer.

Add the aubergines, kaffir lime leaves, sliced red chillies and pea aubergines if using and simmer for 10 minutes until the aubergines are tender and the sauce has reduced. Stir in the lime juice and basil and serve.

Roasted fish with a hot, sour and sweet sauce

SERVES 4

Instead of roasting, as in the recipe here, you could also barbecue or grill the fish, or even deep-fry it, as the Thais love to do, at 190°C for 5–6 minutes until crisp and golden. Whichever you choose, this dish is very simple and completely delicious. Serve it with steamed bok choi and Thai jasmine rice.

4 gurnard, sea bass, silver perch or sea bream, each weighing about 300–400g, scaled and trimmed
75ml fish sauce, plus extra if needed
Vegetable oil
50g shallots, thinly sliced
25g garlic, thinly sliced
3 red bird's eye chillies, thinly sliced
50g palm sugar
30g piece of seedless tamarind pulp

Preheat the oven to 220°C/Gas Mark 7. Make 3 slashes on either side of each fish and place them in a shallow dish. Pour over the fish sauce and work it into the slashes and the belly cavity. Pour the excess off into a small pan. You should be left with about 50ml but, if not, make up to this amount. Set the fish to one side while you make the sauce.

Heat 1cm oil in a medium-sized frying pan over a medium-high heat. Add the sliced shallots and fry them, stirring now and then, until they are crisp and golden. Lift out with a slotted spoon onto kitchen paper and leave to drain. Add the sliced garlic to the oil and fry until crisp and golden. Lift out and leave to cool and drain alongside the shallots. Add the sliced chillies and fry for a few seconds until lightly golden. Remove and leave to drain too.

Add the sugar, tamarind pulp and 4 tablespoons water to the small pan containing the fish sauce. Bring to the boil, stirring to break up the tamarind pulp and simmer for about 1 minute until thickened. Pass through a sieve into a bowl, pressing out as much liquid as you can with a wooden spoon. Return to a clean pan and set aside.

Transfer the fish to a lightly oiled roasting tin and roast for 12 minutes or until the flesh at the thickest part, just behind the head, is opaque and comes away from the bones easily. It should register 55°C on a thermal probe (page 315).

Bring the sauce back to a gentle simmer and stir in half the fried shallots, garlic and chilli. Lift the fish onto warmed plates and spoon over some of the sauce. Scatter over the remaining fried shallots, garlic and chilli, and serve.

Pad thai noodles from the Ghost Gate

SERVES 2–3 AS PART OF A THAI MEAL

This recipe comes from a slightly macabre part of Bangkok, the Ghost Gate. It's in Mahachai Road, a gate into the crematorium next to the Wat Saket temple where, traditionally, executed criminals were taken, but so too were lots of ordinary people. Unsurprisingly, at a location where family and friends would gather, food stalls sprang up, and now, even though the crematorium has long gone, the best pad thai noodles remain. This dish is originally from China and like so much street food all over Southeast Asia, it is not the cooking of the indigenous population but that of immigrants and itinerant workers, who, as in industrial revolution England, would have had few resources to cook at home. Justifiably, this is one of the most famous Thai dishes, a delicate balance of the soft noodles, the crunch of nuts and bean sprouts, and the yin and yang of sweet, salty, hot and sour flavours. I noticed there that the pad thai seemed a lot redder than other versions – this is simply the addition of sweet chilli sauce, which is why they are often considered sweeter than most other pad thai noodles.

10 large raw unpeeled prawns

3 tbsp vegetable oil

175g dried 5mm-wide flat rice noodles (banh pho)

15g garlic, finely chopped

½ tsp crushed dried chillies

2 eggs, beaten

2 tbsp fish sauce

2 tbsp Tamarind water (page 299)

2 tbsp sweet chilli sauce

1 tbsp palm sugar

1 tbsp dried shrimp

1 tbsp Thai preserved radish, chopped (optional)

50g roasted peanuts, coarsely chopped

4 spring onions, halved, then finely shredded lengthways

50g fresh bean sprouts

2 tbsp roughly chopped coriander

Lime wedges, to serve

Peel the prawns, reserving the heads and shells. Heat the oil in a pan over a medium-high heat, add the prawn heads and shells and fry gently for 2 minutes so the oil takes on the flavour of the prawns. Tip the contents of the pan into a sieve set over a small bowl and press out as much oil as you can with the back of a spoon. Set aside.

Drop the noodles into a pan of unsalted boiling water, turn off the heat and leave them to soak for 3–4 minutes or until just tender. Drain, rinse with hot water and toss with a few drops of oil to stop the strands sticking together.

Heat the prawn-flavoured oil in a wok over a high heat. Add the garlic, crushed dried chillies and prawns and stir-fry for 2 minutes until the prawns are just cooked. Pour in the beaten eggs and stir-fry for a few seconds until they just start to look scrambled.

Lower the heat, add the noodles, fish sauce, tamarind water, chilli sauce and sugar, and toss together for a few seconds until the noodles are heated through. Add the dried shrimps, preserved radish if using, peanuts, spring onions, bean sprouts and coriander and toss for another minute. Spoon onto warmed plates and serve with the lime wedges.

Oyster omelettes from the Sang Thai restaurant

SERVES 2

Oyster omelettes are a famous dish from Hua Hin on the western side of the Gulf of Thailand, about an hour and a half south of Bangkok. I've been there three times in the last twenty years, during which time it has become enormously more touristy, which people generally think of as a bad thing, but it isn't always. The cooking at Sang Thai is better than ever. In the late 1990s, for one of my earlier programmes, called Seafood Odyssey, I spent about three days endlessly cooking on the jetty at the front of the restaurant, all the while getting hot and sweaty. One of my fondest memories from that time is of the lightly salted fresh lime soda we needed to consume every 10 minutes, as well as a recipe for crispy fried fish similar to Crisp fried sea bass with tomato, chilli and kaffir lime leaf sauce on page 84. This omelette, which was a delight, and the fried prawns with crispy garlic and chilli on page 113, were the highlights of this visit.

4 Pacific oysters
3 medium eggs
1½ tsp fish sauce
2 tbsp vegetable oil
2 fat spring onions,
    thinly sliced on
    the diagonal
Thai hot chilli sauce,
    to serve

Open the oysters and remove the meat from the shells. Bring a small shallow pan of water to a simmer, add the oyster meats and simmer them for 10–15 seconds until they have just set. Drain, cut in half and set aside.

Break the eggs into a mixing bowl, add the fish sauce and whisk together really well.

Heat a 20cm frying pan (measured across the base) over a high heat, add the oil and swirl it around to coat the sides. Pour in the beaten eggs and tilt it slightly from side to side to spread out the egg. Scatter over the oysters and spring onions and fry for about 1 minute, moving the egg about with a fork now and then to allow the runny egg to run underneath the cooked egg.

When the omelette is lightly golden on the underside, and almost set on top, slide a fish slice underneath it and flip it over. Cook for a few seconds more, then turn it oyster-side up onto a warmed plate and cut it into quarters. Serve warm with some chilli sauce on the side.

Prawns with crispy garlic and chilli

SERVES 2

As with the oyster omelette on the preceding page, this comes from the Sang Thai in Hua Hin. There they make the dish with mantis shrimps, which we can't get, but ordinary prawns are just as good. I particularly like the dry spiciness of this dish. One of my earlier recipes, for salt and pepper prawns, just called for the prawns to be tossed in a mixture of salt, Sichuan pepper and black pepper after they'd been fried which, because the prawns were still in their shell, flavoured the meat perfectly as you peeled them. The same is true with the crisp garlic, chilli and lime leaf mixture here: dry and spicy. The trick is not to overcook the garlic in the hot oil.

50g garlic
150ml vegetable oil
2 red bird's eye chillies, thinly sliced
4 kaffir lime leaves
¼ tsp caster sugar
12 large raw unpeeled prawns

Put the garlic into a mini food processor and coarsely chop using the pulse button. Place a sieve over a heatproof bowl and have it close to hand.

Heat a wok over a medium heat, add the oil and then the garlic and fry for about 1 minute, stirring the garlic constantly so that it colours evenly, until it is just starting to go golden. Add the chilli and lime leaves and continue to fry for a few seconds more until all the garlic is lightly golden. Tip everything into the sieve set over the bowl and leave to drain. Spread the mixture over a baking tray lined with lots of kitchen paper and leave to cool and go crisp. Then tip into a small bowl and stir in the sugar and ¼ teaspoon salt.

Return the wok to a high heat, add 2 tablespoons of the reserved oil and the prawns and stir-fry them for about 1 minute until crisp and just cooked through. Remove from the heat, add the fried garlic mixture and toss together very briefly. Tip onto a warmed serving plate and serve straight away.

Deep-fried chicken wings with a chilli and tamarind sambal and a mango, mint, coriander and lime salad

I don't know whether these crisp fried chicken wings are authentically Thai. I've had them a few times in America, but they may be as Thai as chicken tikka masala is Indian. However, they are so good, I had to include them. It's important the sambal is thick so that when you coat the crunchy cooked wings with it, it doesn't soften the coating. If you can't get thick tamarind pulp, don't add the water.

1kg large meaty chicken wings
75g cornflour
75g rice flour
Vegetable oil, for deep frying
1 quantity *Chilli and tamarind sambal* (page 304)

For the marinade:
3 tbsp dark soy sauce
2 tbsp fish sauce
Juice of 1 lime
15g garlic, finely chopped
2 red bird's eye chillies, finely chopped
1 tbsp palm sugar

For the mango, mint, coriander and lime salad:
1 firm yet ripe mango, peeled and the flesh cut into pieces 1cm × 3cm
Juice of ½ lime
Small handful of mint and coriander leaves, roughly chopped

For the chicken wings, cut off the wing tips and freeze them for stock if you wish. Cut the remainder in two at the joint and make one long cut through the skin along one side of each piece.

Put all the marinade ingredients together in a bowl, add the wings and stir them around, working the marinade into the cuts with your fingers. Set aside for 1 hour, stirring 2 or 3 times.

For the salad, put the mango into a bowl, sprinkle with ½ teaspoon salt and set aside.

Heat some oil for deep-frying to 170°C. Sift the cornflour and rice flour together into a shallow baking tray. Lift the wings out of the marinade, add them to the flour and turn them over a few times until well coated.

Deep-fry the wings for 6–7 minutes until crisp, brown and cooked through. Lift them out onto a tray lined with plenty of kitchen paper and leave to drain briefly, then place them in a mixing bowl, pour over the sambal and toss together until well coated. Stir the lime juice, mint and coriander into the mango salad. Divide the mango salad between 4 deep bowls, top with the crispy chicken wings and serve.

Stir-fried yellow beef curry

SERVES 3–4

One of the joys of the way we make the TV series is that while researchers go out to the countries in question to find good locations and stories about restaurants, cooks and produce, a lot of what actually gets into the programme happens spontaneously while we are filming. This stir-fry is a case in point. We were driving along the back of Mai Khao beach, at the northern end of the island of Phuket. It's a beach famous for turtle egg-laying. David, the producer, and I spotted a photogenic palm-thatched beach shack and almost in unison said, 'There's got to be some good cooking there.' We have a nose for these things. The dish was cooked in two minutes flat. The beef was a little chewy but because it was so thinly sliced it didn't matter, and yet again I was charmed by the combination of chilli, lemongrass, lime juice, kaffir lime leaves, fish sauce and sugar. But above all I noticed the special taste of fresh turmeric, as opposed to powdered. As we were leaving, a pickup arrived, filled with supplies for all the beach places, so I had a look in the back — ginger, galangal, two-foot-long stalks of lemongrass, garlic chives, lovely purple-skinned shallots, plump garlic, kaffir limes and their leaves, jackfruit, coconuts, palm sugar: all the staples. It seemed a great way to shop for lunch.

600g sirloin steak,
    trimmed of all fat
3 tbsp vegetable oil
25g garlic, finely chopped
1 quantity *Thai yellow curry
    paste* (page 302)
8 kaffir lime leaves
1 tsp palm sugar
3 tbsp light soy sauce
2 tbsp lime juice
1 tbsp fish sauce
Handful of Thai sweet
    basil leaves
Freshly ground black pepper

Slice the piece of steak across into very thin slices.

Heat a wok over a medium heat. Add the oil, then the chopped garlic and stir-fry for a few seconds. Add the curry paste and fry for 2 minutes, stirring all the time, until the paste ingredients start to split away from the oil and the mixture smells aromatic.

Increase the heat, add the beef and kaffir lime leaves and stir-fry for 2 minutes, until all the beef has changed colour. Add the sugar, soy sauce, lime juice, fish sauce and 100ml water and bring to a simmer. Stir in the basil and some black pepper to taste and serve immediately.

Duck noodle soup

SERVES 6

This was a star turn at Or Tor Kor market in Bangkok. David, the director, and I had two bowls each, so excited were we by it, but that led me to think it would be better to serve it as a main course than a soup. This recipe is destined for our café in Padstow.

1 × 2.25kg oven-ready duck
2 tbsp hoisin sauce
Ingredients for *Duck broth*
    (page 300)
Freshly ground black pepper

For the soup:
2 tbsp vegetable oil
40g garlic, thinly sliced
300g dried fine egg noodles
3 tbsp fish sauce
1 tbsp dark soy sauce
4 tsp rice vinegar
1 tbsp palm sugar
1 red bird's eye chilli,
    thinly sliced
15g peeled ginger, finely
    shredded
400g fresh bean sprouts
1 bunch coriander,
    roughly chopped
6 fat spring onions, halved
    lengthways and thinly
    sliced on the diagonal

To serve:
2 red bird's eye chillies,
    thinly sliced
3 tbsp fish sauce
3 tbsp rice vinegar
Dried chilli flakes
Palm sugar

Preheat the oven to 230°C/Gas Mark 8. Pull out and discard any excess fat from the cavity of the duck. Brush 2 teaspoons of the hoisin sauce inside the cavity and season with salt and pepper. Place the duck on a rack in a roasting tin and brush all over with the remaining hoisin sauce and season with salt. Roast for 20 minutes, then lower the temperature to 180°C/Gas Mark 4 and continue to roast for 1 hour 10 minutes, pouring off the fat from the roasting tin into a bowl every 20 minutes or so, until the duck is fully cooked and the juices run clear when the thickest part of the thigh is pierced. Leave to cool. Then cut off the legs, and slice away the breasts in one piece. Pull the meat off the duck legs in bite-sized pieces and use the bones, with the remainder of the duck carcass, to make the broth (page 300). Put the leg meat and breasts onto a plate, cover and chill until required. Bring back to room temperature before using.

For the soup, bring a pan of lightly salted water to the boil. Heat the oil in a small frying pan over a medium heat, add the garlic and fry until crisp and golden. Lift out with a slotted spoon onto kitchen paper. Drop the noodles into the boiling water, turn off the heat and leave to soak for 4 minutes. Drain, mix with a little oil and set aside. Thinly slice the duck breasts.

Bring another pan of water to the boil. Put the duck broth into a pan and bring to the boil. Reduce to a simmer and add the fish sauce, soy sauce, rice vinegar, sugar, chilli and ginger. Leave for 5 minutes to allow the flavours to marry.

For the flavourings to serve alongside, mix 1 sliced bird's eye chilli with the fish sauce and the other with the rice vinegar. Put these and the chilli flakes and sugar into 4 small serving dishes.

Divide the small pieces of duck meat from the broth between 6 warmed, deep, Thai-style soup bowls. Drop the noodles and bean sprouts into the boiling water, then drain immediately and divide between each bowl. Top with the duck breast and leg meat, fried garlic, coriander and spring onions. Pour over the boiling hot duck soup and serve with the flavourings.

Chicken, coconut and galangal soup with chilli and kaffir lime leaves
Tom kha gai

SERVES 4

This is generally held to be the chicken counterpart to the classic hot and sour soup, tom yam gung. Apart from making the Asian chicken stock for it, it is very easy indeed and utterly rewarding. I made this for my sons in my cottage at Padstow and they said, 'This is the real thing, isn't it, Dad?' This soup should also contain coriander root but this is difficult to find in this country. However, if you can get it, use 1 tablespoon in the spice paste.

75g shallots, roughly chopped
40g garlic, roughly chopped
6 fat lemongrass stalks, core roughly chopped
40g peeled galangal or ginger, roughly chopped
800ml coconut milk
1.2 litres *Asian chicken stock* (page 300)
300g chicken thigh fillets, cut into thin slices
8 kaffir lime leaves
4–6 red bird's eye chillies, thinly sliced
6 tbsp fish sauce
6 tbsp lime juice
Small handful of coriander leaves, to garnish

Put the shallots, garlic, lemongrass and galangal into a mini food processor with 3 tablespoons of the coconut milk and grind to a smooth paste.

Put the chicken stock into a pan and bring to a simmer. Add the paste and leave to simmer vigorously for 3 minutes. Pass through a sieve into a bowl, pressing out as much flavour as you can, then return to the washed-out pan and bring back to a simmer.

Add the chicken to the pan with the kaffir lime leaves and ½ teaspoon salt and simmer for a further 2 minutes until the chicken is cooked. Add the rest of the coconut milk, the chillies, fish sauce and lime juice and bring back almost to a simmer. It should taste sour, salty and hot. Serve straight away in warmed bowls, sprinkled with the coriander leaves.

Hot and sour squid salad with chilli, lime leaf, mint and coriander

Yam pla muk

SERVES 4–6

This is a refreshing salad that's remarkably low in calories – there's no fat in it whatsoever. I'm not usually in favour of boiling squid but in this recipe it is dropped into lightly salted boiling water and left for only thirty seconds so that it just cooks through and doesn't toughen up in any way. Also, by scoring it on one side into a diamond-shaped pattern, the wide strips curl up attractively. Presented simply on a white plate with lots of greenery – small lettuce leaves, mint and coriander and shredded spring onions – and a generous sprinkling of sliced red chilli, which accentuates the dazzling whiteness of the squid, it looks very appetizing. You can also make this salad with beef. Rub a 3cm thick, 300g sirloin steak with a little oil, season and cook on a ridged cast-iron griddle over a high heat for 1½ minutes on either side for rare. Remove and leave to cool, then cut across into thin slices. Scatter over the top of the salad (together with a few halved cherry tomatoes if you wish), spoon over the dressing and serve.

400g medium-sized prepared squid or cuttlefish (pouches about 18cm long)
1–2 small lettuces, such as little gem or romaine, broken into pieces
2 spring onions, halved and finely shredded
Small handful each of mint and coriander leaves

For the dressing:
3 tbsp lime juice
3 tbsp fish sauce
1 red bird's eye chilli, thinly sliced
1 tsp palm sugar
10g garlic, finely chopped
2 fat lemongrass stalks, core finely chopped
1 kaffir lime leaf, finely shredded

Slit the body pouches of the squid along one side, open them out flat and score the inner surface into a fine diamond pattern with the tip of a small, sharp knife. Cut the squid pouches lengthways into 4 wide strips, and then each strip across into 3 pieces. Score the fins in the same way and cut each one in half. Separate the tentacles into pairs.

Bring 1.5 litres of water and 2 teaspoons salt to the boil in a pan. Add the pieces of squid a small handful at a time and cook for 30 seconds until it has just turned white and opaque and curled up. Remove with a strainer, rinse briefly under cold water, tip into a colander and leave to drain well. Repeat with the remaining squid, bringing the water back to a gentle boil each time. When all the squid is cooked, leave it to cool to room temperature.

Mix the ingredients for the dressing together in a bowl.

Scatter the lettuce leaves, shredded spring onions and herbs over the base of a serving plate. Mix the dressing into the squid and then spoon it over the top of the salad with the excess dressing. Serve straight away.

Steamed clams with nam prik pao

SERVES 4

In the Basic Recipes chapter you will find a recipe for nam prik pao. This is the most important sauce in Thailand, made by pounding together toasted red chillies, dried shrimp and toasted shrimp paste with garlic, tamarind, fish sauce and sugar. It has a depth and ruggedness unsurpassed in any cuisine, dark, hot and pungent, and is the way in which so many Thai dishes are given intense and robust flavour. This clam dish is no exception, made by steaming clams with nam prik pao, lemongrass, galangal, chilli and Thai holy basil. The result, while hot and aromatic, still allows the taste of the freshly opened clams to shine through.

25g peeled galangal or
 ginger, finely shredded
4 tbsp Nam prik pao
 (page 303)
2 tbsp palm sugar
4 tbsp Tamarind water
 (page 299)
2kg small clams, such
 as carpetshell clams,
 scrubbed clean
4 fat lemongrass stalks,
 core finely chopped
1 medium-hot red chilli,
 halved lengthways,
 seeded and thinly sliced
4 kaffir lime leaves, finely
 shredded
Large handful of Thai
 holy basil leaves

Put the shredded galangal or ginger into a mortar or coffee mug and bruise with the pestle or the end of a rolling pin. Mix the nam prik pao, sugar and tamarind water in a small bowl.

Heat a large, dry pan over a high heat, add the clams, cover and cook for 1 minute. Uncover, add the galangal, lemongrass, chilli and half the shredded kaffir lime leaves. Cover again and shake over a high heat for another 1–2 minutes until the clams have opened.

Pour the nam prik pao mixture over the clams and stir together well. Add the Thai holy basil and the remaining kaffir lime leaves, stir together briefly and serve.

Grilled seafood with a coconut and fish sauce marinade

SERVES 4

Once again the versatility of fish sauce is evident in this delicious way of preparing shellfish for grilling. You simply marinate it in a mixture of fish sauce, coconut cream and a little sugar, which enhances the natural sweetness of prawns or lobster. I was walking through the excellent Or Tor Kor market in Bangkok with David Thompson, who is probably the world expert outside Thailand on Thai food, when he picked up a couple of mantis shrimps and gave me this quick recipe. Excellent with some ice-cold Singha beer.

16 large raw unpeeled prawns
    or 2 × 750g live lobsters
4 tbsp coconut cream
    (or the thick 'cream'
    from the top of a chilled
    can of coconut milk)
2 tbsp fish sauce
½ tsp sugar

If using prawns, make a slit through the shell along the underbelly of each one and put them into a bowl. If using live lobsters, put them into the freezer 2 hours before cooking. This will kill them painlessly. Then lay them belly-side down on a board, with the legs pushed out to either side, and cut them in half, first through the middle of the head between the eyes. Turn them around and finish cutting them in half through the tail. Remove the stomach sac, a slightly clear pouch that will now be in halves, from each head section, and remove the dark, thread-like intestinal tract from each tail section.

Mix the coconut cream with the fish sauce and sugar. If using prawns, add them to the bowl and work the mixture into the cuts in the shell with your fingers. If using lobsters, brush the mixture generously over the meat. Set aside for up to 15 minutes.

Preheat a grill or barbecue to medium-high (a disposable foil-tray barbecue would be ideal). Cook the prawns for 3 minutes, turning them once, or the lobsters shell-side down for 8–10 minutes, then serve at once.

Green papaya salad
Som tum

SERVES 1

I originally wrote a recipe for this in Seafood Odyssey, which came out over ten years ago, and I thought I would probably be able to come up with a newer version after my many subsequent trips to Thailand. But I'm pleased to say it is what it is. It's such a classic there's nothing really to add or take away: slightly acidic crunchy papaya, green beans, dried shrimp, peanuts, tomatoes, dressed with garlic, chilli, palm sugar, tamarind, fish sauce and lime.

1 small green papaya
1 tsp palm sugar
Pinch of chopped garlic
Pinch of finely chopped
    red bird's eye chilli
5 × 10cm pieces of snake
    bean or 5 French beans,
    halved lengthways
A few roasted peanuts,
    coarsely chopped
Pinch of chopped dried
    shrimp
1 tbsp fish sauce
1 tbsp *Tamarind water*
    (page 299)
4 cherry plum tomatoes,
    halved
Juice of 1 lime

Peel the papaya and shred it using a mandolin, shredder (page 315) or a large, sharp knife. Work your way round the fruit until you get to the core and seeds, which you discard. Moisten the palm sugar with a little cold water.

Put the garlic, red chilli and green beans into a mortar or mixing bowl and lightly bruise with the pestle or the end of a rolling pin. Add the sugar, peanuts, shrimp, fish sauce, tamarind water, tomatoes and lime juice and bruise everything once more, turning the mixture over with a fork as you do so.

Add a good handful of the shredded papaya, about 50g, turn everything over and bruise one last time. Serve straight away.

Thai fish curry, 'jungle' style
Geng Par Pla

SERVES 4

Two strong memories from a recent visit to Phuket: first, an enormous picture on a billboard just outside the airport of Keith Floyd holding a glass of champagne, dressed in his chefs whites with rather improbable deep-red cuffs, sort of Paul Smith gone wrong; and second, a trip through the market and a discussion about the most common curry pastes in Thailand. I was intrigued by one, called a jungle curry paste, which I discovered was searingly hot and used in curries without coconut milk. It's the sort of paste favoured by rural communities who don't have access to the sophisticated range of ingredients available in the cities. By chance, a bit later on, I found Keith's version of a jungle curry paste in his book Far Flung Floyd, where he describes it as being used in this part of the world for curries made with 'snake, frog, wild boar, assorted birds and unspecified furry creatures'. I've always admired his robust sense of humour. And, I might add to the list, it is also extremely good with fish. It is uncompromisingly hot.

500g boneless fish fillets, such as sea trout, salmon, monkfish, ling, blue-eye trevalla, john dory or a combination
1 tbsp vegetable oil
1 quantity Thai jungle curry paste (page 302)
250ml Asian chicken stock (page 300)
1 tbsp fish sauce
2 tsp palm sugar
2 tbsp Tamarind water (page 299), or lime juice
4 tbsp Crisp fried shallots (page 299)
Handful of coriander leaves, roughly chopped

Cut the fish fillets into 1.5cm-thick slices. Heat the oil in a deep-sided frying pan over a medium heat. Add the jungle curry paste and fry for 2–3 minutes until it smells nicely aromatic. Add the chicken stock and simmer for 1 minute. Stir in the fish sauce, sugar and tamarind water.

Add the pieces of fish to the pan skin-side up, spoon over some of the sauce if they are not quite submerged and simmer for 3–4 minutes or until just cooked through.

Stir in the crisp fried shallots and adjust the fish sauce, sugar, tamarind water and seasoning to taste – it should taste chilli-hot, salty and sour. Scatter over the coriander and serve straight away.

Green mango salad with pork, dried anchovies and deep-fried garlic

SERVES 2

This is rather like a green mango salad we filmed at the Sala Bai cookery school in Siem Reap in Cambodia. The salad is traditionally made with lesser galangal, which is not always easy to come by, but if you can get hold of it, it adds an almost menthol flavour to the finished dish. This is quite chilli-hot. If you'd prefer it milder, use a medium-hot red chilli instead and seed it first.

1 green mango
50g *Vietnamese cooked belly pork* (page 300)
Vegetable oil, for shallow-frying
15–20g dried anchovies (silverfish), or to taste as they are quite 'fishy'
15g peeled lesser galangal or ginger, finely shredded
50g shallots, very thinly sliced
1½ tbsp *Crisp fried garlic* (page 299)
25g roasted peanuts, coarsely chopped
Small bundle of Thai sweet basil leaves, finely shredded

For the dressing:
1½ tbsp lime juice
1½ tbsp fish sauce
½ tsp palm sugar
1 red bird's eye chilli, finely chopped

Peel the green mango and finely shred the flesh away from either side of the thin flat stone in the middle, using either a traditional green papaya shredder (page 315) or a mandolin. You should be left with about 175g. Cut the cold belly pork across into thin slices and then the slices into thin strips.

Heat 1cm oil in a small frying pan, add the dried anchovies and fry them for a few seconds until richly golden. Remove them with a slotted spoon and leave to drain on kitchen paper. Then crumble into small pieces.

Put the green mango into a bowl with all the other ingredients and toss together well.

Mix the ingredients for the dressing together in a small bowl, toss through the salad and serve straight away.

Hainanese chicken rice
Khao man gai

SERVES 4–6

This chicken rice, like babi guling, the slow-roasted pig from Bali on page 177, is a dish I would cross continents for. It appears in various forms all over the Far East, especially Malaysia and Singapore. There are people who wouldn't let a day go by without a plate of chicken rice, and I can perfectly understand why. It's the moistness of the chicken that gets to you; that and the texture of the rice, made silky by first being fried in some of the chicken fat from the cavity of the bird.

1 × 1.5kg free-range chicken
Freshly ground white pepper
25g peeled ginger, thickly
    sliced
15g garlic cloves
6 spring onions, trimmed
Ginger and chilli dipping sauce
    (page 304)
½ cucumber, peeled, halved
    lengthways and sliced
Handful of roughly chopped
    fresh coriander

For the rice:
1 tbsp vegetable oil
350g Thai jasmine rice,
    rinsed
1 tsp sesame oil
1 pandan leaf, tied into
    a knot (optional)

Remove the fat from the cavity of the chicken and set aside. Season the chicken inside and out with salt and white pepper. Lightly bruise the ginger, garlic and 4 of the spring onions with a rolling pin and push inside the cavity. Set aside for 1 hour.

Bring 4–5 litres of water (enough to cover the chicken) to the boil in a large, deep pan in which the chicken will fit snugly. If the pan is too large, the amount of water needed to cover the bird will produce a watery stock. Immerse the chicken in the water, bring almost back to the boil and leave to simmer very gently for 15 minutes. Turn off the heat, cover and leave for 30 minutes, then remove the chicken, cover and set it aside. Skim the fat from the stock and boil until reduced to 1.2 litres.

For the rice, heat the vegetable oil in a medium-sized pan over a medium heat. Add the reserved chicken fat and leave for 2–3 minutes until melted. Remove from the heat, and lift out and discard any bits. You should be left with about 3 tablespoons fat. Return to a medium heat, add the rice and stir-fry for a couple of minutes to coat the grains. Add 600ml of the hot chicken stock and bring back to the boil. Add the sesame oil and ½ teaspoon salt. Stir once, add the pandan leaf if using, cover, lower the heat and leave to cook for 10 minutes. Turn off the heat and leave to sit, still covered, for 10 more minutes, while you remove the chicken from the bones and cut it up into small pieces. Halve the remaining spring onions and thinly shred them lengthways. Divide the ginger and chilli sauce between dipping bowls.

Spoon some of the cooked rice onto each plate, top with the cooked chicken and garnish with the cucumber. Reheat the remaining chicken stock and season to taste. Ladle into small soup bowls and sprinkle in the coriander and the shredded spring onion. Place a plate of chicken rice, dipping sauce and a bowl of soup in front of each person, and tuck in.

CHAPTER FOUR

مليسيا

MALAYSIA

I would like to be able to sum up the cuisine of Malaysia but it's practically impossible. Malaysia is a crossroads where so many different nations have had influence – Indians, Chinese, Portuguese, Dutch, British, Indonesian, Thai and Burmese – that no clear identity arises. This leads to a wonderfully diverse cuisine whose main constituent parts are Malay, Indian, Chinese, nyonya and Eurasian. You're never quite sure what is what. I remember an Indian restaurant in Penang called the Hameediyah, where a chef was making charcoal-scented naan bread and chicken in a tandoor at the front. There were numerous Indian dishes like biryani, tarka dal and mutton korma, but in addition they had a beef rendang, deep brown in colour and rich in coconut milk, cooked down to a thick sauce aromatic with spice and lemongrass. The restaurant specialized in the Malaysian meal, nasi campur, where coconut rice is served with various curries, satays, samosas, sambals and bhajis, normally on a banana leaf. To drink there was Indian lassi and chai, tea sweetened with condensed milk, a local iced cordial made with fresh nutmeg, and, to complete the multinational influence, Coca-cola.

The Hameediyah was packed all day with Malaysians indulging in their most important activity: eating little and often through the day. I have a friend who lives on the island of Langkawi, Narelle McMurtie; she's Australian, but when you've lived there for a while the food quest takes over. Gastronomic trips with her were a whirlwind of tasting sensations. She took me to a lunch restaurant called Siti

Fatima near the resort hotel she owns, the Bon Ton. We arrived at midday to find about eighty dishes already laid out on tables spread with pink and green plastic tablecloths. There was a hot and sour fish curry with tamarind; another fish dish, ikan bakar, large mackerel split open and spread with a spice paste of chilli, garlic, turmeric, shrimp paste and ginger and grilled over charcoal; there was a beef curry, deep red and marinated with dark soy, honey and five-spice powder, like the Chinese barbecued pork, char siu. There were numerous salads. I recall one with bean sprouts and coconut and a green mango one with mint and coriander. I remember a variety of hot chilli sauces, such as sambal belacan, pounded chilli and shrimp paste, and sambal oelek, chilli with vinegar and salt. There was ayam pechak, fried ginger, chilli and coconut chicken, and an enormous bowl of herbs gathered from the jungle. You chose as many things as you liked, added steamed rice and paid. It was about two pounds. This was all Malay cooking, not Chinese, Indian or nyonya.

To me Malaysia is a perfect introduction to the food of Southeast Asia. There's such a variety of vibrant food, it's easy to get around and the people have their priorities right: an everlasting love affair with food. It's where I go for holidays.

Malaysian fish curry with tomato and okra

SERVES 4

In Malaysia and Singapore, this is normally fish head curry. Initially I was keen to include it exactly like that but gauging from the reaction of many of my friends, if I didn't modify the recipe, it would never be used. So I've written it using whole mackerel instead; it would work equally well with some small bass or even gurnard too. It looks really special as I've separately made a basic curry, with its deep orange colour from fresh turmeric and kashmiri chillies, and then poured it over the fish laid out head to tail in a roasting tin. But if you are adventurous, do try making this with fish heads, such as salmon, cod or, if you can get them, grouper. Some of the meat in the head of a fish is extraordinarily good, especially that found in the cheeks, and I confess to an enthusiasm for fish eyes too. I can only say they are deliciously fatty. Try asking your fishmonger to save you some fish heads. They are always available if there is a Chinese community near by. Per person you will need a head weighing about 300g, but if they are bigger than this get your fishmonger to halve them with a cleaver so they sit in the sauce easily and cook evenly.

4 × 300g prepared mackerel
3 tbsp vegetable oil
250g onion, halved and
    thinly sliced
1 quantity *Fish curry paste*
    (page 301)
24 curry leaves (about 2 sprigs)
1 × 250g aubergine
400ml coconut milk
2 red and 2 green medium-hot
    chillies, cut on the diagonal
    into 1cm-thick slices
175g okra
3 medium-sized tomatoes,
    each cut into 6 wedges
1 quantity *Tamarind water*
    (page 299)
Leaves from a small bunch
    of coriander

Preheat the oven to 200°C/Gas Mark 6. Sprinkle the fish with salt inside and out and set aside for 20 minutes. Meanwhile, heat the oil in a large pan, add the onion, sprinkle with salt and fry until it begins to brown.

Lower the heat, add the curry paste and curry leaves and continue to fry gently for another 2–3 minutes, stirring occasionally. Meanwhile, slice the aubergine lengthways into 4 wedges, then each wedge across into slices 1cm thick. Add the coconut milk, 500ml water, chillies, okra, aubergine, tomatoes, tamarind water and 2 teaspoons salt and simmer for 15 minutes.

Put the mackerel side by side in a deep roasting tin in which they fit quite snugly. Pour over the curry sauce (it should almost cover the fish), cover tightly with foil and transfer to the oven. Bake for 30–35 minutes, until the fish are cooked through. Remove, season to taste with more salt if necessary, and garnish with a sprinkling of coriander leaves.

Penang Road laksa
Laksa asam Penang

SERVES 4

I went to a Penang Road laksa restaurant because the foodie who took me there, Fuan, had said it was the best in Georgetown. The night before, he had taken me to Mama's nyonya restaurant, where we had the prawns on page 146. I was slightly in awe of Fuan so when, just before we tasted the laksa, he said, 'I don't really care for the Penang version of laksa,' I thought it was going to be awful. But one taste and I said to him: 'I can't believe you don't like this.' He then agreed he'd been a bit hasty in his judgement. We got on fine after that. I've included both Singapore laksa and this one in the book because they are both so different, and so special. What I love about this one is the intensity of what they call the 'laksa gravy', the soup base of a spiced, sour fish stock, flavoured with lemongrass, galangal, chillies, shrimp paste, tamarind, sugar and laksa leaves (a.k.a. Vietnamese mint or Polygonum odoratum).

2 × 350g sea bass or snapper, scaled and trimmed

2 fat lemongrass stalks, bruised

1 quantity *Penang laksa spice paste* (page 301)

1 quantity *Tamarind water* (page 299)

3 tbsp fish sauce

2 tsp palm sugar

300g fresh round rice noodles or 175g dried 5mm-wide flat rice noodles (banh pho)

For the toppings:

¼ cucumber

¼ small fresh pineapple, removed as a wedge

1 small crisp lettuce, sliced across into 1cm-wide strips

100g shallots or 1 small red onion, thinly sliced

2 red bird's eye chillies, sliced

Handful of mint leaves, such as Vietnamese

½ quantity *Rojak dressing* (page 152), optional

Bring 1.5 litres of water to the boil in a large pan. Add the fish, bruised lemongrass and 1½ teaspoons salt, bring back to a simmer and cook the fish for just 10 minutes. Then lift onto a plate and leave to cool slightly. Add the spice paste, tamarind water, fish sauce and sugar to the pan, cover and simmer for 30 minutes. Strain the laksa 'gravy' through a sieve into a bowl, pressing out as much flavour as you can, then return to a cleaned-out pan, bring back to a simmer and keep hot.

Meanwhile, flake the flesh from the fish, discarding the bones and skin. Cut the pieces of cucumber and pineapple into 5cm-long, thin strips. Arrange the fish and all the topping ingredients on 1 large serving plate or in separate small bowls.

Bring a pan of unsalted water to the boil. If using dried noodles, drop them into the boiling water, turn off the heat and leave to soak for 3–4 minutes or until just tender, then drain. If using fresh noodles, simply drop them into the boiling water, leave for a few seconds to heat through, then drain.

Divide the noodles between 4 large, deep soup bowls and ladle over the hot laksa gravy. Add your desired toppings, some flaked fish and serve, with a spoonful of rojak dressing, if you wish.

Singapore laksa with prawns and coconut milk

SERVES 4

This is what most people in the West regard as the classic laksa, but in fact in Malaysia there is no such thing as a 'real' laksa. Every hawker on every street has his own version. This one has a deep, sweet flavour of prawn and coconut, the former enhanced by frying the prawn shells at the beginning of making the stock. Equally important are the extras that go on at the end: mint and coriander, cucumber, bean sprouts, chilli, crisp fried shallots (page 299) and, if you can get them, little deep-fried silver anchovies.

250g raw unpeeled prawns

4 tbsp vegetable oil

½ quantity *Singapore laksa spice paste* (page 301)

400ml coconut milk

2 tbsp fish sauce

1 tbsp palm sugar, or to taste

300g fresh round rice noodles or 175g dried 5mm-wide flat rice noodles (banh pho)

225g bamboo shoots, drained, rinsed and sliced

100g fresh bean sprouts

150g piece cucumber, halved then cut lengthways into thin strips

3 spring onions, trimmed and thinly sliced on the diagonal

4 tbsp *Crisp fried shallots* (page 299)

Handful of Vietnamese mint or a mixture of coriander and ordinary mint leaves

Lime wedges and thinly sliced bird's eye chilli, to serve

Peel the prawns, reserving the heads and shells. Heat 1 tablespoon of the oil in a medium-sized pan, add the heads and shells and stir-fry for a couple of minutes until crisp and golden. Add 1.2 litres of water, bring to the boil and leave to simmer for 1 hour until reduced to 750ml. Strain and set aside. Bring a pan of unsalted water to the boil for the noodles.

Heat the remaining oil in a large pan, add the spice paste and fry over a low heat for 2–3 minutes until it smells fragrant. Add the coconut milk, reserved prawn stock, fish sauce, sugar and 1½ teaspoons salt (or to taste). Simmer for 3 minutes.

Meanwhile, if using dried noodles, drop them into the boiling water, take off the heat and leave to soak for 3–4 minutes or until just tender, then drain. If using fresh noodles, simply drop them into the boiling water, leave for a few seconds to heat through, then drain.

Add the prawns to the soup and simmer for 1 minute. Divide the noodles between 4 large, deep soup bowls. Top with the bamboo shoots, then ladle over the soup, trying to distribute the prawns evenly between each bowl. Top with the bean sprouts, cucumber, spring onions, fried shallots and herbs, and serve straight away with the lime wedges and sliced chilli.

Devil's curry
Curry debal

SERVES 4

This is not a curry as we know it. It's quite unusual, hot with chilli and mustard and slightly sour with vinegar and tomato. It's described as a Eurasian dish and I imagine the Europeans in this amalgam were the Portuguese, since it's the same sort of dish, with its inclusion of vinegar, as the Goan vindaloo. I wouldn't mind betting, too, that our own devilled dishes, made with ingredients such as kidneys, which also use vinegar, mustard and cayenne pepper, are a derivation of this. It tastes to me like a dish you would find on a Victorian breakfast sideboard in Kuala Lumpur or Singapore. I suggest serving it with plain rice, or perhaps even the Indonesian fragrant rice on page 182. I've only put one bird's eye chilli in the final phase because it's hot enough, but since it's supposed to be a dish that is devilishly hot, do add more if you like.

2 tbsp dark soy sauce

2 tbsp rice vinegar

2 tsp sugar

1 × 1.5kg chicken, jointed into 8 pieces

2 tbsp yellow mustard seeds

3 tbsp vegetable oil

100g shallots or onions, thinly sliced

20g garlic, thinly sliced

1 quantity *Devil's curry spice paste* (page 301)

6 small waxy potatoes such as Charlotte, peeled and halved

300g tomatoes, cut into quarters

1 red bird's eye chilli, thinly sliced

Mix the soy sauce, rice vinegar, sugar and 1 teaspoon salt together in a large bowl. Add the chicken pieces, turn them over once or twice and set aside to marinate at room temperature for 30 minutes, turning them over every now and then. Put the mustard seeds into a spice grinder, grind briefly into a coarse powder and set aside.

Heat the oil in a large heavy-based pan over a medium-high heat, add the shallots and garlic and fry until lightly browned. Add the spice paste and fry for 5 minutes until it smells aromatic. Stir in the chicken and its marinade, the ground mustard seeds, potatoes, tomatoes and 450ml water and simmer, uncovered, for 30 minutes until the chicken and potatoes are cooked and the sauce has reduced slightly and thickened.

Stir in the sliced bird's eye chilli, simmer for 1 minute, then serve.

Nyonya prawns with fried cashew nuts, garlic and shallots

SERVES 2–3

This recipe comes from a very well-respected nyonya restaurant in Penang called Mama's. We filmed the owner and head cook making the dish and it was rather charming. I think nyonya food is the slow-cooking of Malaysia; in other words, a classic cuisine jealously guarded by a sisterhood of mothers and grandmothers keen to preserve traditional Malaysian life. Though the word nyonya refers to a style of cooking, combining Chinese and native Malay flavours, the word actually means 'females'. This is a very simple dish but I think typical of nyonya cooking in that it contains Malay ingredients such as shrimp paste, lemongrass, chilli and tamarind in a Chinese style stir-fry. What I like about this is the addition at the end of fried cashew nuts, garlic and crisp shallots.

5 tbsp vegetable oil
6 fat lemongrass stalks, core finely chopped
1 tsp shrimp paste
25g shelled unsalted cashew nuts, split in half if whole
25g garlic, thinly sliced
50g shallots, thinly sliced
12 large raw peeled prawns
1 tbsp *Tamarind water* (page 299)
100ml coconut milk
½ tsp palm sugar
3 medium-hot red chillies, halved lengthways, seeded and thinly sliced
1 red bird's eye chilli, thinly sliced

Heat 1 tablespoon of the oil in a deep, medium-sized frying pan over a low heat. Add the lemongrass and shrimp paste and fry gently for 1 minute. Scoop out into a small dish and set aside.

Increase the heat slightly and add another 3–4 tablespoons oil to the pan. Fry the cashew nuts, garlic and shallots separately, one after the other, scooping each out in turn with a slotted spoon and leaving to drain on a tray lined with kitchen paper.

Pour away all but 1 tablespoon oil from the pan. Add the prawns and stir-fry for 1 minute. Return the fried lemongrass and shrimp paste mixture to the pan with the tamarind water, coconut milk, sugar, sliced medium-hot chillies and 50ml water, and simmer vigorously for 2 minutes until the prawns are cooked and the sauce has reduced slightly. Season to taste with salt. Tip the prawns into a serving dish, scatter over the sliced bird's eye chilli, fried cashew nuts, garlic and shallots and serve.

Chef Wan's prawn and rice noodle salad

SERVES 4

Chef Wan is a massively famous TV cook in Malaysia. We filmed with him in Malacca, and everywhere we went, people, mostly ladies, were rushing up to get his autograph. He is a national institution, the Jamie Oliver of the Far East but a tad older. If you wanted an example of how incredibly hard-working people are in this part of the world, you need look no further. I was made dizzy by the stories of the number of days TV he does every year – something like 190, and on top of that books and personal appearances. He's a whirling dervish; completely over-the-top, hilarious and incredibly talented. He made this salad on the terrace at the Majestic Hotel, which is well worth staying at if you are in Malacca. It's a typically Southeast Asian salad, hot, sweet, spicy and sour, but it also contains a lot of fresh tomato, quite unusual for this part of the world, and which adds a pleasing freshness and scent.

125g dried rice vermicelli
    noodles
300g large cooked peeled
    prawns
150g shallots, thinly sliced
Large handful of mixed fresh
    coriander leaves, mint
    leaves and chives, torn
40g *Crisp fried shallots*
    (page 299)
90g roasted peanuts,
    coarsely chopped
4 kaffir lime leaves,
    finely shredded
Juice of 2 limes
3 tbsp fish sauce

For the spice paste:
6 medium-hot red chillies,
    seeded and thinly sliced
2 red bird's eye chillies, sliced
15g garlic, roughly chopped
25g dried shrimp, soaked
    in hot water for 30
    minutes then drained
3 vine-ripened tomatoes,
    sliced
4 tbsp palm sugar

Bring a pan of unsalted water to the boil. Meanwhile, put the ingredients for the spice paste into a mini food processor and grind, using the pulse button, into a coarse paste.

Drop the noodles into the pan of boiling water, remove from the heat and leave to soak for 1½ minutes until only just tender. Don't overcook them as they will soften a little more in the salad later on. Drain and refresh under cold water. Toss with a few drops of oil to stop the strands sticking together, then spread out on a clean tea towel or plenty of kitchen paper and leave to drain really well.

Put the noodles into a bowl and add the spice paste, followed by the other ingredients one by one, mixing them in briefly before adding the next, teasing the noodle strands apart as you do so, as they have a tendency to stick together in one clump. Serve immediately.

Amy's spicy nyonya chicken

SERVES 4

This recipe is from another nyonya restaurant, this time in Malacca. As with the recipe for stir-fried prawns on page 146, all the cooks in Amy's restaurant were women, again identifying the strong sense of matriarchal influence in this cooking that is special to Malaysia. This is very easy to make. I have slightly reduced the amount of shrimp paste from the original, but – here's a note of caution – I haven't reduced the amount of chilli. Amy, who is a delightfully understated ambassador for nyonya cooking, says she often stirs in a little lime juice and coconut milk at the end to 'wake up the curry'.

2 tbsp vegetable oil
1 × 1.5kg chicken, jointed
    into 8 pieces
2 lemongrass stalks,
    bruised with a rolling
    pin then cut in half
4 kaffir lime leaves
1 tsp palm sugar
Juice of 1 lime

For the spice paste:
6 dried red kashmiri chillies,
    soaked in hot water for
    30 minutes then drained
75g shallots, thinly sliced
3 fat lemongrass stalks,
    core chopped
40g garlic, roughly chopped
1 tsp shrimp paste
25g peeled galangal or
    ginger, roughly chopped
2 tbsp vegetable oil

Put all the ingredients for the spice paste into a mini food processor and blend together until smooth.

Heat the vegetable oil in a medium-sized pan or deep frying pan over a medium heat, add the chicken and fry until lightly golden all over. Add the spice paste to the pan and fry for a couple of minutes. Add the bruised lemongrass stalks, kaffir lime leaves and 200ml water and leave to simmer for 30–40 minutes, turning the chicken pieces over now and then, until the chicken is cooked and the sauce has reduced by about half.

Stir in the sugar, lime juice and some salt to taste and serve.

Malay lamb korma
Gulai kambing

SERVES 6

Some of the Indian-style curries of Southeast Asia are the most surprising dishes you'll find there because, although essentially like the curries of the subcontinent, they are intriguingly different by their use of very local ingredients, in this case nutmeg, lemongrass, coconut, coconut milk and palm sugar, in addition to more normal ingredients like coriander, cumin, cinnamon, cloves and kashmiri chillies. This is a typical curry that is served as part of nasi campur, where a group of people will choose three or four curries, such as this one, maybe a curry debal (page 143), a fish curry (page 138), a vegetable dish and maybe a salad like the Indonesian lawar on page 203. These are all served around a big bowl of steamed rice with, of course, a searingly hot sambal and a bowl of pickles called achar (page 158).

1kg boneless shoulder of lamb
5 tbsp vegetable oil
1 quantity *Malay korma curry paste* (page 301)
125ml coconut milk
2 tomatoes, cut into wedges
4 fat lemongrass stalks, core finely chopped
2 tsp palm sugar

To finish:
15g garlic, sliced
1 tsp cumin seeds
2 dried red chillies, halved
24 curry leaves (about 2 sprigs)
½ quantity *Crisp fried shallots* (page 299)
2 tbsp roughly chopped Chinese celery

Trim the excess fat from the lamb and cut the remainder into approximately 4cm pieces. Heat 2 tablespoons of the oil in a large, heavy-based pan over a medium-low heat. Add the spice paste and fry for 2–3 minutes until it smells fragrant and the spices start to split away from the oil. Add the lamb and fry for about 2 more minutes. Add 500ml water and 1 teaspoon salt, lower the heat and leave to simmer, uncovered, for 1 hour, stirring every now and then.

Add the coconut milk, tomatoes, lemongrass and sugar, and continue to simmer for 30 minutes or until the lamb is tender.

To finish the curry, heat the remaining 3 tablespoons of oil in a frying pan over a medium heat. Add the garlic and allow it to fry for a few seconds until it starts to turn golden, then add the cumin seeds, dried chillies and curry leaves. Leave to sizzle for a few more seconds, then tip everything into the curry and stir in. Serve the curry sprinkled with the crisp fried shallots and chopped Chinese celery.

Malaysian fruit salad with tamarind, chilli and palm sugar dressing
Rojak

SERVES 4

I think it's fair to say that rojak causes more controversy among Westerners visiting Malaysia than any other dish. It's hard for us to get our heads around the idea of a fresh fruit salad with a chilli and lime-based dressing that also contains shrimp paste. I must say I've been a great fan of fruit and chilli ever since I bought a bag of orange segments dusted in chilli powder at an Aztec ruin in Mexico, and I find a bit of shrimp paste in the background intriguing too. The point of the sauce, though, is that it's very sweet but pleasingly sour with lime and tamarind too. Maybe, rather than a dessert, think of it more as something to be enjoyed mid-afternoon or even with some barbecued chicken.

400g prepared pineapple
(about 1 small pineapple)
½ cucumber, peeled
1 mango
2 nashi pears (Asian pears),
or Granny Smith apples

For the rojak dressing:
25g shrimp paste
3 red bird's eye chillies,
thinly sliced
4 tbsp seedless
tamarind pulp
Juice of 2 limes
125g dark palm sugar

For the topping:
1 tbsp sesame seeds
40g roasted peanuts

For the dressing, put the shrimp paste, chillies, tamarind pulp, lime juice and 120ml water into a mini food processor and whiz together until it is as smooth as possible. Scrape the mixture into a small saucepan and add the sugar and another 100ml water. Bring to the boil and simmer gently for 10 minutes until the sauce thickly coats the back of a wooden spoon. Pass through a sieve into a bowl and leave to cool. Don't refrigerate as it will get too thick.

For the toppings, lightly toast the sesame seeds in a dry frying pan until lightly golden. Tip into a bowl and leave to cool. Coarsely chop the peanuts.

For the salad, cut the pineapple into 2cm pieces. Cut the cucumber in half lengthways and then across into 1cm-thick slices. Peel the mango and cut into similarly sized pieces. Peel the nashi pears or apples, core and cut into thin wedges.

Arrange the fruit on 4 plates and drizzle over the sauce. Sprinkle with the peanuts and sesame seeds and serve.

Street hawkers' prawn noodle soup
Sup mee udang

SERVES 4

In Penang there's a hokkien noodle soup stall just opposite the Pulau Tikus police station. I was taken there by Fay Khoo, who is an amazingly productive cook, businesswoman and writer. She also writes a guide to Kuala Lumpur's restaurants, does TV and about six other jobs – fairly typical of busy Malaysians. They put us all to shame. She explained that what appeared to be a single restaurant was in fact four kiosks, and that the kiosks were operated by different food businesses during the course of the day. The men who made our superb hokkien noodles, having finished their early morning stint, then went off to deal on the local stock exchange. Like all the best food outlets in Southeast Asia, or so it seems to me, décor and smart waiters are anathema to the patrons, who in this case just want a bowl of deeply flavoured stock perfumed with prawn shells and brimming with a mix of both egg and rice noodles, garlic and five-spice-flavoured pork, prawns, morning glory leaves, crisp onions and hard-boiled eggs. The stock base for this soup is also often made with pork ribs, which are sometimes served in the soup too. Feel free to add some to the pot when making the stock.

300g large raw unpeeled
    prawns
10 dried red kashmiri chillies,
    soaked in hot water for
    30 minutes then drained
150g shallots, chopped
30g garlic, roughly chopped
1 tbsp sugar
4 tbsp vegetable oil
1.5 litres Asian chicken stock
    (page 300)

To serve:
100g dried or 200g fresh fine
    egg noodles (hokkien mee)
100g dried rice vermicelli
    noodles
75g morning glory leaves
    or leaf spinach
75g fresh bean sprouts
125g Vietnamese cooked belly pork
    (page 300), thinly sliced
2 hard-boiled eggs, quartered
Crisp fried shallots (page 299)

Peel the prawns, reserving the heads and shells. Put the soaked chillies into a mini food processor with the shallots, garlic, sugar and 1 teaspoon salt and grind until smooth. Heat the oil in a wok or medium-sized pan over a low heat, add the paste and fry for 8 minutes, stirring regularly, until it becomes jam-like in consistency. Scoop half into a small serving bowl and set aside.

Add the prawn shells and heads to the remaining paste in the pan and fry gently for 5 minutes. Add the stock and 1 more teaspoon salt, bring to the boil and simmer for 15 minutes. Strain into a clean pan, pressing as much flavour as you can from the shells and heads, and bring back to a gentle simmer.

Bring a pan of unsalted water to the boil. If using dried noodles, add them to the boiling water, cook for 2 minutes, then lift out and drain. If using fresh egg noodles, add them to the pan, leave for a few seconds to heat through, then lift out and drain. Add the rice vermicelli to the hot water, take the pan off the heat, leave to soak for 2 minutes, then drain.

Add the peeled prawns to the stock and simmer for 1 minute. Divide both types of noodles, the green leaves and bean sprouts between 4 deep soup bowls and ladle over the hot stock and prawns, dividing the prawns between each bowl. Top each one with some sliced pork, 2 egg quarters, some fried shallots and a spoonful of extra chilli paste.

Chicken curry kapitan

SERVES 6

I'm mindful that many of the curries in this book require a lot of preparation. I'm afraid it's essential, but I'm always keen to include a selection of easy dishes too, and this is one of them. All the ingredients can readily be bought at a supermarket. The name kapitan refers to the Chinese official, the main man within the Chinese communities, who acted as the go-between between the Chinese and Malay rulers. He was therefore a man of enormous importance, and this is the 'captain's' curry. No better example of nyonya cuisine exists. A delightful combination of chicken with coconut, palm sugar, cinnamon, ginger and star anise.

1kg skinned and boneless chicken thighs
4 heaped tbsp desiccated coconut
2 tbsp vegetable oil
1 quantity *Malaysian kapitan curry paste* (page 301)
400ml coconut milk
2 × 7.5cm cinnamon sticks
2 tsp palm sugar
Juice of ½ lime
Handful of coriander leaves, roughly chopped, to garnish

Cut the chicken thigh fillets into chunky strips. Heat a large, deep, heavy-based frying pan over a medium heat, add the coconut and stir it around for a few minutes until lightly golden. Tip onto a plate and leave to cool, then tip into a mini food processor and grind quite finely.

Return the frying pan to a low heat and add the oil. Add the spice paste and fry gently for 5 minutes, stirring every now and then. Add the chicken strips and fry for 2–3 minutes more.

Add the coconut milk, cinnamon sticks, sugar and 1 teaspoon salt and simmer for 30 minutes until the chicken is tender and the sauce has reduced and thickened slightly. Add the lime juice and toasted ground coconut and simmer for 1 more minute. Serve straight away scattered with the chopped coriander.

Stir-fried duck with garlic, ginger, mushrooms and five-spice, wrapped in lettuce leaves
Sang choi bau

SERVES 4 AS A STARTER

I find it amazing that one of the most popular dishes in Chinese restaurants in Australia should be so little known in the UK. Maybe there's an idea for a small chain of Chinese tapas bars here? Quite simply, I adore it. In Australia, it normally comes as a second course, where the first course is Peking duck pancakes, the little thin ones served with Hoisin sauce, spring onions and cucumber. In the UK these pancakes are made with the whole duck, which has been deep-fried and shredded, and are called crispy aromatic duck pancakes. Back in Australia, the duck in Peking duck pancakes consists of just some deliciously crisp skin and a few thin slices of the breast meat. The rest of the duck meat is finely chopped up and stir-fried with Chinese mushrooms, bean sprouts, bamboo shoots and other flavourings and served in a crisp lettuce leaf, which you wrap up with great enthusiasm and devour. These can also be made with finely chopped cooked pork; the Chinese red roast pork on page 300 is especially good. I ate this with Narelle McMurtie in Langkawi.

1 small iceberg lettuce
200g roasted duck meat
   or *Chinese red roast pork*
   (page 300)
2 tbsp vegetable oil
2 tsp sesame oil
15g garlic, finely chopped
2 tsp ginger, finely chopped
65g celery, finely chopped
65g shiitake mushrooms,
   fresh or reconstituted
   dried ones, finely shredded
4 spring onions, trimmed
   and thinly sliced
65g bamboo shoots,
   cut into 5mm dice
65g fresh bean sprouts,
   roughly chopped
¼ tsp crushed dried chilli
¼ tsp five-spice powder
4 tsp dark soy sauce
2 tsp Chinese rice wine
2 tbsp chopped fresh mint
2 tbsp chopped fresh coriander

This dish is made very quickly so make sure you have everything prepared before you start. Break the iceberg lettuce into separate cup-shaped leaves and set them aside on a plate. Cut the roasted duck or red roast pork into 5mm dice.

Heat a wok over a high heat, add the vegetable and sesame oil, swiftly followed by the chopped garlic and ginger and then the pork or duck, and stir-fry for 1 minute until the meat is heated through. Add all the other ingredients and toss together for 10–15 seconds, but don't overcook it or the vegetables will lose their crunch.

To serve, you can either spoon some of the mixture straight away into each lettuce cup and take them to the table, or spoon the stir-fried mixture onto a warmed serving plate and take it to the table with the plate of lettuce leaves and let people make up their own. You simply wrap the mixture up in the lettuce leaves and eat – slightly messy, but delicious.

Malaysian vegetable pickle
Achar

MAKES 3 × 500ML JAM JARS

Some sort of pickle is always present at meals all over Southeast Asia. Sometimes it is simply salted, sliced cucumber, onion and carrot dressed with vinegar, sugar and maybe a little chilli, but this achar – and there are lots of different ones – is special. I often wonder if our piccalilli is descended from it, because it is popular not only in Asia but all over the Indian subcontinent too. It's less assertive than piccalilli but still carries quite a punch with the vinegar and chilli, and also has that characteristic bright yellow colour from the turmeric. It's sweet, hot and sour but the most pleasurable thing about it is the nuttiness from the roasted sesame seeds and chopped peanuts. In Malaysia it would be served with curry, but it is excellent with grilled meats, cold cuts and pâté too.

1 cucumber

4 × medium-sized
(50g each) carrots

175g wedge of white cabbage

150g shallots

125g cauliflower, broken
into tiny florets

75g fine green beans,
cut into 2.5cm pieces

15g medium-hot red chillies,
seeded and sliced

15g green chillies, seeded
and sliced

500ml distilled vinegar

3 dried red kashmiri chillies,
soaked in hot water for
30 minutes

50g peeled ginger, roughly
chopped

1½ tsp turmeric powder

2 tbsp vegetable oil

2 tbsp palm sugar

2 tbsp toasted sesame seeds

100g roasted peanuts,
coarsely chopped

Halve the cucumber lengthways and scrape out the seeds with a teaspoon. Cut lengthways into quarters, then across into slices 5mm thick. Peel the carrots, halve lengthways and cut across into slices 5mm thick. Cut the piece of cabbage into slices 1cm thick and then across into similar-sized pieces. Halve the shallots lengthways and then cut across into slices 3mm thick. Toss the cucumber, carrots, cabbage, shallots, cauliflower, green beans and red and green chillies with 1 tablespoon salt, tip into a colander positioned over a bowl and set aside for 1 hour.

Bring the vinegar and 225ml water to the boil in a large pan, add a third of the salted vegetables, bring back to the boil and boil vigorously for 1 minute. Remove with a slotted spoon to another colander set over a bowl and repeat with the remainder. Discard the remaining blanching liquid.

Drain the soaked chillies and put them into a mini food processor with the ginger, turmeric, 1 tablespoon of the oil and 2 tablespoons water and grind into a smooth paste. Heat the remaining oil in a small frying pan over a low heat, add the spice paste and fry gently for 5 minutes. Leave to cool, then mix into the vegetables with the sugar, another ½ teaspoon salt, the sesame seeds and peanuts and stir together well. Transfer to three sterilized 500ml jam jars, seal and store in the fridge for a day or two before using. Keeps for up to a month in the fridge.

Coconut rice with tamarind prawns, anchovy peanut sambal, eggs and cucumber
Nasi lemak

SERVES 4

This dish centres around coconut rice flavoured with pandan leaf. In Malaysia the rice is either sold in banana-leaf packages, called ketupat, from stalls and coffee shops for breakfast, or served on a plate with a selection of other dishes (like a nasi campur) that offer a variety of contrasting textures and flavours. A typical plate might include a curry or two like the one on page 151, some fried fish or chicken, a hard-boiled egg, fried egg or omelette, one or two chilli-hot sambals, some chopped roasted peanuts, maybe a vegetable pickle similar to the achar on page 158, and always cucumber. Short-grain rice is preferred for this dish because of its greater ability to absorb liquid and its slightly sticky texture, which holds it together in its traditional banana-leaf package, but use long-grain if you prefer.

350g short-grain rice or
   long-grain rice
400ml coconut milk
1 pandan leaf, tied into knot,
   or a few drops of pandan
   essence (optional)
Freshly ground black pepper

For the tamarind prawns:
16 large raw unpeeled prawns
1 quantity *Tamarind water*
   (page 299)
1 tbsp kecap manis
1 tsp palm sugar
Vegetable oil, for frying

To serve:
4 eggs, cooked to your liking
   (see above)
Sambal ikan bilis (page 305)
Sambal oelek
Achar (page 158)
½ cucumber, peeled and
   thickly sliced

For the tamarind prawns, make a slit through the shell along the underside of each prawn. Mix the tamarind water, kecap manis, sugar, ½ teaspoon salt and plenty of freshly ground black pepper together in a bowl. Add the prawns and work the marinade into the incisions in the shell. Set aside to marinate for at least 1 hour.

Put the rice into a non-stick pan and add the coconut milk, 300ml water and ½ teaspoon salt. Bring to the boil, stir once, add the pandan leaf or essence, if using, then cover, lower the heat and leave to cook gently for 10 minutes. Turn off the heat and leave for a further 10 minutes without removing the lid.

Heat some oil in a wok or frying pan, or heat a ridged cast-iron griddle, then brush with a little oil. Stir-fry or griddle the prawns for about 2 minutes until cooked through. Serve with the coconut rice, eggs, sambals, achar and sliced cucumber.

Beef rendang

SERVES 6

I wrote a recipe for beef rendang in an earlier book, Food Heroes, Another Helping. I have cooked it on a number of occasions since then and I'm very happy with it. Needless to say, however, as with almost any dish in Southeast Asia, there are many regional variations. My first version came from Indonesia, where the spicy coconut curry sauce is cooked until it entirely disappears, becoming a coating for the now very tender meat, which is then allowed to fry in the residual coconut oil. Before refrigeration, large amounts of buffalo meat could be cooked in this way and kept for many months. In Penang, I came across this Malaysian version, which is much wetter, and I think is great with rice. It is hotter and spicier and has the addition of kaffir lime leaves and a lot of fresh galangal, which you can now buy relatively easily in the UK. There's nothing quite like a rendang: hot and spicy but rich in coconut with a delightful sweet-and-sourness from tamarind and palm sugar. Serve it with steamed jasmine rice.

3 tbsp coconut or vegetable oil
1.5kg blade or chuck steak, cut into 5–6cm chunks
1 quantity *Rendang spice paste* (page 302)
800ml coconut milk
4 fat lemongrass stalks, bruised
12 kaffir lime leaves
2 × 7.5cm cinnamon sticks
125ml *Tamarind water* (page 299), made with 50g seedless tamarind pulp
1 tbsp palm sugar

For the cucumber salad:
1 cucumber
75g finely grated fresh coconut
100g shallots, halved and thinly sliced
1 medium-hot red chilli, seeded and thinly sliced
4 tbsp coconut milk (page 299)
1 tbsp lime juice
1 tsp white sugar

Heat the coconut oil or vegetable oil in a large, heavy-based pan. Add the beef and fry briefly until it has all changed colour but not browned. Add the spice paste, coconut milk, lemongrass, lime leaves, cinnamon sticks and 1½ teaspoons salt. Bring to the boil, reduce the heat, add the tamarind water and leave to simmer, uncovered, for 2½ hours, stirring occasionally, and then more frequently towards the end of cooking, until the beef is tender and the sauce has reduced and thickened.

Half an hour before serving, make the cucumber salad. Peel the cucumber, cut it in half lengthways, scoop out the seeds with a teaspoon and then slice. Toss with ½ teaspoon salt and leave it to drain in a colander for 20 minutes. Heat a dry, heavy-based frying pan over a medium heat, add the grated coconut and shake it around for a few minutes until lightly golden. Tip onto a plate and leave to cool. Mix the cucumber in a bowl with the shallots, red chilli and toasted coconut. Add the coconut milk, lime juice and sugar and toss together well. Season to taste with a little more salt if you wish.

Remove the lemongrass from the rendang, and stir in the sugar and seasoning to taste. Serve with the cucumber salad.

Malaccan black pepper crab with black beans, ginger, garlic and curry leaves

SERVES 2

If Singapore chilli crab is the star in Singapore, black pepper crab is easily its equal in Kuala Lumpur. But this particular version comes from Malacca. The city was enormously important in the sixteenth and seventeenth centuries because of its strategic position overlooking the straits (of Malacca). The spice trade was as important then as oil is now, and most of it passed through this city. It's now a pretty relaxed place, where you can indulge yourself in one of the best dishes of Southeast Asia. This recipe comes from Charmaine Solomon's Encyclopedia of Asian Food; now sadly out of print, though you can get hold of second-hand copies.

1kg raw or cooked whole crabs, such as brown crab, mud crab or blue swimmer

1 tbsp kecap manis

1 tbsp Chinese fermented salted black beans, rinsed and chopped

1 tsp palm sugar

Vegetable oil, for frying

5 spring onions, thinly sliced on the diagonal

25g peeled ginger, finely shredded

15g garlic, finely chopped

20 curry leaves (about 2 sprigs)

1 tbsp black peppercorns, coarsely crushed

15g butter

1 medium-hot red chilli, halved lengthways and thinly sliced

To prepare the crabs, follow the instructions on page 42. Mix the kecap manis, black beans, sugar and 3 tablespoons water together in a bowl and set aside. Heat 75ml oil in a large wok. Add the pieces of crab and stir-fry for 3 minutes, until the crab is half cooked. Lift the pieces out into a bowl and pour away all but 1½ tablespoons of the oil.

Return the wok to a medium heat, add 4 of the sliced spring onions, the ginger, garlic and curry leaves and stir-fry gently for 1 minute, taking care not to let anything brown. Add the black pepper and, after a few seconds, the black bean mixture. Return the crab pieces to the wok, turn over once or twice to coat in the mixture, then cover with a lid and leave to cook for 5 minutes if the crab is raw, 2–3 minutes if using cooked crab.

When the crab is cooked, uncover and add the butter and sliced red chilli to the wok. Turn over once more to coat the crab in the sauce, then spoon onto 1 large serving plate or 2 soup plates, scatter with the remaining spring onion and serve.

Indian-style stir-fried noodles
Mee goreng

SERVES 4

Mee goreng is the noodle version of Indonesian nasi goreng, which is made with rice, and as such is a put-anything-you-want-in-it sort of recipe, within reason. But what it must always have is egg noodles, chilli, shallots and garlic, a little protein and a lot of vegetables cut into small strips or dice, some chilli and soy sauce and, for my money, a couple of beaten eggs poured into the bottom of the wok at the last minute. It's a rugged street-food dish, hence the tomato ketchup. I've suggested the classic accompaniments of crisp fried shallots and lime, but if you don't want to go to the bother of doing the shallots, leave them out. This sweet and spicy dish is much loved by my fiancée Sarah's children, Zach and Olivia. Indeed, I doubt there's a child on this planet who doesn't love mee goreng. And in Olivia's case, even if they were a bit too spicy, she would put on a brave face.

1 × 150–200g potato, peeled

250g firm tofu

4 tbsp vegetable oil

400g fresh medium-thick egg noodles (hokkien mee) or 200g dried egg noodles

3 tbsp tomato ketchup

2 tbsp sweet chilli sauce

2 tbsp dark soy sauce

150g shallots, thinly sliced

10g garlic, thinly sliced

1 tbsp chilli paste, such as sambal oelek

175g chicken breast fillet, cut into 1cm-wide strips

100g large raw peeled prawns

100g bok choi, cut across into 2.5cm-wide strips

1 tsp sugar

2 eggs, beaten

4 spring onions, sliced

100g fresh bean sprouts

50g Crisp fried shallots (page 299)

1 medium-hot chilli, seeded if you wish, thinly sliced

2 limes, halved

Cut the potato and the tofu into 1.5cm cubes. Drop the potato into a small pan of boiling salted water and cook for a few minutes or until just tender. Drain and set aside. Heat 2 tablespoons of the oil in a wok or deep frying pan, then fry the tofu until crisp and golden. Lift out and drain on kitchen paper.

If you are using fresh noodles, simply put them into a bowl, pour over boiling water, drain, rinse and set aside. If using dried noodles, drop them into a pan of boiling unsalted water and cook them for 2 minutes, drain and set aside.

Mix the tomato ketchup with the sweet chilli sauce and soy sauce. Set aside.

Heat the remaining 2 tablespoons of oil in the wok or frying pan, add the shallots and garlic and fry until golden. Add the chilli paste, chicken and prawns and fry for 2 minutes or until just cooked. Add the bok choi and fry for a few seconds more until it has wilted, then add the noodles, diced potatoes, fried tofu, the tomato ketchup mixture, the sugar and some salt to taste. Toss together over a high heat until heated through.

Tilt the wok or pan, push the noodles to one side, pour in the egg, then cover with the noodles and leave to set for about 30 seconds. Add the spring onions and bean sprouts and toss together well. Divide between warmed plates and sprinkle with the fried shallots and sliced chilli. Serve with a squeeze of lime.

Charcoal-grilled skewers of squid with cumin, coriander, lime juice and chilli
Satay sotong

SERVES 4

These satays come from Langkawi. I ate them at a night market, the evening after I'd been out fishing with squid boats off the island. The fishermen go out at dusk and hook the squid with a cluster of barbless hooks on a line called a jig, which they jerk up and down in the water. Essential for jigging success is a bright light, which attracts the squid to the surface. A myriad of small, brightly painted boats on a calm sea, each shining a small light into the darkness, the deeper black outline of the island behind, intermittent warm tropical rain – it's a happy memory, and gave me lots of enthusiasm to try these satays the next evening.

750g cleaned medium-sized squid (pouches about 18cm long)

For the marinade:
1 tsp cumin seeds
2 tsp coriander seeds
1 dried red kashmiri chilli
3 tbsp fish sauce
2 tsp lime juice
1 tbsp palm sugar

For the dipping sauce:
2 tbsp vegetable oil
7g garlic, finely chopped
15g peeled ginger, finely chopped
1 red bird's eye chilli, finely chopped
3 tbsp lime juice
3 tbsp fish sauce
2½ tbsp palm sugar
25g roasted peanuts, finely chopped
2 tbsp chopped fresh coriander

Cover 16 × 18cm bamboo skewers with water and leave them to soak for 30 minutes. Preheat your barbecue to high.

Slit the squid pouches along one side and open them out flat. Cut each one lengthways into 4 strips about 2cm wide, and across into pieces 3cm long. Cut the squid tentacles into pairs. Thread 5–6 pieces of squid tightly onto each bamboo skewer, finishing with a small bundle of the tentacles. Set to one side.

For the marinade, heat a small dry frying pan over a medium-high heat. Add the cumin seeds, coriander seeds and chilli and shake them around for a few seconds until they darken slightly and smell aromatic. Tip into a spice grinder, leave to cool, then grind into a fine powder. Tip the mixture into a shallow rectangular dish, add the fish sauce, lime juice and sugar and mix together well. Add the skewers of squid to the marinade and turn them over in the mixture a few times until well coated.

For the dipping sauce, heat the oil in a small pan over a medium heat, add the garlic, ginger and chilli and cook gently for 1–2 minutes until soft and just beginning to brown. Transfer to a small bowl and leave to cool, then stir in the lime juice, fish sauce, palm sugar, roasted peanuts, fresh coriander and 1 tablespoon water. Divide between 4 small dipping saucers.

Lift the squid satay out of the marinade and barbecue for 1–1½ minutes on each side, brushing with the leftover marinade now and then, until cooked through and nicely browned. Serve hot with the dipping sauce.

Stir-fried beef with black beans, Chinese greens and bamboo shoots

SERVES 4

On the face of it, this might appear to be a classic Chinese stir-fry, but it has some very Malaysian features, namely lemongrass and shrimp paste. With its use of salted black beans and bamboo shoots, it tastes marvellously exotic, yet, like most stir-fries, it is simple to prepare and cook.

500g slice of rump steak, trimmed of all fat

4 tbsp Chinese fermented salted black beans

4 tsp palm sugar

2 tbsp sesame oil

½ tsp shrimp paste

2 tsp cornflour

6 tbsp *Chicken stock* (page 300)

2 tbsp vegetable oil

50g peeled ginger, finely shredded

15g garlic, finely chopped

2 medium-hot red chillies, halved lengthways, seeded and sliced

4 fat lemongrass stalks, core finely chopped

2 tbsp Chinese rice wine

225g bok choi, cut across into 2.5cm-wide strips

225g bamboo shoots, drained, rinsed and sliced

2 tbsp kecap manis

Finely cut the steak across the grain into strips 5mm thick. Put the black beans, sugar, sesame oil and shrimp paste into a small bowl and crush with the back of a spoon into a coarse paste. Mix the cornflour with the stock and set aside.

Heat a wok over a high heat until just smoking, then add the oil and swirl it around. Add the ginger, garlic and chilli, and as soon as the ginger and garlic start to colour, add the black bean paste and stir to mix. Add the beef and lemongrass and stir-fry until it has all changed colour.

Add the Chinese rice wine, reduce the heat slightly and add the bok choi and bamboo shoots. Stir-fry for a few seconds more until the bok choi has wilted.

Add the kecap manis and the cornflour and stock mixture to the wok and toss together until the sauce has thickened. Adjust the seasoning to taste – it should be salty and sweet – also adding a little more stock if the mixture looks a little dry. Spoon onto a plate and serve.

CHAPTER FIVE

BALI

Warung Babi Guling in the town of Ubud has been run by Ibu Oka and her family for over forty years. It is a restaurant specializing in roast pork. The lean pigs are reared in the hills above the town, and killed and cooked at Ibu Oka's compound just down the road from the restaurant. At 5 a.m. every morning up to seven pigs are killed and then stuffed with basa gede, the basic spice paste of Indonesia, known locally as bumbu bali, which traditionally contains the four rhizomes of ginger, turmeric, galangal and lesser galangal (known in Bali as kencur). The paste goes into the belly cavity, the pigs are sewn up, then they are spit-roasted over coffee wood from 7 until 10.30 a.m. Each pig has an attendant to turn the spit, exactly in the same way as was done for the roasts of old England in Tudor times. They carefully rotate the pigs over the embers, brushing them with a mixture of coconut oil and turmeric as they cook, and they have a little pan of water to throw on the logs if they flare up from the fat dripping from the pig. It has a fantastically earthy atmosphere, where the processes won't have changed at all, ever. The pigs, now a deep bronze colour, are carried on long metal trays down to the restaurant, where they are quickly carved and everyone gets a large piece of the light crisp crackling, some lean and fatty meat and a spoonful of the stuffing. I would cross continents to eat there again.

Quite soon after that gastronomic delight I was lucky enough to watch the making of bebek betutu, where a duck is stuffed with the same basa gede, wrapped in banana leaves and cooked under a dome of smouldering coconut husks. Basa gede is to me the flavour of Bali. In addition to the rhizomes, it contains candle nuts, nutmeg, shallots, garlic, lemongrass, shrimp paste, sugar and lime. Nearly half the recipes in this chapter contain it, though we suggest alternatives to the candle nuts, which are hard to find here. I don't think it's saying too much to claim that making it will give you a route into Balinese culture. One of the reasons the markets there are so fascinating is that not only is food on sale for eating, it's also being offered to the Hindu gods, together with flowers. Indeed, the charm of Bali is the relationship between the practical and the spiritual. A town like Ubud has a strange spiritual quality, because everywhere you look there are buildings that serve no purpose other than to delight the eye. The sacred colours of black, white, red and yellow are consciously included in much of the food: yellow in the form of turmeric, and black, white and red in the different coloured rice grown on the island. Red is also evident in lawar, a dish served at religious ceremonies, where a salad of green beans and grated coconut is made red by pig's blood. I have included a recipe here without the blood; it's lovely.

Indonesian stir-fried rice
Nasi goreng

SERVES 4

I've worked with the same TV crew now for over ten years and we are like a family – and, as with all families, some things can really irritate you. I'm not saying I don't love an English breakfast, because I do, but why order one in Malacca, Penang or Ubud when you can have nasi goreng? This rice, stir-fried with a spice paste, vegetables and prawns, is, like a full English, one of the world's great comfort foods. I always point out to David, Chris and Pete, you get a fried egg on top anyway. Arezoo, the assistant producer, and I have spent many an early morning looking at those boys disdainfully as we enjoy our authentic Far Eastern breakfast.

300g long-grain rice
100g fine green beans,
    cut into 2.5cm pieces
2 tbsp vegetable oil
125g skinned and boneless
    chicken, cut into 1cm
    pieces
125g large raw peeled prawns,
    cut into 1cm pieces
200g shallots, thinly sliced
20g garlic, finely chopped
2 medium-hot red chillies,
    seeded and finely chopped
1 red bird's eye chilli, sliced
1 medium carrot, thinly sliced
½ quantity *Balinese spice paste*
    (*basa gede*, see page 302)
1 tbsp tomato purée
1 tbsp kecap manis
1 tbsp light soy sauce
8 spring onions, thinly sliced

To serve:
2 tbsp vegetable oil
4 large eggs
¼ cucumber, sliced
2 medium tomatoes, sliced
½ quantity *Crisp fried shallots*
    (page 299)
Prawn crackers
Achar (page 158)

Put the rice into a 20cm heavy-based saucepan and add 520ml water. Quickly bring to the boil, stir once, cover with a tight-fitting lid, then reduce the heat to low and cook for 10 minutes. Uncover, fluff up the grains of rice with a fork and spread the rice over a tray. Set aside to cool.

Drop the beans into a pan of boiling salted water and cook for 3 minutes. Drain, refresh under cold water and set aside.

Heat the oil in a wok or large, deep frying pan until almost smoking. Add the chicken and prawns and stir-fry for 1 minute. Add the shallots, garlic, chillies and carrots and stir-fry for a further 2 minutes until the carrot is just tender. Add the spice paste and stir-fry for another minute. Add the tomato purée, kecap manis, cooked rice and green beans and stir-fry over a high heat for 2 minutes. Add the soy sauce and spring onions and toss together. Remove from the heat, cover and keep hot.

Heat the oil in a large frying pan, crack in the eggs and fry for a couple of minutes, spooning hot oil over the yolks as they cook. Spoon the nasi goreng onto warmed plates and top each one with a fried egg. Overlap the cucumber and tomato to the side of each plate. Sprinkle the crisp fried shallots over the eggs and fried rice and serve with prawn crackers and achar pickles.

Ibu Oka's Balinese slow-roast pork
Babi guling

SERVES 8

I'm sure that when the TV series accompanying this book is broadcast, the making of babi guling will stand out (see also page 174). I was so over-excited after the first couple of mouthfuls that I said it was worth crossing continents for. My domesticated version, using shoulder of pork stuffed and tied into a long roll, is certainly worth making. It's normal to serve it with steamed white rice and the bean and coconut salad on page 184, but I think that if you served it with apple sauce, roast potatoes, green beans and a gravy made from the pan juices it would be equally sensational.

2.25kg piece of boned shoulder of pork, skin scored at 1cm intervals
1 quantity *Balinese spice paste* (*basa gede*, see page 302)
2 tbsp vegetable oil
½ tsp turmeric powder

Place the pork skin-side down on the work surface and spread the fleshy side with the spice paste, then roll up into a neat joint and tie it at 2.5cm intervals along its length with string. Set aside for at least 1 hour or overnight, uncovered, to dry off the skin.

Preheat the oven to 220°C/Gas Mark 7. Weigh the stuffed joint and calculate the cooking time at 25 minutes per 450g. Mix the oil with the turmeric and brush some over the skin of the pork. Sprinkle all over with salt, put the joint onto a rack set in the base of a roasting tin and roast for 20 minutes. Then lower the heat to 180°C/Gas Mark 4 and cook for the calculated cooking time – approximately 2 hours – brushing the skin every 20 minutes or so with more of the turmeric oil to give it a crisp, golden skin.

Remove the joint from the oven, lift it onto a board and leave it to rest for 15 minutes. Then slice the crackling away from the joint and cut it into pieces with a sharp knife. Carve the meat into thin slices and serve with the crackling.

Slow-cooked lightly smoked duck stuffed with garlic, chilli, lemongrass and galangal
Bebek betutu

SERVES 4–6

You might think that a roasted duck with crisp skin and faintly pink flesh, with potatoes roasted in duck fat and fresh peas, is perfection. I say to you, bebek betutu might just tip the balance. It is, I think, as famous as Ibu Oka's spit-roast pork on page 177. This superb, slow-cooked recipe – for which, by the way, you will need a large roasting bag – is a wonder. Though the meat is almost falling off the bone after four hours of cooking, it is astonishingly moist, and the stuffing of the Balinese spice paste (basa gede), made with garlic, chilli, lemongrass, shallots, galangal and ginger, acts almost like a relish that can be served on the side. The perfect accompaniments to the dish are the fragrant yellow rice on page 182 and an Indonesian salad such as the one on page 206.

1 × 2kg duck
1½ tbsp Tamarind water
    (page 299)
2 tsp shrimp paste
5 tbsp vegetable oil
1 quantity Balinese spice paste
    (basa gede, see page 302)
1 tbsp kecap manis

Sprinkle a 2.5cm-thick layer of hardwood sawdust or hickory chips into a wok and rest a petal steamer over the top. Place the wok over a high heat until the sawdust begins to smoke, then reduce the heat to low. Put the duck onto the steamer, cover the wok with a lid or some foil, and leave the duck to smoke for 5 minutes, or up to 15 minutes more if you really like the taste of smoke, then remove. Put the duck into a shallow dish.

Preheat the oven to 120°C/Gas Mark ½. Mix 2 teaspoons of the tamarind water with 1½ teaspoons salt, the shrimp paste and 2 tablespoons of the oil. Rub the skin of the duck with this mixture. Set aside.

Put the spice paste into a bowl and mix in the rest of the tamarind water, the remaining oil and the kecap manis. Push two-thirds of the spice paste into the cavity of the duck and secure the opening with a fine skewer. Spread the rest over the outside of the bird, then slide it into a roasting bag and pour in 300ml water. Seal the bag so the water can't escape, then place it on a rack set in a roasting tin. Roast for 4 hours.

Slit open the roasting bag and lift the duck onto a carving board. Pour the cooking juices into a jug, leave them to settle, then skim off the fat into a small bowl. Reserve the fat for frying, if you wish. Pour the juices into a small pan and reheat briefly.

To serve, break the duck meat into portion-sized pieces and arrange on a large serving plate. Pour the juices into 4–6 small bowls for spooning over your duck and rice or for eating like a soup, and take to the table together with the rice and salad.

Fragrant yellow rice
Nasi kuning

SERVES 4–6

This fragrant rice says 'Bali on a plate' to me. That might seem debatable, when the cooking from Bali is usually so infused with spicy flavours like galangal, chilli and shrimp paste, but there's something about the beautiful etherealness of this dish that in my mind strikes a chord with the enviable spirituality of the Balinese people. And it is not without good reason that this is a celebratory dish at festivals, with its perfume of lemongrass, galangal and lime leaves. Janet de Neefe, whose book Fragrant Rice has been a source of great inspiration to me, tells the story of how she once ordered a birthday cake for a girlfriend and asked her brother-in-law to make something grand and colourful. She returned to collect it the next day to find 'perched on a painted wooden pedestal, a huge cone of yellow rice. Its peak was covered in a banana leaf and its base was decorated with bright red chillies that looked like spidery flowers, carved tomatoes in the shape of luscious red roses, sprigs of lemon basil and fried peanuts'. This recipe, though much influenced by Janet's, is more everyday than the high-days-and-holidays version in her book.

350g long-grain rice
400ml coconut milk
1 tsp turmeric powder
4 kaffir lime leaves,
    finely shredded
2 lemongrass stalks,
    halved and bruised
25g peeled galangal
    or ginger, thinly
    sliced lengthways

Put the rice into a medium-sized non-stick pan and add the coconut milk, 300ml water, turmeric, kaffir lime leaves, lemongrass stalks, galangal or ginger and ½ teaspoon salt. Bring to the boil, stir once, reduce the heat to low and cover with a tight-fitting lid. Leave to cook for 10 minutes, then remove from the heat and leave undisturbed for another 10 minutes.

Uncover the rice, discard the lemongrass and sliced galangal and fluff up the grains with a fork. Serve straight away.

Green bean and fresh coconut salad with crisp fried shallots, garlic and chilli
Urap buncis

SERVES 4

Much as I like the hustle and bustle of street markets, I find it rewarding to take a common dish like urab, which is often thrown together in extreme haste, and produce it with some care and attention to detail. In this case it will involve blanching the beans until they soften but retain a significant bite, grating fresh coconut and striving to attain the delicious crispness of fried thinly sliced shallots and garlic with chilli and shrimp paste. So much do I enjoy this, that I would suggest it's the perfect accompaniment to something Western like a barbecued spatchcocked chicken.

250g fine green beans,
    cut into 3cm pieces
150g fresh coconut,
    finely grated
2 tbsp vegetable oil
1 medium-hot red chilli,
    seeded and chopped
100g bean sprouts
2 kaffir lime leaves,
    finely shredded
25g *Crisp fried shallots*
    (page 299)
15g *Crisp fried garlic*
    (page 299)
2 red bird's eye chillies,
    thinly sliced

For the dressing:
½ tsp shrimp paste
4 tsp lime juice
1 tbsp vegetable oil
2 tsp palm sugar

Bring a pan of salted water to the boil. Add the green beans and cook for 2 minutes. Drain and refresh under cold water. Dry well on kitchen paper. Remove the fresh coconut from its shell, peel off the brown skin with a potato peeler and finely grate the flesh: the easiest way is by using the finest grating blade of your food processor (page 299). Heat the oil in a small frying pan, add the chopped red chilli and fry gently for a few seconds until just beginning to colour. Scoop onto a plate and leave to cool.

Tip the blanched beans into a bowl and add the grated coconut, bean sprouts, lime leaves, fried red chilli, crisp fried shallots and garlic and sliced bird's eye chilli. Mix together well.

For the dressing, blend the shrimp paste with the lime juice in a small bowl, then whisk in the oil, sugar and ½ teaspoon salt. Add to the bowl, toss everything together and serve.

Char-grilled butterflied fish

Ikan bakar

SERVES 4

This is another popular dish in Indonesia, where they also use steaks or fillets from larger fish, or smaller whole fish that have been slashed two or three times on either side to allow the flavours of the marinade to permeate the flesh. The marinade can be just a simple mixture of fresh or powdered turmeric mixed with salt and crushed garlic, but I like the slightly more complex flavours of the marinade below. The Balinese cook has prepared the fish in the picture by splitting it down the backbone from the head to the tail, gutting it and opening it flat still joined at the belly. You could try this if you haven't got your fish ready gutted from the fishmonger. For a gutted fish, butterfly it as described in the recipe.

4 × 350g sea bream, snapper, silver perch or sea bass, gutted and scaled

For the marinade:
25g shallots, roughly chopped
15g garlic, roughly chopped
1 red bird's eye chilli, thinly sliced
15g peeled ginger, roughly chopped
7g peeled galangal or extra ginger, roughly chopped
10g peeled fresh turmeric, roughly chopped, or ½ tsp turmeric powder
2 tbsp *Tamarind water* (page 299)
4 tbsp vegetable oil

Sambal matah (page 305), to serve

Trim the fins from the fish, then working with one fish at a time, open up the belly cavity down to the tail. Split the head almost in half by cutting from under the mouth up towards the top of the head but not quite all the way through. Open up and press firmly along the backbone until the fish is completely flat.

For the marinade, put the shallots, garlic, chilli, ginger, galangal, turmeric, tamarind water and ½ teaspoon salt into a mini food processor and blend to a smooth paste. Tip into a small bowl and stir in 2 tablespoons of the oil.

Paint some of the marinade over both sides of each fish and leave for 10 minutes while you preheat your barbecue or grill to medium-high. Stir the remaining vegetable oil into the remaining marinade.

If you have one, place the fish in a lightly oiled wire fish grill: this makes turning it easier. Otherwise, simply place the fish on the oiled bars of the barbecue or the rack of the grill pan, skin-side up. Cook for 4 minutes on each side, basting regularly with the leftover marinade, until slightly charred and cooked through. Serve straight away with the sambal matah.

Heinz's assorted seafood braised in coconut milk

SERVES 4

Heinz von Holzen has a Balinese restaurant and cookery school called Bumbu Bali. He treated us to a really good nasi campur, the combination of rice with two or three curries, some satay, sambals and a salad such as a lawar (page 203). After lunch I went to his cookery school, where he prepared and cooked this seafood dish: Indonesian in its flavours from the spice paste flavoured with ginger and galangal, but European in its execution in that he cooked the fish very delicately. I must confess I've taken his recipe and used it at the Seafood Restaurant, served with the green bean and fresh coconut salad on page 184, which is going down a storm.

400g fish fillets, such as monkfish, john dory, barramundi, gurnard or sea bass, taken from a medium-sized fish
250g prepared medium-sized squid (pouches about 18cm long)
12 large raw peeled prawns
Freshly ground white pepper
1 tbsp lime juice
200g (8 heaped tbsp) *Balinese spice paste (basa gede, see page 302)*
2 tbsp vegetable oil
4 kaffir lime leaves, torn into small pieces
2 fat lemongrass stalks, halved and bruised
120ml *Asian chicken stock* (page 300)
250ml coconut milk

Cut the fish into 3–4cm chunks. Slit the body pouches of the squid along one side, open them out flat and score the inside into a fine diamond pattern with the tip of a small, sharp knife. Cut the squid pouches lengthways into 4 wide strips, and then each strip across into 3 pieces. This helps the pieces to curl attractively during cooking. Score the fins in the same way and cut each one in half. Separate the tentacles into pairs.

Put the fish and squid into a shallow bowl with the peeled prawns and sprinkle with ½ teaspoon salt, some pepper and the lime juice. Mix together well. Then add half the spice paste and rub it well all over the pieces of seafood.

Heat the oil in a large, deep frying pan over a medium heat. Add the remaining spice paste and fry gently for 2–3 minutes until it starts to smell fragrant. Add the kaffir lime leaves, lemongrass and stock and simmer for 1 minute.

Add the pieces of fish (not the squid or the prawns) to the pan and leave to cook for 1 minute, then turn them over and cook for a further minute. Add the coconut milk to the pan, together with the squid and prawns, and simmer for 2 minutes until all the seafood is just cooked. Season to taste with a little more salt and lime juice to taste if you wish and serve.

Seafood satay
Satai lilit

SERVES 4 / MAKES 16

In Bali, there are two types of satay: one made from small chunks of marinated meat threaded onto skewers, and the other from minced meat or seafood moulded onto lemongrass stalks or small skewers. These seafood satay are made extra special by being a mixture of white fish and raw prawns, which gives them a lovely succulent sweetness with the aromatic local spice paste. The mixture for these can also be shaped into small fishcakes, shallow-fried in vegetable oil for one minute on each side and served with the same classic dipping sauce. For skewers, use 16 long thin lemongrass stalks from which you have removed a couple of outer layers, or else 18cm bamboo skewers soaked in water for half an hour beforehand.

350g skinned and boned
 white fish fillet, such as
 haddock, coley, flathead
 or silver perch
100g large raw peeled prawns
6 tbsp *Balinese spice paste (basa
 gede,* see page 302)
4 kaffir lime leaves, finely
 shredded
4 tbsp coconut cream
 (or the thick cream from
 the top of a chilled can
 of coconut milk)
2 tsp palm sugar
1 quantity *Southeast Asian
 dipping sauce* (page 304),
 to serve
Vegetable oil, for brushing

Cut the fish and prawns into small chunks and put into the bowl of a food processor with the spice paste, lime leaves, coconut cream, sugar and ½ teaspoon salt. Process together into a thick paste.

If using lemongrass stalks, make a shallow slit in the thicker end of each one and lightly bruise with a rolling pin. This will help to release their flavour. Take a well-heaped tablespoon of the mixture and form it around each lemongrass stalk or soaked bamboo skewer, shaping it slightly fatter at the top, a little like a drumstick. You should make about 16 satays.

Make the dipping sauce and divide it between 4 small dipping saucers.

Preheat the barbecue or grill to medium-high; a disposable foil-tray barbecue would be ideal for this. Brush the satay lightly with vegetable oil and barbecue or grill for 5–6 minutes, turning frequently, until golden brown all over and cooked through. Serve hot with the dipping sauce.

Beef satay
Satai sapi

SERVES 4/MAKES 16

The first time I tasted satay, in Singapore in 1987, I truly believed nothing else could ever taste so amazing. It was a defining moment in my culinary education. But now they don't seem to be as good any more. Maybe it's over-familiarity, as you can now buy them anywhere from Melbourne to Maidenhead, or maybe they're not made quite as carefully as they once were, when I marvelled at their economy as the street hawkers made the embers of charcoal glow with paper fans. But given some special treatment like this, marinating first with chilli, palm sugar, kecap manis and roasted coriander, the romance of the famous dish returns. Satay such as these are also traditionally made with lean pork: fillet would be ideal.

500g lean beef, such as sirloin or fillet steak, well trimmed of all fat
1 tbsp coriander seeds
½ tsp cumin seeds
1 tsp black peppercorns
25g garlic, roughly chopped
3 medium-hot red chillies, halved lengthways, seeded and roughly chopped
2 tsp lime juice
2 tsp palm sugar
1 tbsp kecap manis
1 tbsp vegetable oil, plus extra for brushing
1 quantity *Kecap manis and lime dipping sauce* (page 304), to serve

Soak 16 × 18cm bamboo skewers in cold water for 30 minutes. Cut the beef into 2cm pieces and place them in a bowl.

Heat a dry, heavy-based frying pan over a medium heat, add the coriander seeds, cumin seeds and peppercorns and shake them around for a few seconds until they darken slightly and start to smell aromatic. Tip them into a spice grinder and grind them to a fine powder. Tip the spice powder into a mini food processor and add the garlic, chillies, lime juice, sugar, kecap manis, oil and a teaspoon salt, and grind everything together into a smooth paste.

Add the spice paste to the beef and mix together well. Set aside to marinate for about 15 minutes.

Thread 5 pieces of the beef onto each bamboo skewer. Preheat the barbecue or grill to medium-high; a disposable foil-tray barbecue would be ideal for this. Brush the satay lightly with a little more oil and barbecue or grill for about 4 minutes, turning once, until just cooked through. Serve straight away while still hot with the kecap manis and lime dipping sauce.

Chicken satay with kecap manis, lime leaves and cracked black pepper

Satai ayam

SERVES 4/MAKES 16

This dish posed a problem for me in that the marinade went to waste. Of course, in Bali they would be using the marinade all night long at the food stall. I suggest that, instead of discarding the marinade, you bring it to the boil in a small pan, boil vigorously for 3 minutes while the chicken is grilling, then serve it alongside the chicken.

500g skinned boneless chicken (a mixture of thigh and breast meat)
3 tbsp vegetable oil
50g shallots, finely chopped
20g garlic, crushed
1 tsp soy sauce
1 tbsp kecap manis
2 tsp coarsely ground black pepper
3 kaffir lime leaves, finely shredded
1 quantity *Peanut sauce* (page 304), to serve

Soak 16 × 18cm bamboo skewers in cold water for 30 minutes. Cut the chicken into 2 × 2cm pieces.

Heat the oil in a small frying pan, add the shallots and fry over a medium heat until richly golden. Tip the oil and shallots into a small mixing bowl and leave to cool. Then stir in the crushed garlic, soy sauce, kecap manis, black pepper and kaffir lime leaves. Add the chicken, mix together well and leave to marinate for at least 10 minutes.

Thread 5 pieces of chicken onto each bamboo skewer. Preheat the barbecue or grill to medium high; a disposable foil-tray barbecue would be ideal for this. Brush the satay lightly with a little more oil and barbecue or grill for about 6–8 minutes, turning once, until cooked through. Serve straight away with the peanut sauce.

Baked spiced fish
Pepes ikan

SERVES 4

This traditional way of cooking fish uses a banana-leaf parcel roasted over a charcoal fire. The banana leaf not only imparts a subtle flavour to the fish but also keeps it succulent and moist. However, many of us are not going to be able to get banana leaves, so I've baked the fish in the oven instead, wrapped in foil. This produces more of a sauce than the traditional method, which is perfect when the fish is served with plenty of steamed rice.

4 × 150–175g fillets
    of firm fish, such as
    monkfish or snapper
8 tsp *Balinese spice paste*
    (*basa gede*, see page 302)
8 kaffir lime leaves,
    finely shredded

Preheat the oven to 240ºC/Gas Mark 9. Cut out four 30cm squares of foil. Place a piece of fish in the centre of each square and spread 1 teaspoon of the spice paste over each side. Season with salt, sprinkle over the shredded kaffir lime leaves, then bring the edges of the foil together over the fish and seal to form a watertight parcel.

Place the foil parcels side by side on a baking tray and bake for 10 minutes. Transfer the parcels to warmed plates and let each diner open up his own.

Slow-cooked pork with ginger, chilli and sweet soy sauce
Babi kecap

SERVES 6

I would call this braised pork dish, hot with chilli, sour with tamarind and sweet with palm sugar, a celebration of kecap manis. This is the soy sauce unique to Indonesia, which is made thick, sweet and syrupy by the addition of a generous quantity of the almost fudge-like sugar made from a local palm. This was the star dish at the Bumbu Bali restaurant (see also page 190), where I was served a nasi campur, a selection of curries, sambals, satays, salads and grills with rice.

2 tbsp vegetable oil

100g shallots, thinly sliced

50g garlic, crushed

25g peeled ginger, finely grated

1.25kg lean pork shoulder, cut into 3cm chunks

4 tbsp kecap manis

2 tbsp dark soy sauce

3 tbsp *Tamarind water* (page 299)

½ tsp freshly ground black pepper

3–4 medium-hot chillies, seeded and chopped

4 red bird's eye chillies, left whole

500ml *Asian chicken stock* (page 300)

Crisp fried shallots (page 299), to garnish

Heat the oil in a large, heavy-based pan over a medium heat. Add the shallots and fry until they are soft and richly golden. Add the crushed garlic, ginger and ½ teaspoon salt and cook for 1 minute.

Add the pork to the pan and fry for 2 minutes until lightly coloured. Add the kecap manis, dark soy sauce, tamarind water, pepper, chopped and whole chillies and stock. Leave to simmer, uncovered, for about 1½ hours, stirring now and then towards the end of cooking, until the pork is tender.

Lift the pork out of the sauce with a slotted spoon onto a plate. Boil the cooking liquid until it has reduced to a well-flavoured, slightly thickened, shiny, dark brown sauce. Season to taste with salt, return the pork to the pan and stir in.

Spoon the pork onto a warmed serving plate, scatter with the crisp fried shallots and serve.

Chicken braised in coconut milk
Opor ayam

SERVES 4

This comes from yet another trip to a Balinese market, this time to a night market in Gianyar. 'Night market' is a bit of a misnomer because in my experience while yes, you can buy cheap sneakers and sarongs, they're primarily about hot and cold food stalls, where you can always find very exciting dishes. I got the idea for this simple curry from a stall selling ayam goreng, the local deep-fried chicken. This is a favourite dish in Bali. The chicken is first simmered with coconut milk and the local spice paste, basa gede, that is used everywhere in Bali. The chicken cooked in this fragrant curry is delicious in itself but the locals prefer the chicken fried in hot oil until crisp and light brown and the curry sauce served as an accompaniment. It seems to me, however, that the curry is so excellent it's hardly necessary to fry the chicken, certainly when making the dish at home. But, of course, do so if you have a hankering for some great fried chicken.

1 × 1.5kg chicken, jointed
    into 8 pieces
1 quantity Balinese spice paste
    (basa gede, see page 302)
400ml coconut milk
1 lemongrass stalk,
    lightly bruised

Sprinkle the pieces of chicken on both sides with a little salt and set aside for 30 minutes.

Put the spice mixture into a medium-sized pan and add the coconut milk, lemongrass stalk and 1 teaspoon salt. Bring slowly to the boil, then add the chicken pieces and simmer uncovered, stirring every now and then, for 1 hour until the chicken is tender and the sauce has thickened.

Green bean salad with a chicken and coconut dressing
Lawar buncis

SERVES 6–8

Lawar is a sacred dish in Bali, cooked by men under the guidance of a ritual cooking specialist, a Belawa. I had two versions of this salad: the one below made with chicken (you can also make it with minced pork), which is lovely, and another at a wedding in the village of Padangkerta, which I felt might not be to everyone's taste. On that occasion, the men of the village slaughtered a pig, butchered it and reserved the blood in buckets. The pork they turned into satays, and some of the blood they mixed with the lawar in quantities specified by the Belawa. However, I found their hospitality to be infectious and their keenness to ply me with yet another glass of tuac – the local fermented palm juice that tasted a bit like my brother's homemade wine, which we drank in copious quantities from the demi-johns dotted all over his kitchen in Oxford in the late 1960s, sour, cloudy and yeasty – was irresistible. They were a bit like the locals at the Cornish Arms in St Merryn, very jolly and full of bonhomie. At the time, the red-coloured lawar seemed perfectly nice. The next morning, however, I felt slightly the worse for wear. Was it the lawar or the tuac? Who knows?

500g dwarf green beans, topped and tailed

2 tbsp vegetable oil

3 tbsp *Balinese spice paste* (basa gede, see page 302)

4 kaffir lime leaves, 2 finely shredded and 2 left whole

1 lemongrass stalk, halved and bruised

100g finely chopped chicken

125ml coconut milk

150g fresh coconut, finely grated

3 tbsp *Crisp fried shallots* (page 299)

1 red bird's eye chilli, finely chopped

2 tsp lime juice

Drop the beans into a pan of boiling salted water and cook for 4–5 minutes or until just tender. Drain and refresh under cold water, leave to cool, then chop into 2.5cm pieces.

For the chicken and coconut dressing, heat the oil in a pan over a medium heat, add the spice paste, the 2 whole lime leaves and the bruised lemongrass and fry gently for 1 minute. Add the minced chicken and cook for 2–3 minutes, breaking it up with a wooden spoon as it browns. Add 5 tablespoons water and simmer for about 15 minutes until well reduced and almost dry. This allows time for the kaffir lime leaves and lemongrass to perfume the sauce. Remove and discard the lemongrass and lime leaves and add the coconut milk. Bring back to the boil, lower the heat and simmer for another 10–12 minutes until it has reduced by half and is thick and creamy. Remove from the heat and leave to go cold – it will thicken considerably as it cools.

Tip the green beans into a bowl and mix in the grated coconut, the shredded lime leaves, crisp fried shallots, chilli, lime juice and the dressing. Serve straight away, at room temperature.

A salad of green beans, potatoes, spinach and hard-boiled eggs with a spicy peanut sauce
Gado-gado

SERVES 4

The most memorable part of this famous Indonesian dish is the sweet, limey and spicy peanut sauce you drizzle over the salad just before it's served. You can use almost any combination of cooked vegetables, though I do think the pairing of morning glory and bean sprouts that I saw in Ubud in Bali was too simple. This is an occasion for taking some trouble with just the right vegetables. You need softness and crunch: always some green beans, I think, and some potatoes. I also like to add some par-boiled and refreshed carrot and cauliflower florets. I prefer cauliflower to the sliced cabbage that so often appears in the inferior versions, which are often little more than cabbage with a dressing of peanut butter, sugar and vinegar.

150g new potatoes, peeled and quartered lengthways

150g cauliflower, broken into tiny florets

150g carrots, thickly sliced on the diagonal

150g fine green beans, topped and tailed

100g morning glory or leaf spinach

100g green mango or green papaya (optional)

150g piece of cucumber, peeled

Vegetable oil, for deep-frying

200–250g block of firm tofu, drained

4 eggs

1 quantity Peanut sauce (page 304)

100g bean sprouts

½ quantity Crisp fried shallots (page 299)

Prawn crackers, to serve

Cook the potatoes in boiling salted water for 8 minutes or until tender, then remove with a slotted spoon and leave to cool.

Add the cauliflower to the water, bring back to the boil and cook for 1½ minutes, then drain and refresh under cold water. Repeat with the carrots, cooking them for 4 minutes, the beans for 4 minutes and the morning glory or spinach for just 20 seconds. Set aside to drain on kitchen paper.

Finely shred the green mango or papaya, if using. Cut the cucumber in half lengthways, then across into slices 1cm thick.

Heat some oil for deep-frying to 190ºC. Deep-fry the piece of tofu for 5 minutes until golden brown. Lift out and drain on kitchen paper and, when cool, cut into small, 1cm-thick pieces.

Hard-boil the eggs for 8 minutes, then drain, cover with cold water and, when cool, peel and cut into quarters.

Thin down the peanut sauce with a little water to a thick pouring consistency.

Arrange the cooked vegetables in one large or 4 individual wide shallow bowls with the bean sprouts, shredded mango or papaya if using, cucumber, tofu and hard-boiled eggs. Drizzle with the peanut sauce, scatter over the crisp fried shallots and serve with the prawn crackers.

Aubergine curry with chilli, tomato and kaffir lime leaves
Terung belado

SERVES 4

But for the inclusion of half a teaspoon of shrimp paste, this is a very pleasant vegetarian curry. It bears no resemblance to an Indian curry, but I can't think of any better way of describing it because it's chilli-hot, has lots of ginger and garlic and you can easily serve it on its own with rice. It's the kaffir lime leaves, kecap manis, sugar and lime juice that make it unique to Indonesia.

2 medium-sized aubergines
7 tbsp vegetable oil
200g shallots, thinly sliced
25g garlic, thinly sliced
25g peeled ginger, finely
    chopped
2 medium-hot red chillies,
    seeded if you wish,
    then thinly sliced
½ tsp shrimp paste
200g chopped tomatoes,
    canned or fresh
4 kaffir lime leaves
1 tbsp kecap manis
1 tbsp dark soy sauce
1 tsp palm sugar
Juice of ½ lime

Cut the aubergines in half lengthways and then across into slices 1cm thick. Toss with 1 teaspoon salt and set aside in a colander for 30 minutes.

Heat 5 tablespoons of the oil in a wok or large deep frying pan. Add the aubergines and stir-fry for 6 minutes until lightly golden. Lift out with a slotted spoon onto a plate and set aside.

Add the remaining oil to the pan, add the shallots and garlic and fry until golden. Add the ginger, chillies, shrimp paste and tomatoes and cook for a few seconds more until the tomatoes have softened. Return the aubergines to the pan with the lime leaves and 6 tablespoons water. Simmer for 2 minutes until the aubergines are tender and the sauce has reduced slightly.

Stir in the kecap manis, dark soy sauce, sugar, lime juice and ½ teaspoon salt or to taste, and serve.

Balinese chicken noodle soup
Soto ayam

SERVES 4

This is a popular soup across the whole Indonesian archipelago, but varies a little from one island to another. Sometimes the slices of potato are deep-fried instead of boiled, sometimes there are no noodles, sometimes the soup is made without coconut milk. But there are always slices of hard-boiled egg, fresh bean sprouts and crispy fried shallots to garnish. It's a bit like a Malaysian laksa except that it's flavoured with the local spice paste, and uses fine rice vermicelli noodles instead of thick ones.

2 chicken legs

225g small waxy potatoes, such as Charlotte, peeled

2 tbsp vegetable oil

5 tbsp Balinese spice paste (basa gede, see page 302)

2 kaffir lime leaves

250ml coconut milk

130g rice vermicelli noodles

100g fresh bean sprouts

2 hard-boiled eggs, thickly sliced

4 tbsp Crisp fried shallots (page 299)

Small handful of coriander leaves

2 limes, cut into wedges

Sambal oelek, to serve (optional)

Put the chicken legs into a pan with 1 litre of water and 1 teaspoon salt, bring to the boil, cover and simmer for 25 minutes until the chicken is tender. Meanwhile, cook the potatoes in a pan of boiling salted water until tender – about 15–20 minutes. Drain and thickly slice.

When the chicken is cooked, strain the stock into a bowl. Leave the chicken until it is cool enough to handle, then discard the skin and bones and pull the meat into fine shreds. Cover and set aside. Wipe the pan so you can use it in the next step.

Heat the oil in the cleaned-out pan over a medium heat, add the spice paste and fry gently for 3 minutes. Add the chicken stock and kaffir lime leaves, bring to the boil, cover and leave to simmer for 5 minutes. Add the coconut milk and bring almost back to the boil. Season to taste with salt, cover and keep hot.

Drop the noodles into a pan of boiling unsalted water, remove the pan from the heat and leave them to soak for 2 minutes. Drain.

Divide the noodles, cooked chicken, sliced potatoes and bean sprouts between 4 warmed large, deep bowls. Ladle over the hot soup stock and garnish with the sliced hard-boiled eggs, crisp fried shallots and coriander leaves. Serve with the lime wedges and some sambal oelek if you wish.

Spicy shredded chicken salad with chilli and lime

Ayam sambal mentah

SERVES 6

This is the sort of recipe I would love to find at a wedding buffet. Spatchcock a chicken, season it with salt, pepper and chilli flakes, grill it, then shred it while still warm. Mix it with some crisp fried shallots and garlic, grated coconut, fresh chilli, shredded lime leaves, bean sprouts and cucumber and finally toss with a dressing of shrimp paste, palm sugar, lime juice, lemongrass and coconut milk.

1 small chicken (weighing about 1.2kg)
2 tbsp vegetable oil
Freshly ground white pepper
½ tsp crushed dried chillies
150g fresh coconut, finely grated
4 tbsp *Crisp fried shallots* (page 299)
2 tbsp *Crisp fried garlic* (page 299)
2 red bird's eye chillies (or to taste), finely chopped
2 kaffir lime leaves, finely shredded
150g bean sprouts
½ cucumber, peeled, halved lengthways, seeded and thinly sliced

For the dressing:
1 tsp shrimp paste
2 tsp palm sugar
2 tbsp lime juice
6 tbsp coconut milk
2 fat lemongrass stalks, core finely chopped

Spatchcock the chicken: place it breast-side down on a chopping board and, using strong kitchen scissors or poultry shears, cut along either side of the backbone and remove it. Open up the chicken, turn it over and press down firmly on the breastbone to flatten it. Brush the chicken with a little oil and season well on both sides with salt and white pepper and the crushed dried chillies.

Preheat the grill to medium. Place the chicken on the rack of the grill pan, skin-side down, and grill it about 15cm away from the heat for 15–20 minutes. Then turn it over and grill for a further 15 minutes or until cooked through and the juices run clear. Remove and leave to cool.

When the chicken is cool, remove the meat from the bones and pull into long thin pieces. Place in a bowl with the grated coconut, fried shallots, fried garlic, chilli, lime leaves, bean sprouts and cucumber. Mix together well.

For the dressing, mix the shrimp paste with ½ teaspoon salt, the sugar and the lime juice into a smooth paste. Add the coconut milk and chopped lemongrass and season to taste with white pepper. Toss the dressing with the salad just before serving.

CHAPTER SIX

SRI LANKA

Nowhere on earth is perfect. In Sri Lanka the roads are terrible, it takes hours to get anywhere because of the traffic, and at first you think you are going to be in a major accident every five minutes. Before you even get there, you worry that you will be involved in some terrorist activity. But after a day or so the enormous fertility of this tropical island, the immense bounty of fish from the Indian ocean and the dreamy quality of the climate start to affect you in a positive and optimistic way. There's an abundance of food; rice, of course, is the main crop but the markets are filled with the most exciting colours and shapes of vegetables and fruit. I've never been to a country where there is no shortage of seafood before. The market on the beach at Negombo, just north of Colombo, had no refrigeration that I could see anywhere, but the fish freshly landed that morning were a seafood lover's delight. Darshan, the half Japanese, half Sri Lankan chef who took me round, pointed out three different types of snapper, scabbard fish, garfish with their long pointed beaks, half beaks (with only half a beak), tuna, swordfish, and all the mackerel-related fish such as bonito, Spanish mackerel and kingfish. Squid and cuttlefish still alive so that when you touched them their colour changed with the imprint of your finger; also alive, tiny shrimps right up to prawns the size of small lobsters, and not a farmed one amongst them. Indeed not a farmed fish anywhere. To me it was like the fish Garden of Eden, in spite of the recent horrors of the tsunami and political troubles. Not just the fish but all the produce of the island seemed to me to reflect a time before the mass production of food, where everything tasted better than ever before.

When I started to eat Sri Lankan food, it reinforced the superb quality of the raw materials: the vegetable and fruit curries, finger aubergines, cashew nut, pineapple, jackfruit, asparagus, beetroot and even mundane-sounding ones like tomato and potato were so good you almost questioned the need for meat. The fisherman's curry I ate in a simple village on the beach, fragrant with the taste of curry leaves, pandan leaf, cinnamon, tomato and green chilli, had a sophistication in its cooking that made me realize how important food was to everyone there.

To me the essential flavours of Sri Lankan cooking are coconut, pandan and curry leaves, cinnamon – the whole bark, just broken up a little – and a roasted and ground spice mix that contains coriander, cumin, fennel, cinnamon, cloves, chilli and a few other spices. As with all South Asian meals, rice is the most important element, and what lovely rice dishes they cook, such as the ghee rice on page 306. Like everywhere else a meal would consist of three or four curries, a Sri Lankan 'salad' – not like ours, but of just warmed, roughly chopped herbs with coconut, lime and chilli – and a couple of fiery sambols. What I finally learnt about all food in the Far East is that no dish is the star. The sum of all the parts is what eating there is all about.

Chef Publis's devilled prawns with tomato

SERVES 4

T. Publis Silva is the head chef of the Mount Lavinia hotel in Colombo. Naturally, with a name like that, he is of Portuguese extraction, but he is always referred to rather formally as Chef Publis. He has worked at the hotel for over fifty years and, now in his seventies, he still controls the kitchen perfectly as well as finding time to appear regularly on his own cooking show on local TV. This dish is also known as 'tempered prawns', from the Portuguese temperado, meaning to fry and season, and highlights the Portuguese influences in the dish, notably the absence of any coconut milk. Mount Lavinia is, incidentally, one of those great old colonial-style hotels in the same vein as the Metropole in Hanoi, the Majestic in Ho Chi Minh city, the E&O in Penang and, of course, Raffles in Singapore. However, like many grumpy old men, I enjoy saying I preferred Raffles before it was done up, complete with air-conditioning with the volume of an outboard motor, and if you are a little older than me, a live tiger in the bar. This dish, pictured on the right, which Chef Publis cooked at the beach restaurant in front of the hotel, shows off the two main ingredients in Sri Lankan cooking: seafood and vegetables.

20 large raw peeled prawns
¼ tsp turmeric powder
450g ripe vine tomatoes
60ml coconut or vegetable oil
75g onions or shallots,
    thinly sliced
15g garlic, finely chopped
15g peeled ginger, finely
    chopped
5 × 1cm pieces pandan leaf
20 curry leaves
1 tsp crushed dried kashmiri
    chillies
10cm cinnamon stick, broken
1 green cayenne chilli, thinly
    sliced on the diagonal
100g white of leek, sliced
    on the diagonal
½ tsp freshly ground black
    pepper
100g green pepper, seeded,
    then sliced on the diagonal
Juice of 1 lime
Small handful of fresh
    mint leaves

Toss the prawns with the turmeric and ½ teaspoon salt. Set aside. Finely chop half the tomatoes and cut the rest into wedges. Set aside.

Heat the oil in a large, deep frying pan. Add the onions or shallots and fry for 5 minutes until soft and translucent.

Add the garlic, ginger, pieces of pandan leaf and curry leaves and stir-fry for 1 minute. Add the crushed dried chillies and pieces of cinnamon and stir-fry for another 2 minutes until the mixture smells aromatic.

Add the finely chopped tomatoes, green chilli, leek, black pepper and 1 teaspoon salt and stir-fry for 5 minutes. Add the prawns, green pepper and tomato wedges and cook for another 5 minutes until the prawns are cooked. Stir in the lime juice, scatter over the mint leaves and serve.

Potato mustard curry

SERVES 4–6

I remember watching this potato curry being cooked for me at the Mount Lavinia hotel in Colombo, mostly because the night before the Tamil Tigers had bombed Colombo. Well, to say 'bombed' is an overstatement. They flew over in two homemade kit-planes, apparently constructed from bits smuggled into the island and launched from a tiny airstrip somewhere in the forest in the north. Whether they dropped the bombs out of the side windows I don't know, but it all seemed rather pathetically tragic, and sadly two pilots and two people on the ground were killed. I also believe they managed to demolish one or two floors of the tax office, which one or two locals expressed some satisfaction with. From our hotel, we just thought it was a firework display – and the next day this delicious potato curry.

500g small, evenly sized waxy new potatoes, such as Charlotte
1½ tsp coriander seeds
1 tsp cumin seeds
¼ tsp fennel seeds
1 tbsp yellow mustard seeds
3 tbsp vegetable oil
100g onions or shallots, halved and thinly sliced
4 green cayenne chillies, thinly sliced
4 × 2.5cm pieces pandan leaf
10–12 curry leaves
10cm cinnamon stick, broken into smaller pieces
10g Maldive fish flakes or bonito flakes
25g garlic, finely chopped
½ tsp turmeric powder
Pinch of fenugreek seeds
120ml coconut milk
1 tbsp lime juice

Put the potatoes into a pan of cold salted water, bring to the boil, then leave to simmer for 10–12 minutes or until tender. Drain and set aside.

Meanwhile, put the coriander, cumin and fennel seeds into a spice grinder and grind to a fine powder. Put the mustard seeds into a mortar and coarsely grind with the pestle.

Heat the oil in a shallow, medium-sized pan. Add the onions or shallots and chillies and fry gently for 2–3 minutes. Add the pandan leaf, curry leaves, pieces of cinnamon stick and ½ teaspoon salt and fry gently for another minute.

Add the Maldive fish or bonito flakes, garlic, powdered spices and turmeric and cook for 1 minute. Add the fenugreek seeds, potatoes, coconut milk, ground mustard seeds and 200ml water and bring to a simmer. Add another ½ teaspoon salt and the lime juice, simmer for 1–2 minutes, then serve.

Pineapple curry

SERVES 6–8

This curry comes from the Sun House in Galle. The cooking here and at the Dutch House just across the road, both owned by Geoffrey Dobbs, is exceptional, particularly the vegetable curries. I was reassured to see, when I watched the chefs make this and the 'white' pumpkin curry on page 254, how simple these dishes really are. I have nostalgic memories of sitting outside under the frangipane trees with a choice of possibly ten curries and sambols in front of me, and a steady stream of ice-cold Lion beers coming from Dick's Bar near by. To me the Sun House was perfection; a bright airy bedroom with a breeze blowing right through it, whirling punkah fans overhead rather than air-conditioning, bookshelves filled with well-thumbed Penguin novels from the 1960s and 1970s like Somerset Maugham, Graham Greene and Anthony Powell, and downstairs in Dick's Bar, Eartha Kitt, Shirley Bassey, Ray Charles, and Andy Williams singing 'Music To Watch Girls By'.

4 tbsp vegetable oil

25g garlic, finely chopped

100g onions or shallots, halved and thinly sliced

5cm cinnamon stick, broken into smaller pieces

24 curry leaves

6 × 2.5cm pieces pandan leaf

3 tbsp Roasted Sri Lankan curry powder (page 303)

1 tsp turmeric powder

400ml coconut milk

650g prepared pineapple chunks (about 1 medium-sized pineapple)

4 green cayenne chillies, thinly sliced

Heat the oil in a large deep frying pan. Add the garlic and leave it to sizzle for 1 minute, then add the onions or shallots, cinnamon, curry leaves and pandan leaf and fry gently for 3 minutes.

Add the roasted curry powder and turmeric and fry for 1 minute until the mixture smells nicely aromatic. Add the coconut milk, bring to the boil and leave to simmer for a couple of minutes.

Add the pineapple chunks, green chillies and 1½ teaspoons salt, bring back to the boil and simmer for 5 minutes. Serve.

Sri Lankan chicken curry

SERVES 4

As an introduction to the food of Sri Lanka, a chicken curry is a perfect choice. Needless to say it contains the holy trinity – to me – of cinnamon bark, pandan leaf and curry leaves, and also tomato, coconut milk and roasted curry powder. Make this curry and you'll be hooked on all the others in this chapter.

2 tbsp coconut or vegetable oil

1 × 1.5kg chicken, jointed
 into 8 pieces

Freshly ground black pepper

15cm cinnamon stick, broken
 into smaller pieces

10 green cardamom pods,
 bruised

10 cloves

350g onions or shallots,
 halved and thinly sliced

40g garlic, crushed

25g peeled ginger, finely
 grated

2 tbsp *Roasted Sri Lankan curry
 powder* (page 303)

1 tsp kashmiri chilli powder

1 tsp turmeric powder

200g chopped tomatoes,
 fresh or from a can

20 curry leaves

4 × 4cm pieces pandan leaf

1 fat lemongrass stalk,
 halved and lightly bruised

3 green cayenne chillies,
 slit open lengthways

400ml coconut milk

1 tbsp lime juice

Heat the oil in a large, deep, heavy-based frying pan. Season the chicken pieces on both sides with salt and pepper, add them to the pan and fry over a medium heat for 5 minutes on each side until golden brown. Lift onto a plate.

Add the cinnamon, cardamom pods and cloves to the oil left in the pan and leave them to sizzle for a few seconds. Add the onions or shallots and fry gently for 5 minutes until soft and lightly browned. Add the garlic and ginger and fry for 2 minutes. Add the roasted curry powder, chilli powder and turmeric and fry for 1 minute more.

Return the chicken pieces to the pan with the tomatoes, curry leaves, pieces of pandan leaf, lemongrass, chillies and 1 teaspoon salt. Cover and cook gently over a medium-low heat for 25 minutes or until the chicken is tender.

Uncover, add the coconut milk, cover again and simmer for 5 minutes more. Stir in the lime juice and serve.

Fisherman's layered curry
with tomato, chilli and ginger

SERVES 6

I went out with the fishermen of Pelana village early one morning. They were hoping to catch parawer, the most prized fish on the south coast of the island. About a mile offshore, I watched them play out a net from one boat into a large circle, which was then pulled in by hand from another boat. I was much enthused by their spirit, cheerfulness and skilful cooperation in the tricky work of pulling in the net using nothing other than muscle power. Then I went back to their house and watched Chandrika, the aunt of Lasantha, head fisherman, prepare this curry. She sliced garlic, red onions and ginger against a large blade, which she held between her feet as she sat on the floor of the tiny kitchen area. Pictures of three of her family – Lasantha's mother, daughter and baby niece – lost in the tsunami, were on the table in the front room where we all later sat to eat the fish. I was taken with the sophistication of the dish, where the fish was cooked with a little coconut vinegar, turmeric, chilli powder and water, then layered with a stir-fry of onions, garlic, green chillies, cinnamon, curry leaves and roasted spice. She explained how it was important for this to be left for at least 10 minutes before being eaten with rice, so that the flavours of the vegetables infused the fish. I felt very privileged to be there; they also taught me how to eat with my fingers. Having moulded the fish into a ball with a little rice, you scoop it up in three fingers, place them to your lips and then use your thumb to push the food into your mouth.

1kg thick gurnard, grey mullet, sea bass or snapper fillet, cut into large 3cm chunks

3 tbsp coconut vinegar

2 tsp turmeric powder

1 tsp kashmiri chilli powder

3 tbsp coconut oil

25g peeled ginger, finely shredded

25g garlic, thinly sliced

200g red onions or shallots, thinly sliced

4 green cayenne chillies, thinly sliced

1 tsp black mustard seeds

1 tsp freshly ground black pepper

300g plum tomatoes, sliced

20 curry leaves

Put the fish into a large shallow pan with 2 tablespoons of the vinegar, 1 teaspoon of the turmeric, the chilli powder, 1 teaspoon salt and 200ml water. Bring to a simmer, cover and cook for 3 minutes, turning the pieces of fish over halfway through, until just cooked. Remove from the heat and set aside.

Heat the coconut oil in a wok or large deep frying pan over a medium heat. Add the ginger and garlic and fry for 1 minute. Add the onions or shallots, chillies, the remaining teaspoon of turmeric, the mustard seeds, black pepper and 1 teaspoon salt, and stir-fry for 4 minutes until the onion is just soft. Add the remaining tablespoon of vinegar, the sliced tomatoes, curry leaves and the liquid from the cooked fish, and continue to stir-fry for 6 minutes or until the tomatoes have broken down and the mixture is moist but not too wet.

Place one third of the stir-fried vegetables over the base of a serving plate and arrange half the pieces of cooked fish on top. Cover with another third of the vegetables, the remaining fish and the rest of the vegetables, and set aside for 10 minutes before serving.

Coconut dal with tomatoes and curry leaves

Parippu

SERVES 6–8

This dal is very common in Sri Lanka and tastes exactly as you might expect, like an Indian dal but noticeably flavoured with coconut, cinnamon, pandan leaf and curry leaves. As in the rest of the Indian subcontinent, you would almost always expect to have dal as part of any meal.

250g red lentils (*masoor dal*)
1 green cayenne chilli, sliced
½ tsp turmeric powder
4 × 2.5cm pieces pandan leaf
200ml coconut milk
3 tbsp coconut or vegetable oil
100g onions or shallots, finely chopped
15g garlic, crushed
3 dried red kashmiri chillies, broken into small pieces
12 curry leaves
1 tsp cumin seeds
1 tsp black mustard seeds
7.5cm cinnamon stick
1 tsp freshly ground coriander seeds
150g tomatoes, roughly chopped

Put the lentils into a pan with the green chilli, turmeric, pandan leaf and 1 litre of water. Bring to the boil and simmer, uncovered, for 40 minutes or until the lentils have broken down and the mixture has reduced and thickened quite considerably.

Add the coconut milk and leave to simmer, stirring now and then, for another 15–20 minutes or until it has thickened once more.

When the dal is cooked, heat the oil in a small frying pan. Add the onion and garlic and fry gently, stirring now and then, until golden brown. Add the dried red chillies, curry leaves, cumin seeds, mustard seeds, cinnamon stick and ground coriander and fry gently for 1 minute. Add the tomatoes and cook for another 1–2 minutes until they have just softened.

Tip the mixture into the dal, stir well and season with 1 teaspoon salt or to taste. Simmer for 5 minutes then serve.

Sour blackened fish curry
Ambul thiyal

SERVES 6 AS PART OF A MIXED CURRY MEAL

One of the things that most impressed me about Sri Lanka was the abundance of fish. Wherever there was a coast road, every half a mile or so there would be a stand where someone was selling fish straight out of the Indian Ocean: tuna, bonito, kingfish, sardines, swordfish, mahi mahi, and many more. I remember our car being stopped by one fisherman who was holding a plate piled high with live prawns the size of small lobsters. None of this fish is farmed; it is all wild and all superb. The dish of ambul thiyal is designed as a means of preservation as well as a fish curry, and is generally made with tuna. As there's little refrigeration, and oily fish goes off quickly in tropical temperatures, the most popular thing to do is to cook it at once, particularly with something sour like goraka, a yellow fruit that they sun-dry until it turns black and which has a delicious smoky sourness somewhat like tamarind. This produces a dry, black, sour and spicy curry, which is traditionally taken by people who live by the sea as a present to their relatives inland. I don't honestly think it works on its own, but in a family meal together with maybe a chicken curry, a couple of vegetable curries, some rice and perhaps a hot fiery sambol, such as the seeni sambol on page 305, it is a very pleasant dish.

175g onions, roughly chopped

20g peeled ginger, roughly chopped

20g garlic, crushed

2 fat lemongrass stalks, core thinly sliced

1½ tbsp *Roasted Sri Lankan curry powder* (page 303)

20g goraka pieces (see above), or 4 tbsp *Tamarind water* (page 299)

10cm cinnamon stick, broken into smaller pieces

2 tsp kashmiri chilli powder

4 green cayenne chillies, thinly sliced

24 curry leaves

24 × 1cm pieces pandan leaf

4 tbsp vegetable oil

1 tsp freshly ground black pepper

500g piece of tuna loin fillet

Preheat the oven to 200°C/Gas Mark 6. Put the onion, ginger, garlic, lemongrass, curry powder, the pieces of goraka or the tamarind water, cinnamon, chilli powder, cayenne chillies, curry leaves, pandan leaf, oil, black pepper, 2 tablespoons water and 2 teaspoons salt into a mini food processor and blend to a smooth paste. Transfer to a small bowl.

Cut the tuna fish into 3cm pieces and stir it into the paste. Transfer the mixture to a small cast-iron casserole dish and cover with a tight-fitting lid. Bake for 25 minutes until the fish is cooked.

Beetroot curry
Theldala

SERVES 4

I ordered quite a few beetroot curries when I was in Sri Lanka because I am very fond of beetroot and it is a good example of how the Sri Lankans can turn any vegetable into a memorable dish. I liked the creamy dishes with lots of coconut milk, but this was a welcome change, more like a stir-fry, where the beetroot remains slightly crunchy. It's known locally as a theldala. I've used coconut oil but you might find the flavour a little too powerful. If so, use vegetable oil instead. This is also nice made with carrots cut into batons like the beetroot.

750g raw beetroot, trimmed
    of their leaves
3 tbsp coconut or vegetable oil
1 tsp cumin seeds
1 tsp black mustard seeds
7.5cm cinnamon stick,
    broken into smaller pieces
10–12 curry leaves
2 green cayenne chillies,
    thinly sliced
150g onions, finely chopped
15g garlic, crushed
1 tsp Unroasted Sri Lankan
    curry powder (page 303)
1 tsp kashmiri chilli powder
¼ tsp turmeric powder
125g chopped tomatoes,
    fresh or from a can
1 tbsp lime juice

Peel the beetroot and cut them across into 7–8mm thick slices. Then cut each slice into 7–8mm wide batons.

Heat the oil in a large, deep frying pan over a medium heat. Add the cumin seeds, mustard seeds, cinnamon and curry leaves and leave to sizzle for a few seconds until the mustard seeds stop popping. Add the green chillies, onion and garlic and fry for 5–6 minutes until soft and lightly browned. Stir in the curry powder, chilli powder and turmeric, cook for a few seconds then add the beetroot, tomatoes and 1 teaspoon salt. Cover and cook over a medium-low heat for 15 minutes, stirring regularly, until the beetroot is just tender but still very slightly crunchy. Add a couple of tablespoons of water during cooking if it starts sticking to the base of the pan, but ideally leave it to cook in its own juices.

Uncover, stir in the lime juice and serve.

Cashew nut curry

SERVES 6–8

Every time I check into a new hotel room I make a beeline for the mini bar to see if they've got any cashew nuts in the little cupboard above the fridge. They are still an item of luxury to me – hellishly fattening, of course. I soon discovered in Sri Lanka that all the restaurants sell cashew nut curry, cashew nuts being a local crop, and I ordered it all the time because it was so cheap. They use fresh ones, which are deliciously soft, but I've found that by soaking dried nuts in water for about half an hour and then cooking them in the curry for about the same time they become creamy again. I like cashew nut curries that also have a vegetable in them. This was normally snake gourd, but also sometimes snake beans, so I've used green beans instead.

300g unsalted cashew nuts

2 tbsp coconut or vegetable oil

7.5cm cinnamon stick

150g onions, finely chopped

15g garlic, crushed

25g peeled ginger, finely grated

2 green cayenne chillies, thinly sliced

½ tsp turmeric powder

2 tsp *Roasted Sri Lankan curry powder* (page 303)

400ml coconut milk

2 fat lemongrass stalks, core thinly sliced

4 × 3cm pieces pandan leaf

10–12 curry leaves

150g green beans, cut into 3–4cm pieces

1 tsp jaggery or palm sugar

1 tbsp lime juice

Small handful of coriander leaves, roughly chopped

Put the cashew nuts into a bowl, cover with hot water and leave to soak for 30 minutes.

Heat the oil in a medium-sized pan, add the cinnamon and leave it to sizzle for a few seconds, then add the onion and garlic and fry gently for 5 minutes until soft and just beginning to brown. Stir in the ginger, green chillies, turmeric, curry powder, coconut milk, lemongrass, pandan leaf and curry leaves. Cover and leave to simmer for 20 minutes.

Drain the cashew nuts and stir them into the sauce with 150ml water and ½ teaspoon salt. Cover and simmer for a further 20 minutes. Uncover, add the green beans and continue to cook for another 10 minutes or until both the cashew nuts and beans are tender. Uncover the pan towards the end of cooking to reduce the sauce a little if necessary.

Stir in the sugar, lime juice and coriander, and serve.

Tomato curry
Thakkali curry
SERVES 6

This is a lovely fresh-tasting curry, of course, with all those tomatoes in it. I was in two minds when writing this, whether to call for the tomatoes to be skinned or not. I myself don't mind little furls of rolled-up tomato skin in my curry, but feel free to peel the tomatoes first if you wish, by cutting out the stalk, making a shallow cross in the top, lowering them into boiling water and leaving them for 20–30 seconds. I've put whole cloves, cardamoms and cinnamon in the curry and it is quite normal to leave them in, but just as I am an enthusiast for the odd bit of tomato skin, I also enjoy biting on the odd clove or cardamom.

1kg vine-ripened tomatoes
3 tbsp vegetable oil
2 tsp fenugreek seeds
5cm cinnamon stick
6 green cardamom pods,
    lightly bruised
6 cloves
10–12 curry leaves
6 × 2.5cm pieces pandan leaf
15g garlic, finely chopped
20g peeled ginger, finely
    grated
250g onions, halved and
    thinly sliced
2 tsp chilli powder
2 tsp *Unroasted Sri lankan
    curry powder* (page 303)
1 medium-hot green chilli,
    thinly sliced
4 tbsp coconut milk
1 tsp jaggery or palm sugar

Finely chop half the tomatoes and cut the remainder into wedges. Heat the oil in a large, deep frying pan. Add the fenugreek seeds, cinnamon stick, cardamom pods, cloves, curry leaves and pandan leaf and fry gently for 1 minute.

Add the garlic, ginger and onion and fry gently for 4 minutes until softened. Add the chilli powder and curry powder and fry for 1 minute more. Add the chopped tomatoes, green chilli and 150ml water and simmer for 5 minutes until the tomatoes have broken down into a sauce.

Add the tomato wedges, coconut milk, sugar and 1 teaspoon salt and simmer for a further 3 minutes or until the tomato wedges are just tender, then serve.

Coconut chilli crab
Kakuluwo uyala

SERVES 4

I'm not sure this is the precise recipe for Sri Lankan chilli crab from the New Yarl Eating House in Wellawatta, Colombo, pictured on the right, because it was virtually impossible to see what was going into the pan, it was so dark and steamy inside the kitchen. I've never been in a restaurant kitchen before where there was no air extraction whatsoever, and this in a tropical country. There were also three or four enormous gas burners going, cooking food for queues of customers. The temperature must have been way up in the 40s, with high humidity thrown in too. All the chefs, wearing nothing but a dhoti, were full of good humour and enthusiasm for their incredibly macho work, the restaurant was small and packed, and the atmosphere was fabulous. Needless to say, I've never tasted crab so good. The Sri Lankans are proud that they export most of their crab to Malaysia and Thailand. They say the locals won't pay the price, although it seemed pretty cheap to me. Oh and by the way, they didn't cut up the crab for the curry, but I have, to make it a little easier to eat.

1.8kg Asian blue swimming crabs or 2 × 900g brown crabs, live or cooked
3 tbsp vegetable oil
10cm cinnamon stick, broken into smaller pieces
½ tsp fenugreek seeds
200g onions or shallots, finely chopped
50g garlic, crushed
50g peeled ginger, finely grated
½ tsp turmeric powder
2 tsp kashmiri chilli powder
2 tbsp *Roasted Sri Lankan curry powder* (page 303)
150g chopped tomato, fresh or from a can
1 litre coconut milk
10–12 curry leaves
2 green cayenne chillies, slit open lengthways
25g finely grated fresh coconut
1 tbsp uncooked rice
1 tbsp lime juice

To prepare the crabs, follow the instructions on page 42.

Heat the oil in a large, deep pan. Add the cinnamon pieces and fenugreek seeds and leave them to sizzle for a few seconds, then add the onion and cook for 5–6 minutes until lightly golden. Add the garlic and ginger and cook for 2 minutes. Add the turmeric, chilli powder and curry powder and cook for 1 minute. Add the tomatoes and fry for 1–2 minutes until they begin to soften, then add the coconut milk, curry leaves, chillies and 1 teaspoon salt and bring to a simmer. Leave to simmer, uncovered, for 10 minutes.

Meanwhile, heat a dry, heavy-based frying pan over a medium heat. Add the coconut and cook, stirring constantly, until golden brown. Set aside on a plate to cool. Repeat the process with the uncooked rice. When both are cool, tip them into a spice grinder and grind to a fine powder.

Add the crab pieces to the curry sauce, bring to the boil and cook for 10 minutes, turning the pieces over now and then so they cook evenly. To serve, lift the crab into a large, warmed serving bowl. Stir the roasted coconut and rice powder into the sauce and simmer for 2–3 minutes until thickened. Stir in the lime juice, pour back over the crab and serve.

Chilli-spiced cabbage salad
Gova mellum

SERVES 4–6

When I first tasted a mellum, it was made with grated coconut and a salad leaf with an unpronounceable (for me) name, which I later learnt was mukunuwenna. I was not particularly impressed; it tasted dry and stringy. I was told that Sri Lankans don't much enjoy a Western-style salad of raw leaves. They prefer theirs cooked – in the sense that the ingredients are briefly softened over a high heat. However, naturally, once I'd tried a few, I ended up very enthusiastic about mellums, especially this cabbage and coconut-based one. I've also found this is very good made with green beans cut lengthways into long, thin slices.

300g piece of Savoy cabbage
(about half a large cabbage)
2 tsp vegetable oil
1 tsp black mustard seeds
150g onions, halved and
thinly sliced
15g garlic, finely chopped
2 green chillies, seeded
and finely chopped
10–12 curry leaves
¾ tsp turmeric powder
50g fresh coconut,
finely grated
1 tbsp lime juice

Cut the cabbage into quarters and remove and discard the core and thick central ribs. Finely shred the leaves and then wash and drain.

Heat the oil in a wok or large, heavy-based pan. Add the mustard seeds and as soon as they stop popping, add the onion and cook for 3 minutes or until just soft and beginning to brown.

Add the garlic, green chillies, curry leaves, turmeric, cabbage and 1 teaspoon salt. Stir-fry over a high heat for 2 minutes until the cabbage is only just tender.

Take the pan off the heat, add the coconut and toss together well until the coconut absorbs any excess liquid. Toss through the lime juice and serve immediately.

Asparagus curry

SERVES 6

I wouldn't suggest that you make this curry during the first two to three weeks of the asparagus season, when all that asparagus requires is some melted butter and lemon juice, a spoonful of hollandaise, or maybe a lick of olive oil and a few slivers of parmesan. But afterwards, as the first love dies, this curry with tomato and coconut milk is pretty delicious. I discovered it when our supplier of asparagus to the Seafood Restaurant in Padstow asked if I could produce a recipe that would match a beer being brewed for us by Sharp's in Rock, called Chalky's Bark. This is a beer designed to go with food, quite hoppy with a finish that has a faint taste of ginger. Beer is my drink of choice with curry and the match is really rather good, particularly as there is ginger in the curry too.

4 × 175g bunches asparagus
2 tbsp coconut or vegetable oil
5cm cinnamon stick
10–12 curry leaves
3 × 5cm pieces pandan leaf
200g onions, halved and thinly sliced
25g peeled ginger, finely grated
1 green cayenne chilli, finely chopped
1 tsp kashmiri chilli powder
¼ tsp turmeric powder
1 tbsp *Unroasted Sri Lankan curry powder* (page 303)
250g vine-ripened tomato, chopped
300ml coconut milk
10g Maldive fish flakes or bonito flakes
Juice of 1 lime (about 2 tbsp)

Break each asparagus stalk near its base to dispose of the woody part. Cut the remainder into 2.5cm lengths.

Heat the oil in a medium-sized shallow pan over a medium heat. Add the cinnamon stick, curry leaves and pandan leaf and leave them to sizzle for a few seconds, then add the onion and fry until soft and just beginning to brown. Add the ginger, green chilli, chilli powder, turmeric and curry powder and fry for 2–3 minutes more.

Add the tomato and fry for 2 minutes. Add 4 tablespoons water, reduce the heat to a simmer and leave to cook for another 2 minutes until the tomatoes have broken down into a sauce. Stir in the coconut milk and Maldive fish or bonito flakes and bring to a simmer. Add the asparagus and 1½ teaspoons salt and simmer for 5 minutes until the asparagus is tender. Stir in the lime juice and serve.

Stir-fried curried chicken, vegetables and roti bread
Koththu roti

SERVES 4

Koththu roti, a mixture of shredded flatbreads called gothamba roti (page 307), stir-fried vegetables, curried meat such as lamb, chicken or prawns, and eggs, is far and away the most famous street-food dish in Sri Lanka, not least because of the noise made by the two blunt, paddle-shaped metal blades hammering against the griddle plate as they chop the roti into strips. Apparently there are a couple of songs in which the beat of the roti blades is incorporated into the background percussion. I suspect that koththu roti were originally a way of using leftovers, and they would therefore also work equally well made with your own leftover curry, instead of the freshly cooked chicken below.

For the curried chicken:
45g peeled ginger, chopped
25g garlic, crushed
1 green cayenne chilli, chopped
½ tsp *Roasted Sri Lankan curry powder* (page 303)
¼ tsp turmeric powder
1 tsp freshly ground coriander seeds
1 tsp kashmiri chilli powder
3 tbsp coconut milk
Freshly ground black pepper
750g skinned and boneless chicken
10–12 curry leaves

For the stir-fried mixture:
3 medium eggs
3 tbsp vegetable oil
24 curry leaves
250g onions, thinly sliced
15g garlic, crushed
25g peeled ginger, grated
4 green cayenne chillies, sliced
100g finely shredded cabbage
100g carrots, coarsely grated
6 *gothamba rotis* (page 307), cut across into 1cm strips
½ tsp crushed dried chillies

For the curried chicken, preheat the oven to 200°C/Gas Mark 6. Put the ginger, garlic, green chilli, curry powder, turmeric, ground coriander, chilli powder, coconut milk, ½ teaspoon black pepper and 1 teaspoon salt into a mini food processor and grind together into a smooth paste. Cut the chicken breasts in half and put them into a baking dish with the thighs, curry paste and curry leaves and mix together well. Cover the dish tightly with foil and bake for 40 minutes until the chicken is cooked through. Set aside until cool enough to handle, then break the chicken into bite-sized pieces, stir back into the sauce and set aside.

For the stir-fried mixture, beat the eggs with a little black pepper and ½ teaspoon salt and set aside. Heat the oil in a wok or large non-stick frying pan, add the curry leaves, onion, garlic, ginger and green chilli and stir-fry for 5 minutes until the onion is soft. Add the cabbage, carrot and 1 teaspoon salt and stir-fry for another 4 minutes or until all the vegetables are just tender.

Add the strips of roti and the crushed dried chilli and stir-fry for another 2 minutes. Add the curried chicken and its sauce, stir-fry for 1–2 minutes until it has heated through, then pour in the beaten eggs and stir-fry for another minute or until they are lightly set. To serve, spoon one quarter of the mixture into a portion-sized bowl, press down lightly and then invert onto a warmed plate. Repeat with the remaining mixture and serve straight away.

Spicy beef and vegetable-stuffed gothamba rotis

MAKES 12

Street food in Sri Lanka has the rather endearing English name of 'short eats'. Gothamba roti is a classic. Roti bread is rolled out into a thin disc about the size of a dinner plate, then folded round a rectangular block of chopped and cooked vegetables and minced beef flavoured with Sri Lankan curry powder and chilli. You eat them hot from the pan squirted with chilli sauce – a sort of Sri Lankan meat-and-veg pie. The kind of thing you'd be happy to eat at a test match at the Galle Oval.

1 quantity *Gothamba roti dough* (page 307)

3 tbsp vegetable oil

For the filling:

350g peeled floury potatoes, cut into large chunks

3 tbsp vegetable oil, for frying

200g onions, finely chopped

20g garlic, crushed

250g minced beef

1 tsp crushed dried kashmiri chillies

2 tsp *Unroasted Sri Lankan curry powder* (page 303)

75g cabbage, chopped

1 large carrot, coarsely grated

75 leek, chopped

50g frozen peas

½ tsp freshly ground black pepper

Thai hot chilli sauce or sweet chilli sauce, to serve

Make the gothamba roti dough and leave it to rest for at least 30 minutes. Meanwhile, cook the potatoes in a pan of well-salted water for 15–20 minutes until tender. Drain well and mash.

Heat the oil in a medium-sized pan, add the onion and garlic and fry until golden brown. Add the minced beef, increase the heat and fry until nicely browned. Add the crushed dried chilli and curry powder and fry for 1 minute, then add the cabbage, carrot, leek and peas and cook for a further 2 minutes. Season with the black pepper and 1 teaspoon salt, mix in the mashed potatoes and set aside to cool slightly.

Put the vegetable oil into a shallow dish. Divide the roti dough into twelve 50g pieces. Roll each one into a ball, drop into the oil and turn over once. The oil makes it easier to shape the dough. Then take one ball, put it in the centre of a dinner plate and with your fingers smooth and press into an 18–20cm disc. Take 60g of the filling mixture and shape it with a palette knife into a rectangular block 4 × 6cm, and 2cm deep. Slide the block of filling onto the palette knife and place it 2cm up from the lowest edge of the roti disc. Fold over the sides so they overlap, stretch and fold the bottom edge over the filling, then roll it over away from you into a rectangle. Put on a baking tray lined with clingfilm and reshape into a neat block if necessary. Repeat with the remaining pieces of dough and filling.

Heat a large non-stick frying pan over a medium heat. Add 6 of the roti and cook for 3 minutes on one long side until crisp and golden brown. Turn each one onto the next side, cook for another 3 minutes, then turn again, until each of the 4 long sides are cooked. Then stand each one upright and cook for another 3 minutes on each end. Remove and keep hot while you cook the rest. Serve hot or warm, with the chilli sauce.

'Deep-fried' eggs in a tomato and coconut milk curry

Biththara kari

SERVES 4

To me the pleasure of curried eggs is of the same order as egg and chips: simple comfort food. I'm very fond of the way they do an egg curry in Sri Lanka, which is to boil the eggs, peel them and roll them in turmeric, then fry them in oil until the skin is a bit tough, which is very pleasing when eating the curry. I also like the eggs simply broken into the sauce and gently cooked for a few minutes. In this case, make the sauce in a 20cm frying pan and simmer it for a few minutes to thicken it. Make shallow indentations in the mixture, then break in the eggs. Cover the pan and simmer the eggs for six minutes or to your liking.

8 medium eggs

2 tbsp vegetable oil, plus extra for deep-frying the eggs

3cm cinnamon stick, broken into smaller pieces

1 tsp cumin seeds

¼ tsp yellow mustard seeds

½ tsp fenugreek seeds

10–12 curry leaves

50g red onions, finely chopped

2 green cayenne chillies, finely chopped

1 tsp turmeric powder

1 tsp kashmiri chilli powder

1 tsp *Unroasted Sri Lankan curry powder* (page 303)

400g chopped tomatoes, fresh or from a can

200ml coconut milk

Lower the eggs into a pan of boiling water and hard-boil for just 6 minutes. Drain, cover with cold water and leave to cool, then carefully peel and set aside.

For the sauce, heat the oil in a medium-sized pan. Add the cinnamon, cumin seeds, mustard seeds, fenugreek seeds and curry leaves and leave them to sizzle for a few seconds, then add the onion and fry over a medium heat for 3–4 minutes until soft and just beginning to brown.

Add the green chilli, ½ teaspoon of the turmeric, chilli powder, curry powder and tomatoes, and cook briefly until the tomatoes just begin to soften, then stir in the coconut milk and bring to a simmer. Simmer for a few minutes until the sauce has slightly reduced and thickened. Season to taste with salt.

Pour 1cm oil into a medium-sized non-stick frying pan and place over a medium heat. Roll the peeled hard-boiled eggs in the turmeric, then add what's left to the oil and fry the eggs for a couple of minutes, turning them over with a spoon from time to time, until an almost crisp skin has formed and they are lightly golden all over. Lift out with a slotted spoon and drain briefly on kitchen paper, then drop them whole into the sauce.

Stir-fried lamb with sweet peppers, coconut milk and lime

Lamb baduma

SERVES 4

Quite often in Sri Lanka, you feel you are part of Southeast Asia rather than part of the Indian subcontinent. This is not only because of the lush tropical vegetation, endless white sandy beaches and a population of many different races. It's also because the food quite often feels more like that of Malaysia, say, than India. This recipe is a case in point. It's called a baduma, which I would translate as a stir-fry. The green and red peppers used in the recipe are similar to the long thin peppers of the Mediterranean that you can often buy in UK supermarkets now. I think they have a better flavour than the more common bell-shaped peppers.

500g lamb fillet, trimmed
    of excess fat
1 tbsp *Roasted Sri Lankan*
    curry powder (page 303)
1 tsp kashmiri chilli powder
¼ tsp turmeric powder
½ tsp freshly ground
    coriander seeds
15g garlic, crushed
25g peeled ginger,
    finely grated
½ tsp freshly ground
    black pepper
1 × 150g green pepper
1 × 150g red pepper
3 tbsp vegetable oil
10–12 curry leaves
½ tsp fenugreek seeds
4 × 2.5cm pieces pandan leaf
150g red onions, halved
    and thinly sliced
100ml coconut milk
1 tbsp lime juice

Handful of coriander leaves,
    roughly chopped

Cut each lamb fillet across into 2 or 3 pieces, then each piece lengthways into thin strips about 2.5cm wide and 10cm long. Put the lamb strips in a bowl with the curry powder, chilli powder, turmeric, coriander, garlic, ginger, black pepper and 1 teaspoon salt. Mix together well and set aside for at least 20 minutes.

Cut the green and red peppers lengthways in half, remove the seeds and cut across into slices 8mm wide. If you have managed to get long thin peppers, cut them on the diagonal to get longer slices. Set aside with the lamb.

Heat the oil in a wok or large, deep frying pan over a medium-high heat. Add the curry leaves, fenugreek seeds and pandan leaf and allow them to sizzle for just a few seconds, then add the onion and peppers, increase the heat to high and stir-fry for 3 minutes.

Add the marinated lamb and stir-fry for another 3 minutes or until just cooked through and tender. Add the coconut milk, lime juice and coriander, toss together briefly and serve.

Sri Lankan crab omelette with curried coconut gravy

SERVES 4

This recipe comes from Charmaine Solomon's Complete Asian Cookbook. Charmaine is one of the world's leading experts on all Asian cooking. I remember a trip to Australia, where she lives, in the early 1980s, when I was running perilously close to missing my flight back to the UK, so keen was I to get a copy of the book to take home and a pair of R.M. Williams' riding boots. I met her subsequently on a filming trip in the 1990s when she took me around the Vietnamese market in Cabramatta with her very pleasant husband Reuben. The most important thing, however, about Charmaine is that she is Sri Lankan and her recipes are the definitive ones. Somewhat outrageously, I've made a small change to her recipe, which is to put the softened spring onions and chillies into the crab filling rather than into the omelette. This makes little difference to the flavour; it's just that I like the look of the white and the green when you slice the omelette up.

For the omelette:

40g butter or ghee

3 spring onions, thinly sliced

1 medium-hot green chilli, seeded and finely chopped

250g fresh white crab meat

1½ tsp lime or lemon juice

Freshly ground black pepper

4 large eggs

Small handful of coriander leaves, roughly chopped

Lime cheeks, to serve

For the omelette 'gravy':

3 tbsp vegetable oil

100g onions, finely chopped

15g garlic, crushed

30g peeled ginger, grated

10–12 curry leaves

1 lemongrass stalk

10cm cinnamon stick, broken

6 × 2.5cm pieces pandan leaf

½ tsp kashmiri chilli powder

½ tsp turmeric powder

1 tsp *Roasted Sri Lankan curry powder* (page 303)

400ml coconut milk

For the 'gravy', heat the oil in a medium-sized pan over a medium heat. Add the onion, garlic, ginger and curry leaves and fry gently for 5–6 minutes until the onion is very soft and just beginning to go golden. Halve and bruise the lemongrass stalk, and break the cinnamon stick into smaller pieces. Add the lemongrass, cinnamon and pandan leaf to the pan and fry for 1 minute. Add the chilli powder, turmeric and curry powder and fry for 1 minute more. Add the coconut milk and leave to simmer for 5–10 minutes until thickened. Remove the lemongrass and season to taste with salt. Set aside and keep warm.

For the omelette, heat 15g of the butter or ghee in a small frying pan, add the spring onions and chilli and fry for 1 minute until softened. Add the crab meat and toss over a low heat for 1–2 minutes until heated through. Sprinkle over the lime or lemon juice and season to taste with pepper and salt. Keep hot.

Break the eggs into a bowl, season with ½ teaspoon salt and some black pepper and whisk together well. Heat a 25cm non-stick frying pan (measured across the base) over a high heat, add the remaining butter or ghee and, as soon as it is foaming, swirl it to coat the pan, then pour in the eggs. Cook, pulling the egg into the centre with a fork as it sets, until lightly golden underneath but still moist on top. Stir the coriander into the crab meat and spoon it down the centre of the omelette. Fold the sides over the filling and roll the omelette out onto a large serving plate. Slice across into 4 pieces, spoon over some of the gravy and serve with the rest of the gravy and the lime cheeks.

Peter Kuruvita's beef curry

SERVES 8

Peter Kuruvita is the owner and chef of Flying Fish, an excellent seafood restaurant right at the end of a wharf at Pyrmont in Sydney. He is half Sri Lankan and spent much of his childhood there. He has just published a beautiful book called Serendip, one of the old names for Sri Lanka, about his memories of Colombo together with lots of great traditional recipes. This one for his beef curry I particularly liked because, like much of Sri Lankan cooking, it is very simple to make, and flavoured with lots of cinnamon.

1kg chuck steak, cut into
    2cm chunks
2 tsp freshly ground
    cumin seeds
2 tsp freshly ground
    coriander seeds
1 tbsp kashmiri chilli powder
8 cloves
5 tsp *Roasted Sri Lankan*
    curry powder (page 303)
1 tsp fenugreek seeds
4 green cardamom pods,
    lightly bruised
2 × 10cm cinnamon sticks,
    broken into smaller pieces
1 tsp turmeric powder
4 × 2.5cm pieces pandan leaf
65g peeled ginger, thinly sliced
4 tbsp vegetable oil
350g onions, finely chopped
35g garlic, thinly sliced
24 curry leaves
2 tbsp tomato purée
1 tsp freshly ground
    black pepper

Put the meat into a bowl with all the spices, pieces of pandan leaf and ginger and mix together well.

Heat the oil in a large, heavy-based pan, add the onion, garlic and curry leaves and cook for 5 minutes until soft but not browned. Increase the heat to high, add the meat and stir-fry for another 5 minutes until the beef is evenly coloured.

Cover with 1 litre of water and add the tomato purée, black pepper and 2 teaspoons salt. Bring to the boil, lower the heat, part-cover and leave to simmer for 2 hours, stirring now and then, until the beef is tender and the sauce has reduced and thickened.

Egg hoppers
Bittara appa

MAKES 12

Sometimes, with recipes I'm very excited about but which are unusual, I worry if people will bother to do them. This is the case with egg hoppers. You have to make a yeast batter with rice flour, then cook a pancake in a small, wok-shaped pan, so that the finished pancake has sides to it, within which you cook a whole egg. You then sprinkle the egg with one or two fiery sambols like those on page 305 and eat it for breakfast. All I can say is that egg hoppers are great fun but sadly not easy to do. The first time I tested the recipe in Sydney, all worked beautifully. Back in Cornwall, I couldn't get the pancakes crisp enough. Something to do with a different rice flour, I guess. The point of using yeast in the batter is that it creates a delightful laciness in the pancakes from the air bubbles, and, if you leave it to mature in a warm place for 3–4 hours, the finished pancakes have something of the flavour of sour dough.

400ml coconut milk
250g rice flour
¼ tsp easy-blend dried yeast
13 medium eggs, 1 for the batter and 12 for the hoppers
1 tsp jaggery or palm sugar
Vegetable oil, for cooking

Thai hot chilli sauce and a couple of coconut sambols (page 305), to serve

Warm 100ml of the coconut milk very slightly in a pan. Sift the rice flour and yeast into a mixing bowl, make a well in the centre, break in 1 egg and add the warm coconut milk and 200ml water. Add the sugar and gradually whisk everything together to make a smooth batter. Cover and leave somewhere warm for up to 2 hours until the mixture has risen and become frothy. Gradually whisk in the remaining coconut milk, 1 teaspoon salt and up to 100ml water to make a thin batter with the consistency of single cream.

Heat a 20cm non-stick frying pan over a high heat. For the first hopper, measure 3 tablespoons of the batter into a small bowl. As you need to be quick when making hoppers, it is best to have the batter measured out each time so you can add it to the pan in one go. Brush the surface of the pan generously with oil, pour in the batter and quickly swirl it around to coat the base and sides of the pan in a thin, even layer. Return the pan to the heat, break an egg into the centre, cover with a lid and reduce the heat to medium-low. Leave the hopper to cook for 3 minutes until the sides are crisp and golden and the egg is cooked.

Release the hopper from the pan with a palette knife, slide out onto a plate and serve hot. Make the rest of the hoppers in the same way, with the remaining batter and eggs, serving each one as soon as it is cooked. If you are having trouble doing this all in one, make the pancake on its own, fry an egg separately, then add to the hopper.

Pork kalu pol curry

SERVES 8

Kalu pol means 'black coconut' and refers to a special spice powder of dark-roasted coconut, dried chillies, rice and fennel, cumin and mustard seeds, which is used to thicken curries. This curry also uses the dark-roasted Sri Lankan curry powder, giving the finished curry its traditional 'black' colour. It's interesting to see similarities to a classic vindaloo here, another Portuguese-influenced dish, especially in the addition of lots of dried red chilli, spices and a little vinegar. This dish is traditionally served with coconut rice, or kiribath as it is known in Sri Lanka (page 306). This can either be served warm, or smoothed out into a 5cm-high layer on a flat plate, left to cool to room temperature, then cut into diamond-shaped pieces.

3 tbsp vegetable oil

10cm cinnamon stick, broken
    into smaller pieces

6 × 2.5cm pieces pandan leaf

24 curry leaves

250g onions, finely chopped

25g garlic, crushed

65g peeled ginger, grated

2 fat lemongrass stalks,
    core thinly sliced

1 tsp kashmiri chilli powder

1½ tbsp *Roasted Sri Lankan
    curry powder* (page 303)

½ tsp turmeric powder

2 tbsp coconut vinegar

350g chopped tomatoes

1.5kg boned shoulder of pork,
    cut into 2.5cm chunks

½ tsp freshly ground black
    pepper

For the kalu pol:

2 tsp uncooked white rice

15g dried red kashmiri chillies

1 tbsp black mustard seeds

1 tsp fennel seeds

2 tsp cumin seeds

50g fresh coconut, finely
    grated

2 tbsp *Tamarind water*
    (page 299)

Heat the vegetable oil in a large, heavy-based pan over a medium heat. Add the cinnamon, pandan leaf and curry leaves and leave them to sizzle for a few seconds, then add the onion and fry for 6 minutes until lightly browned. Add the garlic, ginger and lemongrass and fry for 2–3 minutes more. Add the chilli powder, curry powder and turmeric and fry for 1 minute. Add the vinegar and let it bubble away for a minute or so. Then add the tomatoes, pork, black pepper, 750ml water and 2 teaspoons salt, and bring to a simmer. Part-cover and cook for 1 hour or until the pork is almost tender and the sauce has reduced and thickened slightly.

Meanwhile, for the kalu pol, heat a dry, heavy-based frying pan over a medium heat. Add the rice and shake it around for about 3 minutes until richly golden. Tip into a bowl, add the chillies to the pan and shake these around for another 3 minutes until they darken slightly, taking care not to let them burn. Add to the bowl with the rice. Now add the mustard, fennel and cumin seeds to the pan, stir them around constantly for 3 minutes until richly browned, then add to the bowl. Put the coconut into the pan and stir it around constantly for about 5 minutes until richly golden. Tip everything into a spice grinder, in batches if necessary, and grind to a fine powder. Return to the bowl and stir in the tamarind water and enough additional water to make a smooth paste.

Add the kalu pol paste to the curry and leave it to simmer, uncovered, for a further 10–15 minutes until the pork is very tender and the sauce has reduced and thickened.

Parsley, coconut and chilli salad

SERVES 4

This is my version of a wonderful salad I ate in Sri Lanka, where it was made with a leafy herb-like vegetable called gotukola, a member of the umbelliferae family (which also includes parsley, carrots, fennel and celery).

1 green cayenne chilli,
    finely chopped
50g flat-leaf parsley leaves,
    roughly chopped
100g red onions, quartered
    and very thinly sliced
50g finely grated fresh coconut
10g Maldive fish flakes
    or bonito flakes
2 tbsp lime juice
Freshly ground black pepper

Put the green chilli, parsley leaves, red onion, coconut and Maldive fish or bonito flakes into a bowl and toss together well. Stir through the lime juice and pepper and salt to taste, and serve within 5 minutes.

'White' pumpkin curry

SERVES 4–6

This is the other curry from the Sun House in Galle (see also page 222), a typically mild, coconut-milk-based vegetable curry known as a 'white' curry because of the use of unroasted curry powder, although it is in fact pale yellow from the turmeric. I was intrigued that they didn't remove the skin from the pumpkin before cooking – and indeed after a period of simmering it becomes perfectly tender and makes a nice contrast to the slightly softer flesh. Though the chefs fried the onion, garlic, pandan leaf, curry leaves and Sri Lankan spice, it's more common for all the ingredients to be simmered together, traditionally in a sealed clay pot, for about fifteen minutes until tender. Incidentally, you can equally well use squash for this curry, which has a slightly firmer texture. Particularly good varieties are crown prince, kabocha and butternut.

750g piece of unpeeled
    pumpkin or squash
100g onions, halved and
    thinly sliced
15g garlic, finely chopped
10–12 curry leaves
4 × 2.5cm pieces pandan leaf
3 green cayenne chillies,
    thinly sliced
1 tbsp *Unroasted Sri Lankan*
    curry powder (page 303)
½ tsp turmeric powder
½ tsp fenugreek seeds
10g Maldive fish flakes
    or bonito flakes
400ml coconut milk

Scoop away and discard the seeds from the pumpkin or squash and cut it through the skin into 2.5 × 4cm chunks.

Put the pumpkin or squash into a pan with the onion, garlic, curry leaves, pandan leaf, chillies, curry powder, turmeric powder, fenugreek, Maldive fish or bonito flakes, coconut milk and 1 teaspoon salt. Bring to a simmer, cover with a tight-fitting lid and leave to simmer for 12–15 minutes or until the pumpkin or squash is tender. Adjust the seasoning to taste and serve.

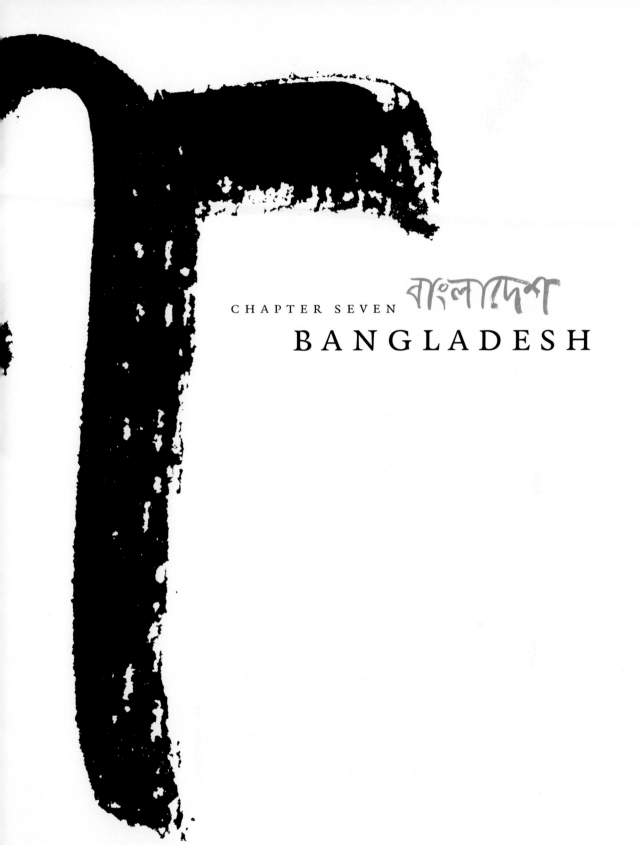

CHAPTER SEVEN বাংলাদেশ
BANGLADESH

The Bangladeshi flag is a red disc on a green background, meaning an enormously green country and a very hot sun. The reason it is so green is that the mighty Ganges, Brahmaputra, and Meghna rivers and their tributaries criss-cross the entire country. Most of Bangladesh, 80 per cent of the land area, is covered with water from the monsoons. The perception of the country from the West is of somewhere lurching from one natural disaster to another, but while it is true that the occasional cyclone is catastrophic, the benefit of an annual covering of nutrient-rich water means fertile soil and an unbelievable abundance of freshwater fish. We went to a market in a village by a river where there must have been thirty varieties, some of them enormous, almost a metre in length. Thus the most important foods in Bangladesh are fish and rice, and a quarter of the recipes here are for fish.

For me the biggest surprise was how far the received view of Bangladesh was from the reality. I expected to find catastrophe and grinding poverty. I found a country certainly amongst the poorest in the world but full of spectacular beauty. Driving through green countryside and observing village life in the Indian subcontinent is immensely calming, not only to me but also I suspect to a lot of people: a panorama of paddy fields, water buffalos with a white egret or two on their back, men and women planting rice, and the villages themselves, gardens filled with banana plants or fruit trees, wooden houses near rivers, and children shouting and scampering with innocent freedom.

You often read of Bangladeshis saying their cuisine is not worth making a fuss about, that it's just the sort of stuff they cook at home. Maybe that's why most of the Indian restaurants in the UK, which are owned and run by Bangladeshis, tend to feature the cuisine of the rest of India and Pakistan. But I found the local food fascinating and good. The important thing to know about Bangladesh is that it is influenced by culinary ideas from much further north. You could almost say that fish, rice and dals are village food, but in addition to these most people eat a whole variety of meat and rice dishes with northern Indian and Persian influence. I'm thinking particularly of the biryani I had in Dhaka, the chicken pilau and a couple of restaurant dishes, such as a creamy chicken korma and a magnificent Moghul lamb rezala. Much of the cooking is done with the clarified butter, ghee, and dairy produce appears also in the form of yogurt in a lot of the dishes. The day I arrived one of the most typical flavourings in Bangladeshi food was driven home forcefully when I watched someone cook three fish dishes all with mustard oil and mustard seeds. I suppose if you ask me for three or four of the most distinctive flavours of Bangladeshi cooking, I'd say mustard, ghee and a particular spice mix, panch phoran, unusual in that the combination of mustard, nigella, cumin, fennel and fenugreek seeds contains whole rather than powdered spices. I'm still marvelling at the subtlety of the mango chutney I had when eating lunch with a family in Dhaka, a sweet one flavoured with panch phoran.

Toovar dal with tamarind, tomatoes and curry leaves

SERVES 4–6

This dal is unusual in that it is referred to in Bangladesh as 'sour', which often indicates the presence of tomatoes. We don't normally consider tomatoes sour, but actually they are, and together with the tamarind and lime they give the pulses a particularly enjoyable slightly astringent note. Toovar (or toor) dal is a dark ochre-coloured split pea with a rich, earthy flavour.

250g toovar dal
2 tbsp each vegetable oil and mustard oil
100g onions, thinly sliced
15g garlic, crushed
½ tsp turmeric powder
1 tsp freshly ground cumin seeds
1 tsp freshly ground coriander seeds
200g chopped vine-ripened tomatoes
1 tbsp *Tamarind water* (page 299)
4 green cayenne chillies, slit open lengthways
1 large pinch asafoetida
1 tsp black mustard seeds
1 tsp cumin seeds
10–12 curry leaves
4 cloves
10cm cinnamon stick, halved
Lime wedges, to serve

Put the dal into a medium-sized pan with 1 litre of water, bring to the boil, then lower the heat and leave to simmer for about 45 minutes or until the dal is soft and the mixture has reduced and thickened.

When the dal is almost ready, heat 1 tablespoon each of mustard and vegetable oil in a medium-sized pan. Add the onion and fry for 6–8 minutes until soft and lightly golden. Add the garlic, turmeric, cumin and coriander and fry for a further 2–3 minutes. Add the tomatoes and cook until they just begin to soften. Add the mixture to the dal with the tamarind water and green chillies and simmer gently for 3–4 minutes.

Heat the remaining mustard and vegetable oil in a small frying pan over a medium heat. Add the asafoetida, mustard seeds, cumin seeds, curry leaves, cloves and cinnamon, cover with a lid and leave to sizzle for 1 minute until the mustard seeds stop popping. Add to the dal and season to taste with salt. Cover and leave for 5 minutes for the flavours to infuse. Serve with lime wedges.

Mung bean dal with ginger, chilli and mustard seeds
Moong dal

SERVES 4–6

Although dals are common in Bangladesh, they are not as important a source of protein as they are in the rest of the Indian subcontinent because the Bengalis have enormous quantities of freshwater fish available to them. Never the less, I don't think I ate a single meal there where they weren't much in evidence on the menu. They are almost always finished with a tarka: a combination of spices and other flavourings, such as ginger, garlic and mustard leaves, briefly fried in a small amount of hot oil and stirred in at the last minute to give a burst of fresh flavour. This recipe uses moong dal, the husked and split mung bean. On a personal note, my memory of curries goes back to the early 1960s, but it wasn't until I tasted a dal in the early 1970s that I realized how strange and fascinating Indian food could be. I first tasted the bland yet hot earthiness of a dal in Newlyn in Cornwall, of all places, where a friend of Pat Phoenix, who played Elsie Tanner in Coronation Street, made four curries, a dal and a fresh chutney for us all one evening and that's when I said to myself, 'Now, that is interesting food!'

250g moong dal
½ tsp turmeric powder
1½ tbsp vegetable oil
1 pinch asafoetida
¼ tsp crushed dried
    kashmiri chillies
1 tsp black mustard seeds
20g peeled ginger, finely
    chopped
6 curry leaves
1 tbsp ghee
Jaggery or palm sugar,
    to taste

Put the moong dal into a colander and rinse under cold running water until the water runs clear. Put into a pan with 750ml water and the turmeric and simmer for 10–15 minutes or until the dal is soft and the mixture has reduced and thickened.

For the tarka, heat the oil in a small frying pan over a medium heat. Add the asafoetida, crushed dried chillies and, as soon as they start to darken slightly, add the mustard seeds. When they stop spluttering, add the ginger and curry leaves and cook for 1 minute. Add the ghee and pour the mixture immediately into the dal. Add 1 teaspoon salt, or to taste, and a little sugar if you wish, cook for 3–4 minutes, then serve.

Fish khatta with tomatoes

SERVES 4

This curry was cooked for me in Badeh Shahr, the family village of my host in Sylhet, Kamran Choudhury. The original settlers in that part of Bangladesh were from Afghanistan, and much of the food is of Muslim origin via northern India, Afghanistan and Persia. Even this simple dish of fish, spice and tomato shows this influence in the copious quantities of onion and garlic it uses. Khatta means 'sour' and here the sourness comes solely from the tomatoes.

30g peeled ginger, roughly
    chopped
30g garlic, roughly chopped
200g sliced onions
6 tbsp vegetable oil
1½ tsp turmeric powder
1 tbsp freshly ground
    coriander seeds
2 tsp kashmiri chilli powder
500g vine-ripened
    tomatoes, sliced
500g skinned firm white
    fish fillet, such as John
    Dory, sea bass, monkfish
    or snapper
10g fresh coriander,
    roughly chopped

Put the ginger, garlic and onion into a mini food processor and blend to a smooth paste.

Heat the oil in a medium-sized pan over a medium heat, add the ginger, garlic and onion paste and cook gently for 4 minutes. Add the turmeric, coriander, chilli powder and 1 teaspoon salt and fry for 1–2 minutes until the mixture starts to smell aromatic.

Add the tomatoes and 100ml water and cook for 10 minutes until the tomatoes have broken down into a sauce. Cut the fish into roughly 3cm chunks, add to the pan with another 100ml water and bring to a simmer. Cook for 3 minutes until the fish is just cooked. Stir in the chopped coriander and serve.

Beef shatkora

SERVES 6

When I tell you that around Sylhet in Bangladesh there is a popular folk song in praise of the shatkora, a citrus fruit similar in size and flavour to a grapefruit and unique to the countryside around that area, you will understand that this is a very special beef curry. And given that the majority of the Indian restaurants in the UK are run by expats from Sylhet, it will be no surprise to you to learn that you can get these fruit in the UK, both fresh in season and frozen (page 313). I've also used pink grapefruit with good results, though. Like many northern Indian dishes in Bangladesh, there's a lot of ghee in this recipe, a sign of prosperity and generosity there, which is very nice if this is one curry among many at a meal. However, if it is to be the only curry you serve, I recommend you halve the quantity of ghee as it makes it quite rich.

1.5kg chuck or blade steak
150ml mustard or
    vegetable oil
10 cloves
6–8 pieces cassia bark
10 green cardamom pods,
    lightly bruised
225g onions, halved
    and thinly sliced
35g garlic, crushed
50g peeled ginger, finely
    grated
1 tsp turmeric powder
5 tsp kashmiri chilli powder
4 tsp freshly ground
    cumin seeds
4 tsp freshly ground
    coriander seeds
3 tbsp tomato ketchup
100g ghee
1 shatkora or ¼ pink
    grapefruit
½ tsp freshly ground
    black pepper
1 tsp *Garam masala*
    (page 302)

Cut the beef into 3cm pieces, trimming away and discarding any large pieces of fat.

Heat the oil in a large, heavy-based pan over a medium heat. Add the cloves, cassia and cardamom pods and allow them to sizzle for a few seconds. Add the onions and cook gently for 20–30 minutes, stirring now and then, until they are very soft and light brown.

Add the garlic, ginger, turmeric, chilli powder, ground cumin, ground coriander and 2 teaspoons salt and fry for 1 minute. Add the beef and cook, stirring, for 10 minutes. Add the tomato ketchup and ghee and cook for 2–3 minutes. Add 300ml boiling water, cover and simmer for 1½ hours or until the beef is almost tender.

Meanwhile, cut the shatkora or grapefruit in half and squeeze out the juice. Cut into quarters and discard three pieces. Remove the residual flesh from the remaining quarter and slice away most of the white pith. Cut the zest on the diagonal into thin strips.

After the curry has been cooking for 1½ hours, add the shatkora or grapefruit zest and juice and cook, uncovered, for a further 20–30 minutes or until the beef is tender and the gravy has reduced and thickened around the beef. Skim off the excess oil, add the black pepper, garam masala and a little salt to taste, and serve.

Afsaneh's fish curry with potatoes at Badeh Shahr

SERVES 6

Testimony to the importance of fish in Bangladesh is that I have three dishes in this chapter that are based on the local river fish. When you consider that 80 per cent of Bangladesh is under water during the time of the monsoon, and fish swim over millions of acres of what will be land for the rest of the year, you can appreciate how full the markets are of freshwater fish, or 'sweet-water' fish, as they call them, and why some of them are so large. In a market near the little village where this dish was shown to me, I saw some fish weighing 30 to 40 kilograms. This curry is intended to be made with the local fish called rui. However, I tested the recipe in Australia using blue-eye trevalla with excellent results, as it has a firm meaty texture. In the UK I would suggest using monkfish. It would also work well with cod, hake or haddock – you would have to be prepared for the chunks of fish to break up a little during cooking, but it wouldn't affect the flavour at all.

175g onions, roughly chopped
40g garlic, roughly chopped
40g peeled ginger, roughly
    chopped
1kg peeled waxy main-crop
    potatoes, such as Desiree
4 tbsp vegetable oil
1 tbsp kashmiri chilli powder
2 tbsp freshly ground
    coriander seeds
1 tbsp turmeric powder
500g monkfish fillet
    (or see above for other
    fish suggestions)
2 tbsp jaggery or palm sugar
1 tbsp lime juice
Large handful of coriander,
    roughly chopped

Put the onion, garlic and ginger into a mini food processor and blend to a smooth paste. Cut the potatoes into small 1cm-thick slices.

Heat the oil in a wide shallow pan. Add the onion paste and fry for 10 minutes until lightly brown. Add the chilli powder, coriander, turmeric and 2 teaspoons salt and fry for another 2–3 minutes until the mixture starts to smell aromatic. Add 100ml water and leave the sauce to simmer, uncovered, for 5 minutes. Add another 300ml water and the potatoes, cover and leave to simmer for 10 minutes or until the potatoes are tender.

Cut the fish into roughly 3cm chunks. Stir them into the curry and leave to simmer for a further 4 minutes or until just cooked through. Stir in the sugar, lime juice and coriander, and serve.

Pork with green chilli and black sesame paste

Dohneiiong

SERVES 6

I'm certainly not going to say that unless you can get hold of black sesame seeds, this dish is not worth making. Toasting the more common, beige-coloured sesame seeds before grinding them produces just as nice a curry, but I did like the fact that when I watched it being made in the Khasia tribal village, the finished dish was strikingly black, almost like a risotto nero in the Mediterranean. You may not care for black food but this dish is quite distinctive, unusual and extremely well flavoured. Black sesame can be found in good Asian grocers, if you decide to seek it out. The original recipe calls for belly pork but I found it a bit too fatty, as the dish was also cooked with copious amounts of mustard oil — which, by the way, I've reduced here — together with the oil yielded by the sesame seeds. Serve with a kachumber salad (page 306).

100g black sesame seeds
2 tbsp vegetable oil
50ml mustard oil
225g shallots or onions, halved and thinly sliced
8 green cayenne chillies, thinly sliced
100g tomatoes, sliced
1kg boned pork shoulder, trimmed of excess fat, then cut into 3cm chunks

For the masala paste:
25g peeled fresh turmeric or 1 tsp turmeric powder
100g peeled ginger, roughly chopped
50g garlic, roughly chopped
25g onions or shallots, roughly chopped
1 tsp freshly ground coriander seeds
1 tsp freshly ground cumin seeds

To make the masala paste, put all the ingredients into a mini food processor with ½ teaspoon salt and blend together until smooth. Put the black sesame seeds into a spice grinder with the vegetable oil and grind to a smooth paste.

Heat the mustard oil in a medium-sized pan. Add the onions or shallots and green chillies and fry gently for 5 minutes until soft. Add the masala paste and another ½ teaspoon salt and fry for a couple of minutes until the mixture smells aromatic. Stir in 100ml water and the tomatoes and cook for 5 minutes until the tomatoes have broken down to form a sauce.

Add the pork, black sesame paste and another 200ml water, part-cover and simmer for 1 hour, stirring now and then until the pork is tender, then serve.

Lightly spiced cauliflower, cabbage and carrots
Chachchari

SERVES 4

This is a very simple Bengali vegetable side dish that would go as well with a roast chicken as it does with curries. This was cooked for me in a private house and it shows how uncomplicated a lot of Bangladeshi cooking is. There is no particular spice in it, there's not a lot of chilli, and you can use any combination of vegetables you wish. Just cook them in order, starting with those that take the longest, and try not to use any water so the vegetables cook in their own juices, to the point where they slightly catch on the base of the pan and start to brown. Potatoes, sweet potatoes, pumpkin, aubergine and spinach leaves are also commonly used.

3 tbsp vegetable oil

1 tsp *Panch phoran* (page 303)

75g onions, thinly sliced

100g carrots, cut into
    sticks 1cm × 3cm

375g cauliflower, broken
    into small florets

150g piece of cabbage,
    core removed and
    leaves sliced across
    into 2cm-wide strips

150g dwarf green beans,
    cut into 3cm pieces

½ tsp turmeric powder

2 green cayenne chillies,
    each cut into 3 pieces

150g prepared butternut
    squash, cut into pieces
    1cm × 3cm

Heat the oil in a large saucepan over a medium heat. Add the panch phoran and leave it to sizzle for a few seconds, then add the onions and a teaspoon salt and fry for 2–3 minutes, stirring.

Add the carrots and cauliflower and cook, stirring and frying all the time, for 3 minutes. Add the cabbage, green beans and turmeric and fry for another 2–3 minutes.

Add the chillies, the squash and another ½ teaspoon salt and cook for 5 minutes. Then cover, lower the heat slightly and leave the vegetables to cook very slowly in their own juices for 5 minutes or until tender and lightly browned here and there.

Shawkat's fish steamed with mustard masala

Bhapa elish sorshey

SERVES 4

The memory of Shawkat Osman cooking this dish on the lawn at the exclusive Dhaka Club is somewhat hazy because we had just arrived from London some hours before, our flight having been delayed by a day. Shawkat has a very successful cookery programme, which he makes in Calcutta and is seen by millions of Indians but, for reasons I don't recall, you can't see it in Bangladesh. He rattled through about four fish dishes in the space of twenty-five minutes and although I seemed to be taking notes, I couldn't read any of them back – except for this dish, which is the preferred way of cooking hilsa fish. This is possibly the most revered fish from all the rivers and lakes in Bangladesh, and is none other than our own shad, which has more bones than you could shake a stick at. I know, because in my jet-lagged state I tried to demonstrate on camera how easy it is to remove bones from your mouth, but afterwards the crew said they wouldn't be showing that piece. This dish, where a steak from a large fish is coated with a masala made with ground black mustard seeds, onions fried in mustard oil, garlic, turmeric and chilli powder, is particularly good, and I liked the way he sprinkled a few thinly sliced red onions and green chilli into the banana leaf parcel before folding it up for steaming. You'll find it quite intensely hot and mustardy, and the tomato-based kachumber salad on page 306 is a vital accompaniment.

4 tsp black mustard seeds

6 tbsp mustard oil

75g onions, halved and thinly sliced

40g garlic, thinly sliced

1 tsp turmeric powder

2 tsp kashmiri chilli powder

4 × 175g steaks hake, cod, barramundi or blue-eye trevalla

50g piece of red onion, thinly sliced

1 green cayenne chilli, thinly sliced

Prepare a steamer ready for cooking (page 315). Put the mustard seeds into a spice grinder and grind to a fine powder.

Heat the mustard oil in a small frying pan, add the onions, garlic, turmeric, chilli powder, mustard powder and 1 teaspoon salt and fry everything gently until soft and lightly browned. Tip the mixture into a mini food processor and blend to a smooth paste. Spread one side of each fish steak with half the paste.

Tear off four 30cm squares of foil (or banana leaf if you can get it). Place one fish steak, paste side down, into the centre of each piece and spread the top with the rest of the paste. Divide the sliced red onion between the fish and sprinkle over the green chilli. Seal each parcel well and put into the steamer. Cover and steam for 20 minutes until cooked through.

Unwrap each parcel and lift the fish onto a warmed plate. Spoon over any cooking juices and serve at once.

Fish dampokht

SERVES 6

One of the pleasures of visiting places to make a TV programme is that doors are opened, in this instance by the Kabir family in Dhaka, whose cook prepared and baked this fragrant dish for us one lunchtime. It's not the sort of food you would find anywhere outside of a family environment, in this case a very long-established, old-money family. You can see the Persian influences: there are almonds, pistachios, sultanas and saffron in the dish, and it seems to me distantly related to the raans of northern India, Pakistan, Iran and Afghanistan, where the same sort of coating, albeit more spicy, is applied to whole legs of lamb. Here a paste of these ingredients, together with garlic, ginger, onion, a modest amount of chilli, cumin and coriander, is spread over a good thick fillet of meaty freshwater fish (rui), and baked in the oven. This is perfect buffet food. Along with the dampokht they served a chicken pilau, a beef curry very similar to the shatkora on page 266 called beef jhalgosht, a kachumber and raita salad and three homemade family chutneys, the like of which I had never tasted before. One that was particularly good was the sweet green mango chutney (page 304). Incidentally, I think the dampokht is almost better served cold or at room temperature the next day.

1kg thick skin-on fillet
    of salmon, snapper
    or barramundi, taken
    from a large fish

For the spice paste:
3 tbsp milk
½ tsp loosely packed
    saffron strands
20g raisins
50g ghee
250g onions, thinly sliced
40g peeled ginger, sliced
30g garlic, roughly chopped
2 tsp kashmiri chilli powder
2 tsp freshly ground
    cumin seeds
2 tsp freshly ground
    coriander seeds
30g shelled unsalted
    pistachio nuts
30g blanched almonds
3 tbsp lime juice
4 tbsp natural yogurt

For the spice paste, warm the milk, add the saffron and set aside to soak. Cover the raisins with hot water and leave them to soak alongside the saffron for 30 minutes. Meanwhile, melt the ghee in a small pan, add the onion and fry gently until very soft and nicely browned.

Heat the oven to 200°C/Gas Mark 6. Drain the raisins. Put them into a mini food processor with the fried onions, saffron milk, the remaining spice paste ingredients and 1½ teaspoons salt, and blend to a smooth paste.

Season the fish fillet on both sides with a little salt. Place the fish skin-side down on a lightly oiled non-stick baking tray and spread with the paste. Bake for 20–25 minutes until cooked through. Lift onto a warmed serving plate.

Aromatic chicken pilau with cinnamon, tomato and nutmeg

SERVES 6–8

This is one of the best dishes in the book for an informal dinner party. It's easy to double up, but make sure you use a wider pan, rather than one that is deeper and taller, as success depends on the rate of evaporation of the liquid. Interestingly, in Indian restaurants, both pilaus and biryanis are made by cooking the rice separately from the meat and amalgamating them at the end, for reasons of timing. While they can be excellent cooked this way, there is nothing to beat cooking chicken, rice and aromatics all together. It is a marvel of endlessly fascinating aromatic flavours and not at all chilli-hot. The cucumber and mint raita on page 306 goes well with this, as does a good quality lime pickle.

750g skinned and boneless
  chicken (a mixture of
  breast and thigh meat)
Freshly ground black pepper
75g ghee
2 × 5cm cinnamon sticks or
  10 pieces of cassia bark
10 cloves
10 green cardamom pods
2 bay leaves
25g garlic, finely chopped
65g peeled ginger, finely
  grated
450g onions, halved and
  thinly sliced
1 tbsp freshly ground
  coriander seeds
2 tsp freshly ground
  cumin seeds
1 tsp freshly grated nutmeg
½ tsp kashmiri chilli powder
400g chopped tomatoes,
  fresh or from a can
1 tsp turmeric powder
400g basmati rice
12 curry leaves
Roughly chopped fresh
  coriander, to garnish

Cut the chicken into 3cm pieces and season lightly with salt and pepper. Preheat the oven to 180°C/Gas Mark 4.

Melt the ghee in a large flameproof casserole over a medium-high heat. Add the whole spices (the cinnamon or cassia, cloves and cardamom pods) and the bay leaves and leave them to sizzle for a few seconds until aromatic. Add the garlic and ginger and cook gently for 2–3 minutes. Add the onion and cook, stirring now and then, for 15 minutes or so until very soft and lightly golden. Add the coriander, cumin, nutmeg and chilli powder and fry for a further 2 minutes.

Stir the chicken into the casserole and cook for 5 minutes until it has lightly coloured all over. Add the tomatoes, turmeric, 500ml water, 1 teaspoon black pepper and 2 teaspoons salt and bring to a gentle simmer. Stir the rice into the casserole with the curry leaves, bring back to a vigorous boil, stir once more and cover with a tight-fitting lid. Transfer to the oven and bake for 20 minutes. (You could also do this on the top of the stove if you can maintain a constant low enough heat.)

When the pilau is cooked, remove it from the oven or the heat and leave to rest for 5 minutes. Then uncover and fluff it up with a fork. Spoon it onto a warmed serving plate and sprinkle with the chopped coriander.

Spicy pea and potato samosas
Aloo matar shinghara

MAKES 20

The filling for these shingharas, photographed on location (opposite), is some simply spiced potatoes and peas, and the pastry deep-fries to a pleasing crispness. The best time for eating these would be, in my mind, at about 9.30 to 10 o'clock at night, after a drinks party, where everybody had arrived at 6.30 or 7 and they were having so much fun they forgot to go home for supper.

For the potato filling:
500g evenly sized waxy
    potatoes, such as Charlotte
4 tbsp vegetable oil, plus
    extra for deep-frying
2 tsp black mustard seeds
275g onions, finely chopped
1 tsp turmeric powder
30g garlic, crushed
4 green cayenne chillies,
    finely chopped
1 tsp kashmiri chilli powder
150g frozen peas, thawed

For the pastry dough:
225g plain flour, plus extra
    for dusting
2 tbsp vegetable oil

For the pastry, sift the flour and ½ teaspoon salt into a bowl. Add the oil and about 150ml warm water and mix together to make a soft, pliable dough, adding a little more water if necessary. Turn out onto a surface lightly dusted with flour and knead for 2–3 minutes until very smooth and elastic. Wrap in clingfilm and set aside to rest for 1 hour.

Meanwhile, for the filling, put the potatoes in a pan, cover with water, add 1 teaspoon salt and bring to the boil. Cook for 20 minutes or until tender. Drain, cover and set aside for 20 minutes. Then peel the potatoes and break into small pieces.

Heat a non-stick frying pan over a medium-high heat. Add the oil, then the mustard seeds, cover with a lid and fry until they have stopped popping. Add the onion and fry for 5–6 minutes, stirring, until soft and lightly browned. Add the turmeric, garlic, green chillies and chilli powder and fry for a few seconds, then add the potatoes, peas and 1 teaspoon salt and mix well.

Unwrap the dough, divide it into 10 evenly sized pieces and shape each piece into a ball. Work with one piece of dough at a time, keeping the others covered with clingfilm so they don't dry out. Roll it into a thin 15cm disc. Cut the disc into two D-shaped pieces and brush half of both the curved and straight edge with a little water. Spoon 1 slightly heaped tablespoon of the filling to one side of the D and fold the other side over so the edges meet. Press together well, then place on a tray lined with greaseproof paper. Continue until you have 20. Set them aside for at least 30 minutes to dry slightly, as this will make for better deep-frying.

Heat some oil for deep-frying to 180°C. Fry the shingharas 1 or 2 at a time for 3 minutes until crisp and golden brown, turning them over now and then as they cook. Lift out with a slotted spoon onto another tray lined with plenty of kitchen paper and leave to drain. Serve hot or warm.

Potatoes and spinach with cumin and mustard seeds

Sag aloo

SERVES 4–6

This is a simple vegetable side dish, but the sort of thing you can find yourself secretly rating as the best of the evening as you leave a good Indian restaurant. The trick is to cook the potatoes in as little water as possible, so that they lightly fry and become crusty with all the spices, before adding the spinach, which only needs brief cooking.

4 tbsp mustard oil
1 tsp black mustard seeds
1 tsp cumin seeds
25g garlic, crushed
30g peeled ginger, finely grated
2 green cayenne chillies, thinly sliced
½ tsp turmeric powder
½ tsp kashmiri chilli powder
700g peeled floury potatoes, cut into 2.5–3cm pieces
250g spinach, washed, drained and cut into rough pieces
½ tsp *Garam masala* (page 302)

Heat the mustard oil in a large pan over a medium-high heat. Add the mustard seeds and cover with a lid. As soon as the seeds stop popping, lower the heat, uncover and add the cumin seeds. Allow them to sizzle for a few seconds until they have darkened slightly, then add the garlic, ginger and green chillies and fry for a further 2 minutes.

Stir in the turmeric and chilli powder, then the potatoes, 5 tablespoons water and 1 teaspoon salt. Cover with a tight-fitting lid and leave to cook over a low heat, shaking the pan every now and then to ensure the potatoes are not sticking, until they are tender. Add a tablespoon or two more water if you need to during cooking.

Uncover the potatoes, stir in the spinach and cook for 1–2 minutes until it has wilted down. Sprinkle over the garam masala and serve.

A wet fish curry with aubergines, potatoes and moong dal

Macher jhol

SERVES 4

This is one of the best-known dishes of Bangladesh but very different from anything you'd find in a restaurant either there or in the UK. One thought I had there was that their local food, so quickly put together from relatively few ingredients, was not the sort of thing you'd expect if you were eating out. Of course, what I'm looking for is precisely the sort of food that people eat at home, like jhol. It's a thin, soupy fish stew with lots of vegetables, but though it tastes light it's packed full of flavour. I feel it's one of those dishes you need to become accustomed to, by which time you will then crave it endlessly.

500g thick white fish fillet, such as hake, haddock or snapper, skin on
2 tsp turmeric powder
3 tbsp vegetable oil
200g peeled small waxy potatoes, such as Charlotte, cut into 1cm-thick slices
100g moong dal
1 tsp *Panch phoran* (page 303)
1 tsp ground ginger
1 tsp kashmiri chilli powder
1 tsp freshly ground cumin seeds
1 tsp freshly ground coriander seeds
150g aubergine, cut into 1cm-thick pieces
4–6 green cayenne chillies, halved lengthways
4 tbsp roughly chopped fresh coriander

Cut the fish across into pieces 2.5cm thick, then dust on both sides with some salt and half the turmeric.

Heat the oil in a medium-sized pan over a medium-high heat. Add the pieces of fish a few at a time and fry for 1 minute on each side until lightly browned. Lift out onto a plate, add the potato slices and fry until golden on each side. Lift out and set aside with the fish.

Add the moong dal to the oil left in the pan and leave to sizzle for a few seconds. Add the panch phoran, the rest of the turmeric and the ground spices, sizzle for a few seconds more, then add 900ml water, the fried potatoes, aubergines, green chillies and 1 teaspoon salt and bring to the boil. Cover and simmer for 10 minutes until the potatoes are tender. Add the pieces of fried fish and simmer for 2 minutes more until the fish is cooked through. Stir in the fresh coriander and serve.

Spicy fried potato curry with paneer cheese and peas

Aloo muttar paneer

SERVES 4–6

When I was watching the three chefs, resplendent in their chef's whites, cook the beef shatkora on page 266, I was intrigued to see they were cooking a couple of other dishes at the same time. This made filming a little tricky as we weren't sure whether the potatoes, peas and paneer were going into the shatkora or not, and we were at a linguistic disadvantage too. But it eventually became clear this was a separate dish, being cooked for some customers in the restaurant, and a very good one too. I was surprised that they stirred some ghee in at the end, but then dairy produce is an important part of the Bangladeshi repertoire. I ordered one when I had dinner in the restaurant that evening and found it delicious.

4 tbsp vegetable oil

250g peeled small waxy potatoes, such as Charlotte, halved lengthways and cut into 1cm-thick slices

250g paneer, cut into pieces 1cm × 2cm

12 curry leaves

1 tsp cumin seeds

100g onions, chopped

15g garlic, crushed

25g peeled ginger, finely grated

½ tsp turmeric powder

3 green cayenne chillies, slit open lengthways

250g vine-ripened tomatoes, chopped

½ tsp Garam masala (page 302)

175g peas, fresh or frozen

15g ghee

Heat 2 tablespoons of the oil in a wide shallow frying pan over a medium heat. Add the potato pieces and fry them for 6–8 minutes, turning them every now and then until they are golden brown all over. Using a slotted spoon, lift out onto a plate. Add another tablespoon of oil and the paneer and fry for 3–4 minutes until these too are golden all over. Set aside with the potatoes.

Add another tablespoon of oil to the pan, add the curry leaves and cumin seeds and allow them to sizzle for a few seconds. Add the onions, garlic and ginger and fry gently for 5 minutes until the onions are soft and just beginning to brown. Add the turmeric, chillies and chopped tomatoes and fry until the tomatoes have broken down to form a sauce.

Add the potatoes, 100ml water and 1 teaspoon salt, cover and simmer for 5 minutes until the potatoes are tender and the liquid has reduced to a thickish sauce. Add the pieces of fried paneer, garam masala and peas, and simmer for 2 minutes or until the peas are just tender. Stir in the ghee and serve.

A rich king prawn and coconut curry
Chingri malai kari

SERVES 4

This excellent north Indian prawn curry is called malai because it is influenced by Malaysian cooking with its use of grated coconut, coconut milk, palm sugar and lime juice.

300g shallots or onions, roughly chopped

40g peeled ginger, roughly chopped

40g garlic, roughly chopped

400g large raw peeled prawns

1 tsp turmeric powder

3 tbsp mustard or vegetable oil

1 tsp cumin seeds

3 bay leaves

10–12 curry leaves

½ tsp kashmiri chilli powder

½ tsp mild paprika

4 green cayenne chillies, slit open lengthways

300ml coconut milk

30g fresh coconut, finely grated

1 tbsp *Garam masala* (page 302)

1 tsp jaggery or palm sugar

1 tbsp lime juice

Put the onion, ginger and garlic into a mini food processor and blend to a smooth paste.

Put the prawns into a bowl and toss them with the turmeric and 1 teaspoon salt. Heat 2 tablespoons of the oil in a large, non-stick frying pan, add the prawns and stir-fry briefly – just 1–2 minutes until they take on some colour. Spoon onto a plate and set aside.

Add the remaining oil to the pan with the cumin seeds, bay leaves and curry leaves and allow them to sizzle for a few seconds. Add the onion paste, chilli powder and paprika and fry gently for 10 minutes, stirring, until the paste is rich and aromatic. Add 150ml water, cover and simmer for 6 minutes, stirring now and then. Stir in the green chillies and simmer for a further 4 minutes.

Add the coconut milk and bring to a simmer. Add the prawns, grated coconut, garam masala and sugar and simmer for 1–2 minutes until the prawns are cooked through. Stir in the lime juice and serve.

Mild lamb curry with yogurt, cardamom and cassia

Rezala

SERVES 6–8

In Bangladesh a rezala more often than not will be made with what they call 'mutton' but is in fact goat. It's moderately easy to get goat in the UK now, but I achieved really good results using a supermarket-bought shoulder of lamb. What I particularly like about this Bangladeshi celebratory dish – it's a high days and holidays curry – is the restraint in the amount of spices: in this case just cardamom and cassia, finished with a little chilli. The taste is incredibly subtle. In some way the cardamom and cassia mixed with the flavour of the lamb cooked in yogurt and some sweet, slowly browned onions is much more than the sum of its parts. I have been really keen in this chapter to pick recipes that demonstrate the enormous range of Indian cooking and this one, I think, is a particularly good example.

600g onions, halved

40g peeled ginger, roughly
    chopped

40g garlic, roughly chopped

100g ghee

10 green cardamom pods

10g cassia bark or pieces
    of cinnamon stick

1.5kg boned shoulder of
    lamb, cut into 4cm cubes

250g natural wholemilk yogurt

2 tsp jaggery or palm sugar

6 dried red kashmiri chillies

½ tsp loosely packed saffron
    strands

5 green cayenne chillies,
    slit open lengthways

1 tbsp lime juice

Thinly slice half the onions. Roughly chop the remainder and put into a mini food processor with the ginger and garlic. Blend to a smooth paste.

Heat the ghee in a heavy-based pan over a medium-high heat. Add the cardamom pods and the cassia or cinnamon and leave to sizzle for a few seconds until they start to smell aromatic. Add the sliced onions and fry for 10 minutes, stirring now and then, until richly golden. Add the onion paste and fry for a further 5 minutes, stirring.

Stir in the lamb and fry for 5 minutes. Now add the yogurt, 1 tablespoon at a time, stirring and frying for 1 minute before adding the next. Once all the yogurt has been added, stir in the sugar and 1 teaspoon salt, cover and leave to simmer for 30 minutes.

Meanwhile, cover the dried red chillies with hot water, and the saffron with 2 tablespoons hot water, and leave both to soak for 30 minutes.

Drain the soaked red chillies and finely chop. Stir them into the lamb with the green chillies and saffron water. Re-cover and simmer for a further 30 minutes or until the lamb is tender. Uncover, stir in the lime juice and another 1 teaspoon salt, or to taste, and serve.

Moghul chicken korma

SERVES 6–8

Most of us who love Indian cooking have an idea of what a korma is: a very mild, creamy curry, often fragrant with cardamom, saffron and rosewater, and in this case pale lemon in colour. In fact, 'korma' refers to the method of cooking – braising – and not to a particular set of ingredients, so it can vary from creamy to light and aromatic or even deep-red and fiery. Never the less, this one, very similar to the one I had in Dhaka, is rich and creamy, thick with ground almonds and poppy seeds.

2 tbsp white poppy seeds

2 tbsp rosewater

½ tsp loosely packed saffron strands

40g peeled ginger, roughly chopped

25g garlic, roughly chopped

2.5cm cinnamon stick

Seeds from 10 green cardamom pods

2 tsp coriander seeds

½ tsp freshly grated nutmeg

250g natural wholemilk yogurt

700g skinned and boneless chicken (a mixture of breast and thigh meat), cut into 5cm pieces

350g onions, roughly chopped

50g ghee

50g ground almonds

½ tsp freshly ground white pepper

3 green cayenne chillies, halved lengthways

75–100ml double cream

Heat a dry, heavy-based frying pan over a medium heat, add the poppy seeds and shake them around for a few seconds until they darken very slightly and smell nutty. Tip into a spice grinder, leave to cool, then grind into a fine powder. Put into a bowl and set aside. Warm the rosewater, add the saffron and set aside to soak.

Put the ginger and garlic into a mini food processor with 3 tablespoons water and blend to a smooth paste. Heat a small, heavy-based pan over a low heat, add the cinnamon, cardamom seeds and coriander seeds and shake them around for a few seconds until they darken slightly and start to smell aromatic. Tip them into a spice grinder and grind them to a fine powder. Put the garlic and ginger paste, ground roasted spices, grated nutmeg, yogurt and 1 teaspoon salt into a bowl and mix together. Stir in the chicken and leave to marinate for 30 minutes.

Meanwhile, put the onion into a food processor and blend to a smooth paste. Heat the ghee in a large, heavy-based pan, add the onion paste and fry gently for 5–6 minutes until it just starts to brown. Add the chicken and all its marinade, the ground almonds, white pepper and 3 tablespoons water. Bring up to a gentle simmer, part-cover and simmer for 25 minutes.

Uncover the chicken, add the green chillies, ground poppy seeds and saffron rosewater and simmer, uncovered, for a further 5 minutes, by which time the sauce should be quite thick. Add the cream and simmer for a further 1–2 minutes, then serve.

Chicken tikka masala

SERVES 4

It's not true to say you wouldn't find chicken tikka masala in any restaurant in the Indian subcontinent – because it was on the menu of one I visited in Sylhet, the Woondal, and cost just £1! Never the less, Britain's favourite dish was invented by an enterprising Bangladeshi chef in the UK. So this is a recipe influenced a little by British restaurants and a little by Bangladesh, but I haven't puréed the final sauce as is normal, and I've thrown in a few fresh green cayenne chillies at the end for a bit of heat. Also, I think it's a good idea to use some sort of food colour for the chicken tikka. A little mixed red and yellow food colourings will do.

750g skinned boned chicken
1½ tbsp lemon juice
1 tsp kashmiri chilli powder
2 tsp mild paprika
1 tsp turmeric powder
A few drops each of red and
 yellow food colouring
2 tsp cumin seeds
Seeds from 12 green
 cardamom pods
25g garlic, roughly chopped
25g peeled ginger, chopped
4 tbsp natural yogurt
25g ghee, melted

For the sauce:
3 tbsp ghee
200g onions, finely sliced
15g garlic, crushed
25g peeled ginger, grated
1½ tsp freshly ground
 coriander seeds
½ tsp kashmiri chilli powder
½ tsp mild paprika
225g tomatoes, finely chopped
1 tbsp tomato purée
1 tbsp ground almonds
120ml single or double cream
3–4 green cayenne chillies
1 tsp *Garam masala* (page 302)
1½ tbsp lemon juice
2 tablespoons chopped fresh
 coriander

Cut the chicken into 4cm chunks, Put into a bowl with the lemon juice, chilli powder, paprika, turmeric, food colourings and 1 teaspoon salt, and toss together well. Set aside for 20 minutes. Meanwhile, heat a dry, heavy-based pan over a medium-high heat. Add the cumin seeds and shake them around for a few seconds until they start to smell aromatic. Grind to a fine powder in a spice grinder. Set aside 1 teaspoon for the sauce. Add the cardamom seeds to the rest and grind once more.

Put the ground cumin and cardamom, garlic, ginger and yogurt into a mini food processor and blend. Stir into the chicken and marinate at room temperature for 30 minutes.

Meanwhile, for the sauce, heat the ghee in a medium-sized pan. Add the sliced onions and fry for 6–8 minutes until soft and richly golden. Add the crushed garlic and grated ginger and cook for 2–3 minutes more. Add the reserved ground cumin, freshly ground coriander, chilli powder and paprika and fry for a further 1–2 minutes. Add the tomatoes and fry until they have broken down into a sauce. Add the tomato purée, ground almonds, 300ml boiling hot water and ½ teaspoon salt and simmer for 10 minutes.

Lift the pieces of chicken out of the marinade and thread onto metal skewers. Stir the remaining yogurt marinade, the cream, green chillies (slit open) and garam masala into the sauce and simmer for 8–10 minutes until a little reduced. Meanwhile, heat a ridged cast-iron griddle over a high heat, lower the heat to medium and brush with a little oil. Brush the chicken on the skewers with melted ghee and cook for about 8 minutes, turning now and then, until the chicken is cooked through and slightly charred in places. Push the pieces of chicken tikka off the skewers into the sauce and bring back to a simmer. Stir in the lemon juice and chopped coriander and simmer for 2–3 minutes, then serve.

Spiced rice with lentils and hard-boiled eggs

Bhuna khichuri

SERVES 4–6

Khichuri, a Bengali national dish, was the inspiration for our own kedgeree. As with everywhere in India, any sort of pulse, such as lentil, is a valuable source of protein for the very poor. Khichuri is often accompanied by crisply fried fillets of fish, aubergines or potatoes, and of course hard-boiled eggs. Where our idea of including poached smoked haddock came from I don't know – unless it was suggested by the yellow colour of the crisp turmeric-fried fish in the Bengali dish. This is really quite easy to make and also good as an alternative to a pilau rice, served with any sort of fish or vegetable curry.

250g moong dal (page 311)

4 tbsp ghee

10cm cinnamon stick, broken into smaller pieces, bruised

6 green cardamom pods, bruised

6 cloves

10–12 curry leaves

30g peeled ginger, finely chopped

½ tsp cumin seeds

2 green cayenne chillies, slit open lengthways

1 tsp turmeric powder

250g basmati rice

1 tsp *Garam masala* (page 302)

2 quantities *Crisp fried shallots* (page 299)

4–6 hard-boiled eggs, quartered

Chopped fresh coriander, to garnish

For the turmeric-fried fish:

600g firm fish fillet, such as John Dory, gurnard, snapper or barramundi

2 tsp turmeric powder

2 tsp kashmiri chilli powder

4 tbsp ghee

For the khichuri, rinse the moong dal chilka in cold water until the water stays relatively clear. Cover with fresh water and leave it to soak for 30 minutes, then drain well.

Heat 2 tablespoons of the ghee in a medium-sized pan over a medium heat. Add the cinnamon, cardamom, cloves and curry leaves and, as soon as they begin to splutter, add the ginger and cumin seeds and fry for 1–2 minutes until the ginger smells 'nutty'.

Add the green chillies, turmeric and rice and fry gently for 2–3 minutes, stirring. Add the dal and 1 teaspoon salt and stir again. Add 850ml boiling-hot water, bring back to the boil and cover with a tight-fitting lid. Lower the heat and leave to cook gently for 10 minutes. Meanwhile, melt the remaining ghee to fork into the rice at the end.

While the khichuri is cooking, fry the fish. Cut the fish into 8–10cm pieces each weighing 30–40g. Mix the turmeric with the chilli powder and 1 teaspoon salt on a plate and dust the pieces of fish on both sides in it. Melt the ghee in a large non-stick frying pan over a medium-high heat, add the pieces of fish and fry for 1 minute on either side until crisp and golden.

Uncover the rice and gently fork in the garam masala, melted ghee, fried shallots and some extra seasoning. Spoon onto a warmed serving plate and garnish with the hard-boiled eggs and chopped coriander. Serve with the fried fish.

Lamb biryani

SERVES 8

The Fakhruddin biryani factory in Dhaka is a food-filmmaker's delight and a triumph of manual labour over machinery, where the cooking of biryanis would not have changed in two thousand years. They make 3,000 biryanis a day. I tried to write down the recipe, but they kept producing buckets of different spices, pails of yogurt, handfuls of saffron, rosewater, and aloo bokhara, a tiny, sour plum. One other ingredient they were insistent upon was long pepper, that looks a bit like a short, brown-black catkin. It's hotter than black pepper and has an almost resinous scent. I ate one of their biryanis, and I've never tasted one better. It was served with a kachumber salad similar to mine on page 306 and a sweet and sour plum chutney.

For the lamb:

20 green cardamom pods

10 cloves

2 × 10cm cinnamon sticks, broken into smaller pieces

4 pieces of blade mace

2 dried kashmiri chillies

350g natural wholemilk yogurt

50g peeled ginger, grated

35g garlic, crushed

1 tsp freshly ground black pepper (long pepper, if possible)

1kg meaty loin lamb chops, trimmed of all excess fat

2 tbsp blanched almonds

For the rice:

½ tsp saffron strands

3 tbsp rosewater

600g basmati rice (unrinsed)

1 tsp cumin seeds

8 green cardamom pods

12 cloves

75g ghee

24 dried aloo bokhara or small dried prunes

4 tbsp sultanas

1 quantity *Crisp fried shallots* (page 299)

250ml full-cream milk

For the lamb, put the cardamom pods, cloves, cinnamon and mace into a spice grinder and grind to a fine powder. Add the dried chillies and blend until finely chopped. Put the yogurt in a bowl and stir in the spices, ginger, garlic, black pepper and 2 teaspoons salt. Add the lamb chops and marinate for 2 hours.

For the rice, put the saffron into a clean mortar and crush it into a powder with the pestle. Stir in the rosewater and set aside.

Preheat the oven to 200°C/Gas Mark 6. Put the blanched almonds into a bowl and cover with hot water. Leave to soak for 30 minutes, then drain and cut lengthways into long shards. Spread the almonds on a small baking sheet and roast in the oven for 6–8 minutes until golden brown. Remove and leave to cool. Reduce the oven temperature to 160°C/Gas Mark 3. To assemble the biryani, put 4 litres of water into a very large pan with the cumin seeds, cardamom pods, cloves and 4 teaspoons salt and bring to a rolling boil. Meanwhile, melt the ghee in a large, 5–6-litre flameproof casserole dish. Spread the meat and its marinade over the base of the pan and sprinkle over the aloo bokhara, sultanas and three-quarters of the crisp fried shallots. Sprinkle the rice into the boiling water, bring back to a vigorous boil, then boil for 3 minutes. Drain well, then quickly spread half the rice over the meat and drizzle over half of the saffron rosewater. Spread over the remaining rice and drizzle over the remaining rosewater. Pour over the milk and cover the pan with foil and then a tight-fitting lid. Place the casserole over a medium-high heat and bring to the boil, then transfer to the oven and cook for 1¾ hours.

Remove the biryani from the oven, spoon onto a large warmed serving platter and sprinkle with the remaining crisp fried shallots, roasted almonds, and serve.

Dry cauliflower curry with mustard seeds, ginger and nigella seed

SERVES 4

I am inordinately fond of dry vegetable curries like this. It is a pleasing addition to a meal that takes in three or four different dishes, making a contrast to the wetter ones. There is a lot of mustard seed in here but it blends in well with the cauliflower. After all, both belong to the same plant genus, the brassicas.

2 tsp yellow mustard seeds

2 tsp black mustard seeds

3 tbsp mustard oil

600g cauliflower, broken into small florets

1 tsp cumin seeds

50g onions, finely chopped

15g garlic, finely chopped

20g peeled ginger, finely chopped

1 tsp turmeric powder

3 mild green chillies, finely chopped

1 tbsp *Tamarind water* (page 299)

2 tsp nigella seed (kalonji)

Put the yellow and black mustard seeds into a mortar and grind to a powder with the pestle, or grind in a spice grinder.

Heat the oil in a large, deep frying pan, add the cauliflower and cumin seeds and shake them around for 2–3 minutes until the cauliflower is coloured with brown spots. Add the onion, garlic, ginger, turmeric, green chillies, tamarind water, 2–3 tablespoons water and 1 teaspoon salt. Cover and fry gently for another 5 minutes until the cauliflower is just tender, but still with a little bit of crunch and the mixture is dry.

Add the mustard powder and nigella seeds and toss together briefly for 1 minute, then serve.

Beef kofta curry

SERVES 6

This is the Indian version of Italian meatballs in tomato sauce to be served with spaghetti. In fact, I sometimes serve this with pasta too.

2 tbsp coriander seeds

1 tbsp cumin seeds

2 tsp *Garam masala* (page 302)

1½ tsp kashmiri chilli powder

2 tsp turmeric powder

135ml vegetable oil

600g onions, finely chopped

25g garlic, crushed

700g minced beef

1½ tbsp beaten egg

8 green cardamom pods

6 cloves

7.5cm cinnamon stick,
    broken into smaller pieces

200g chopped tomatoes,
    fresh or from a can

1 tbsp tomato purée

24 curry leaves

5 green cayenne chillies,
    slit open lengthways

Heat a dry, heavy-based pan over a high heat. Add the coriander and cumin seeds and shake them around for a few seconds until they darken slightly and start to smell aromatic. Tip them into a spice grinder and grind to a fine powder, then mix with the garam masala, chilli powder and turmeric.

Heat 6 tablespoons of the oil in a large saucepan. Add the onions and garlic and fry gently for 10–12 minutes until soft and lightly browned. Add the ground spices and 1 teaspoon salt and cook gently for another 3–4 minutes. Scrape half the mixture into a mixing bowl and leave to cool.

Add the minced beef, beaten egg and 1 teaspoon salt to the spiced onion mixture in the bowl and mix together well. Shape into approximately 28 golfball-sized pieces and set aside.

Add the green cardamom pods, cloves and cinnamon stick to the spiced onion mixture left in the pan together with the tomatoes, tomato purée, 300ml water, curry leaves, chillies and another teaspoon of salt and bring to a gentle simmer.

Meanwhile, heat the remaining oil in a non-stick frying pan. Add the meatballs, in 2 batches if necessary, and fry for 2–3 minutes, turning them now and then until lightly browned all over. Drop them into the sauce, part-cover and simmer for 20 minutes, carefully stirring every now and then, until the meatballs have set and the sauce has reduced and thickened nicely, then serve.

Aubergine curry with tomatoes, ginger and fennel seeds

SERVES 6

If you can get them, use finger aubergines for this. They are shaped rather like a small courgette and hold their shape well during cooking. This is a simple curry, but interesting to me as it uses a lot of fennel seeds, a common flavour in Bangladeshi food. Incidentally, they call them aniseed there, but they're not, because I wandered into a kitchen in Sylhet and tried them. All through India, as indeed in some Indian restaurants in the UK, sugar-coated fennel seeds are offered at the end of a meal as a breath-freshener and digestive.

600g aubergines, ideally Asian finger aubergines
150ml vegetable oil
40g peeled ginger, roughly chopped
40g garlic, roughly chopped
2 green cayenne chillies, finely chopped
2 tsp fennel seeds
1 tsp cumin seeds
1 tbsp freshly ground coriander seeds
½ tsp turmeric powder
400g chopped tomatoes, fresh or from a can
½ tsp freshly ground black pepper
1 tbsp each chopped fresh coriander and mint

Top and tail the aubergines and cut in half lengthways. If using larger, Mediterranean-style aubergines, then cut each one across in half and then each piece lengthways into 6 or 8 wedges. Toss them with ½ teaspoon salt and set aside in a colander for 10 minutes.

Heat a large frying pan over a high heat. Pour the oil into a shallow dish. Brush the aubergine pieces, a few at a time, with oil, put them in the frying pan and cook for 3–4 minutes on each side until richly browned. Cooking the aubergines in this way helps prevent them from absorbing too much oil, which would make the finished dish greasy. Set aside in a bowl and repeat with the remaining aubergines.

Put the ginger, garlic and chilli into a mini food processor with 2–3 tablespoons water and grind to a smooth paste.

Put 2 tablespoons of the remaining oil into the frying pan and add the cumin and fennel seeds. Leave them to sizzle for a few seconds, then add the ginger and garlic paste and leave this to fry for a further 2–3 minutes. Add the coriander and turmeric and fry for 1 minute, then add the tomatoes, black pepper, 3 tablespoons water and ½ teaspoon salt. Cover and leave to simmer for 8–10 minutes until reduced and thickened slightly.

Return the fried aubergine slices to the pan and stir well to coat in the sauce. Simmer for 5 minutes, then stir in the fresh coriander and mint and serve.

BASIC RECIPES

Shallot oil

MAKES 125ML
125ml vegetable oil
100g shallots, finely chopped

Heat the oil in a small frying pan over a medium heat, add the shallots and fry, stirring constantly, until crisp and lightly golden. Transfer immediately to a small bowl and leave to cool.

Chilli oil

MAKES 125ML
125ml vegetable oil
3 tbsp bright red, hot, very fresh dried chilli flakes

Heat the oil in a small pan over a medium heat. Add the dried chilli flakes and leave for 5 minutes. Allow to cool, then transfer to a clean, dry jar, seal and keep in a cool place for several days. Strain, to remove the chilli flakes, before using.

Crisp fried garlic

6 tbsp vegetable oil
50g (about 12) garlic, thinly sliced

Heat the oil in a small frying pan over a medium-high heat, add the sliced garlic and fry until crisp and golden. Lift out onto kitchen paper. When cool, keep in an airtight container.

Crisp fried shallots

Vegetable oil
350g shallots (onions), thinly sliced

Heat 1cm oil in a large frying pan over a medium-high heat. Add the sliced shallots and fry, stirring now and then, until crisp and golden. Lift out onto plenty of kitchen paper and sprinkle with a little salt. When cool, keep in an airtight container.

Roasted rice and roasted rice powder

50g Thai jasmine or long-grain rice

Heat a small, heavy-based frying pan over a medium heat. Add the rice and shake it around for a few minutes until the grains become richly golden brown and smell 'nutty'. For salads, tip the rice into a mortar or coffee mug and, while still hot, pound it with a pestle or the end of a rolling pin to break it up, but don't reduce to a powder. For roasted rice powder, grind in a mini food processor or a spice grinder. When cool, keep in an airtight container.

Tamarind water

Take 60g tamarind pulp (about the size of a tangerine) and put it in a bowl with 150ml hand-hot water. Work the paste with your fingers until it has broken down and the seeds have been released. Strain the slightly syrupy mixture through a fine sieve into another bowl and discard the fibrous material left behind. The water is ready to use and will keep in the fridge for 24 hours.

Coconut flesh

A small coconut yields about 250g flesh, and a large coconut about 300g. Choose a coconut that feels heavy, and shake it to make sure it is still full of water. This means the flesh is fresh and moist and will yield more coconut milk. If you want to save the coconut water from inside, pierce two of the eyes with a thick skewer and drain off the water into a glass. This can be used for cooking or you can simply drink it. Then whack the shell with a hammer once or twice to crack it open, or throw it onto a concrete floor, then prise out the flesh with a round-bladed knife. For coconut flesh that is pristine white, peel off its brown skin using a really sharp potato peeler. It's a bit fiddly but worth the effort. For salads such as the Balinese bean and coconut salad on page 184, I set up my food processor with its finest grating blade and feed the flesh through the tube to get long, thin strands. However, there is no need to remove the skin before making coconut milk (see below) or for preparing grated coconut where the appearance is not crucial, such as in a curry paste. In this case, simply break the unpeeled flesh into small cubes, drop it into a food processor and briefly whiz. Excess coconut can be frozen. Packets of finely grated frozen coconut can be bought from most Indian and Asian supermarkets, and are a great standby.

Coconut milk

Coconut milk is extracted from the flesh. To get about 200ml coconut milk, mix 300g finely grated fresh coconut (i.e. the flesh from 1 large coconut) with 250ml hot water and leave it to stand for about 10 minutes. Then whiz it in a liquidizer or food processor and pour it into a muslin-lined sieve set over a bowl. When most of the liquid has dripped through, twist the muslin around the remaining coconut and squeeze it to extract every last drop of milk. If you leave it to settle for 20 minutes or so, the milk will separate. The thicker opaque liquid that settles on the top is often called the 'cream' and the thinner liquid underneath is the 'milk', but for most of the recipes in this book there is no need to separate the two. If you use canned coconut milk instead, which is far richer than fresh coconut milk, I recommend diluting it with 1 part water to every 3 parts canned milk. So for 400ml coconut milk, mix 300ml canned milk with 100ml water.

Cambodian fish paste sauce Tuk prahoc

2 tbsp prahoc (Cambodian fermented fish paste)

Bring 250ml water to the boil in a pan. Reduce the heat to medium-low, add the prahoc and simmer gently for 10 minutes until the fish has broken down and the water is cloudy. Strain through a sieve into a bowl and discard any solids. Strain once again through a muslin-lined sieve. The liquid is now ready. Keeps for a week in an airtight container in the fridge.

Asian chicken stock

MAKES 1.5–1.75 LITRES

For dishes where you need more depth of flavour and a slightly more 'meaty' taste, especially for soups which include pork as well as seafood, add 500g meaty pork ribs, separated between the bones, to the pot at the beginning of cooking.

2 chicken carcasses or 500g chicken drumsticks or wings
1 bunch spring onions or 1 medium onion, sliced
40g garlic, left whole but lightly bruised
75g peeled ginger, thinly sliced and lightly bruised
1 star anise
1 tsp black or white peppercorns

Put the chicken carcasses or pieces into a pan and cover with 3 litres of cold water. Slowly bring to the boil, skimming off the scum as it rises to the surface, then lower the heat and add the remaining ingredients. Leave to simmer gently for 1½ hours, skimming off any fat. Strain and leave to cool. Freeze for later use.

Asian beef broth

MAKES 2.75 LITRES

40g peeled ginger, cut into 6 pieces
350g shallots, sliced
4 star anise
2 × 7.5cm cinnamon sticks
½ tsp fennel seeds
900g shin of beef
1kg beef marrow bones
2 celery sticks, roughly sliced
2 carrots, roughly sliced
2 onions, roughly sliced
8 cloves
1 tsp black peppercorns

Put the ginger and shallots onto a chopping board and bash them lightly with a rolling pin. Heat a large, dry, heavy-based frying pan over a high heat, add the star anise, cinnamon sticks and fennel seeds and shake them around for a few seconds until they darken slightly and start to smell aromatic. Tip onto a plate, add the bruised ginger and shallots to the frying pan and cook for 10 minutes until nicely toasted. Add to the roasted spices.

Put the shin of beef, beef bones, celery, carrots, onions, cloves, peppercorns, roasted spices, ginger, shallots and 5 litres of water into a large pan. Bring to the boil, skimming off the scum as it rises to the surface. Lower the heat, add 1 tablespoon salt and leave it to simmer very gently for 3–5 hours: the longer, the better.

Strain the broth into a clean pan. If you can, chill overnight, which will enable you to lift off and discard the excess fat from the surface before using. Freeze for later use.

Duck broth

MAKES 2 LITRES

1 large roasted duck carcass
1 bunch spring onions, sliced
25g peeled ginger, sliced
6 black peppercorns
2 star anise
3 cloves
10cm cinnamon stick

Put all the ingredients into a large pan, cover with 3 litres of water and bring to the boil, skimming off any scum as it rises to the surface. Leave to simmer gently for 3 hours, skimming regularly to remove any fat, until the stock has reduced by a third to 2 litres. Strain the stock through a fine sieve into a clean pan. If you have time, chill the stock overnight in the fridge and then skim the congealed fat off the surface. If not, then skim off as much as you can. Freeze for later use.

NOTE: Remove any small pieces of meat from the duck bones and freeze separately. They are wonderful in the Duck Noodle Soup on page 119.

Vietnamese cooked belly pork

The Vietnamese use cooked pork in many dishes. I have found this is the best way to prepare it.

500g boneless belly pork in one piece, skin left unscored

Put the piece of pork into a pan with 1 litre of cold water and 2 teaspoons salt. Bring to the boil, cover and leave to simmer very gently for 1 hour. Lift out and leave to cool before using.

Chinese red roast pork
Char siu

Chinese red roast pork can be made with lean pork fillet or the more fatty belly pork, which produces crisp crackling too. When you buy roast belly pork from Chinatown, the collected roasting juices, flavoured with soy and spices, sometimes come with it. If you wish, leave the roasting juices to cool, then skim off the congealed fat from the surface and reduce them on the top of the stove. Then thicken with ½ teaspoon cornflour slaked with 1 teaspoon water. They make a very good dipping sauce, but hoisin or plum sauce also work very well.

6 garlic cloves (about 40g)
1 tsp finely grated fresh ginger
100ml dark soy sauce
2 tbsp clear honey
1 tbsp Chinese rice wine
1 tbsp five-spice powder
2 tsp natural red food colouring
1kg boneless belly pork in one piece, skin left unscored, or 2 × fat 300g pork fillets

Put the garlic cloves onto a chopping board, sprinkle with 1 teaspoon salt and crush into a paste, using the blade of a large kitchen knife. Scoop the paste into a shallow dish and mix in the ginger, soy sauce, honey, rice wine, five-spice powder and red food colouring. If using belly pork, place it in the dish, skin-side up, and press down into the mixture, taking care not to get any on the skin. If using pork fillets, place them in the dish and turn them over in the mixture until well coated. Set aside in the fridge to marinate for at least 8 hours, or overnight, turning the fillets over in the marinade now and then.

Preheat the oven to 180°C/Gas Mark 4. For the belly pork, pierce the skin with a skewer or small sharp knife at about 3cm intervals, then rub with a little oil and sprinkle with ½ teaspoon salt. Place the fillets, or the belly of pork skin-side up, on a rack set over a roasting tin containing about 1cm water. Roast the fillets for 30–35 minutes and the belly of pork for 2 hours until golden and crispy. Remove from the oven and leave to rest for 15 minutes before slicing.

SPICE PASTES AND BLENDS

Pastes keep perfectly in the fridge for a week. After that, they progressively lose their fragrance. To store them for longer, spoon the paste into small pots or ice-cube trays, cover and freeze.

Cambodian Khmer curry paste *Kroeung*

This is the fresh herb paste used in many Cambodian dishes, which gives their food its special fragrant flavour. There are three different types of kroeung: yellow, red and green, all based on similar combinations but each one tinted by the colour of the predominant ingredient. In this one, it's turmeric (in the red one, it's mild dried red chillies and in the green one lots of fresh lemongrass, leaves as well as stalks).

50g peeled galangal or ginger, roughly chopped
50g peeled fresh turmeric or 2 tsp turmeric powder
40g garlic, roughly chopped
8 fat lemongrass stalks, core chopped
100g shallots, roughly chopped
4 kaffir lime leaves, finely shredded
1 strip pared lime zest (from a kaffir lime if available)
2 tsp Cambodian fermented fish paste (prahoc) or Thai shrimp paste
1 medium-hot red or green chilli, chopped

Traditionally the ingredients are pounded, one by one, in a mortar with a pestle; alternatively, put everything into a mini food processor with about 2 tablespoons water, to help get the paste moving, and process until you have a very smooth paste.

Malaysian fish curry paste

1 tbsp coriander seeds
1 tbsp cumin seeds
1 tbsp fennel seeds
1 tbsp black peppercorns
15g finely grated fresh coconut
7–10g dried kashmiri chillies, soaked in hot water for 30 minutes, drained
25g garlic, roughly chopped
25g peeled ginger, roughly chopped
1 tbsp turmeric powder
1 fat lemongrass stalk, core roughly chopped
1 tsp palm sugar
3 tbsp vegetable oil

Put the coriander, cumin and fennel seeds and black peppercorns into a spice grinder and grind to a powder. Tip the powder into a mini food processor and add the coconut, chillies, garlic, ginger, turmeric, lemongrass, sugar and vegetable oil. Blend to a smooth paste.

Penang laksa spice paste

2 fat lemongrass stalks, core roughly chopped
50g shallots, roughly chopped
30g garlic, sliced
30g peeled galangal or ginger, roughly chopped
10g peeled fresh turmeric, thinly sliced, or ½ tsp turmeric powder
1 tbsp Nam prik pao (page 303)

Put all the ingredients for the laksa spice paste into a mini food processor and blend to a smooth paste.

Singapore laksa spice paste

25g dried shrimps
10 dried red kashmiri chillies, slit open and seeds shaken out
1 tbsp shrimp paste
2 fat lemongrass stalks, core chopped
25g candle nuts, macadamia nuts, unsalted roasted cashew nuts or roasted peanuts
15g garlic, roughly chopped
40g peeled galangal or ginger, roughly chopped
50g peeled fresh turmeric, roughly chopped, or 2 tsp turmeric powder
125g onions or shallots, roughly chopped
1 tbsp freshly ground coriander seeds
3 tbsp vegetable oil

Put the dried shrimps and dried chillies into a bowl. Cover with hot water and leave to soak for 20–30 minutes. Drain, put into a mini food processor with all the other ingredients and blend to a smooth paste.

Malay korma curry paste

80g fresh coconut, finely grated
1 tbsp coriander seeds
2 tsp cumin seeds
2 tsp fennel seeds
3cm cinnamon stick
¼ tsp cloves
¼ tsp cardamom seeds (about 5 green pods)
½ tsp black peppercorns
1 tsp turmeric powder
½ tsp freshly grated nutmeg
4 dried red kashmiri chillies
8 macadamia nuts
300g shallots or onions, roughly chopped
25g peeled ginger, roughly chopped
40g garlic, roughly chopped
2 tbsp vegetable oil

Heat a dry, heavy-based frying pan over a medium-low heat. Add the coconut and shake it for 4–5 minutes until richly golden. Tip onto a plate to cool. Add 1 teaspoon of the coriander seeds, the cumin and fennel seeds to the pan and shake around for a few seconds until they darken slightly and smell aromatic. Tip into a spice grinder, add the remaining coriander seeds and other dry spices, chillies, macadamia nuts and toasted coconut and grind into a powder that will look a bit like wet sand because of oil from the coconut. Tip into a food processor, add the shallots, ginger, garlic and oil and blend to a smooth paste.

Malaysian devil's curry spice paste

15 dried red kashmiri chillies, soaked in hot water for 30 minutes then drained
2 tsp mild paprika
20g peeled ginger, roughly chopped
100g onions or shallots, roughly chopped
20g garlic, roughly chopped
25g candle nuts, macadamia nuts, cashew nuts or peanuts
1 tbsp freshly ground coriander seeds
1 tsp turmeric powder
4 tbsp vegetable oil

Put the ingredients with ½ teaspoon salt into a mini food processor and blend to a smooth paste.

Malaysian kapitan curry paste

6 dried red kashmiri chillies, soaked in hot water for 30 minutes then drained
275g shallots or onions, roughly chopped
2 tsp five-spice powder
2 tsp turmeric powder
25g garlic, roughly chopped
50g peeled fresh ginger
4 fat lemongrass stalks, core chopped
½ tsp shrimp paste
2 tbsp vegetable oil

Put all the ingredients into a mini food processor and blend to a smooth paste.

Rendang spice paste

100g finely grated fresh coconut
8 dried red kashmiri chillies
2 tbsp coriander seeds
1 tsp cumin seeds
25g peeled fresh turmeric, roughly
    chopped, or 1 tsp turmeric powder
225g onions or shallots, roughly chopped
30g garlic, roughly chopped
50g peeled galangal or ginger
6 medium-hot red chillies, seeded
    and roughly chopped

Heat a dry, heavy-based frying pan
over a medium heat. Add the grated
coconut and stir it for a few minutes
until it is richly golden. Tip into a
food processor and leave to cool.
Meanwhile, put the dried chillies,
coriander seeds and cumin seeds
into a spice grinder and grind to
a fine powder. Add this to the food
processor with the rest of the spice
paste ingredients and 100ml water,
and blend to a smooth paste.

Thai mussaman curry paste

10 dried red kashmiri chillies, seeded
    and roughly chopped
2 tbsp coriander seeds
1 tbsp cumin seeds
1 tsp cardamom seeds (from about
    20 green pods)
16 whole cloves
5cm piece cinnamon stick
2 large pieces blade mace
3 tbsp vegetable oil
200g shallots or onions, roughly chopped
25g garlic, roughly chopped
1 tsp shrimp paste
25g peeled fresh ginger, roughly chopped
2 fat lemongrass stalks, core chopped
8 tbsp coconut milk

Heat a dry, heavy-based frying pan
over a medium heat. Add the dried
chillies and shake around for a minute
or two until lightly toasted, then tip
into a spice grinder. Return the pan
to the heat and add the coriander,
cumin and cardamom seeds, cloves,
cinnamon and blade mace and shake
them around for a few seconds until
they darken slightly and start to smell
aromatic. Add to the spice grinder
and grind everything to a fine powder.
    Heat the oil in a frying pan, add the
onion and garlic and fry slowly over a
medium heat, stirring occasionally,
for 20 minutes or until richly
browned. Add the shrimp paste and
ground spices and fry everything for
2–3 minutes more. Tip the mixture
into a mini food processor, add the
remaining ingredients and blend
everything to a smooth paste.

Thai green curry paste

5 fat lemongrass stalks, core chopped
15g peeled galangal or ginger, chopped
2 medium-hot green chillies, chopped
3 kaffir lime leaves, roughly chopped
10 black peppercorns, crushed
50g garlic, roughly chopped
100g shallots, roughly chopped
1 tsp shrimp paste

Put all the ingredients into a mini
food processor with 3 tablespoons
water and ½ teaspoon salt and grind
into a smooth paste.

Thai yellow curry paste

3 dried red kashmiri chillies
1 red bird's eye chilli, roughly chopped
3 fat lemongrass stalks, core chopped
25g peeled fresh galangal or ginger,
    roughly chopped
50g peeled fresh turmeric, chopped,
    or 2 tsp turmeric powder
50g onions or shallots, roughly chopped
30g garlic cloves, roughly chopped
2 tsp shrimp paste

Cover the dried red chillies in hot
water and leave to soak for 30
minutes. Then drain, reserving 2
tablespoons of the liquid. Put the
chillies and reserved liquid into
a mini food processor with the
remaining ingredients and grind
everything into a smooth paste.

Thai jungle curry paste

1 large medium-hot red chilli, roughly
    chopped
2 red bird's eye chillies, roughly chopped
2 green bird's eye chillies, roughly
    chopped
25g peeled galangal or fresh ginger,
    roughly chopped
3 fat lemongrass stalks, core chopped
100g shallots, roughly chopped
25g garlic cloves, roughly chopped
¼ tsp freshly ground coriander seeds
¼ tsp freshly ground cumin seeds
⅛ tsp turmeric powder
1 tsp mild paprika
½ tsp shrimp paste

Put all the ingredients into a mini
processor with ½ teaspoon salt and
blend to a smooth paste.

Balinese spice paste
Basa gede/bumbu bali

(pictured on page 298)
1½ tsp black peppercorns
½ nutmeg
25g candle nuts, macadamia nuts,
    cashew nuts or roasted peanuts
1 tsp sesame seeds
60g shallots, roughly chopped
25g peeled ginger, roughly chopped
40g peeled galangal (or extra ginger),
    roughly chopped
15g peeled fresh turmeric, chopped,
    or 1 tsp turmeric powder
3 fat lemongrass stalks, core chopped
20g garlic
2 medium-hot red chillies, seeded and
    roughly chopped
3 red bird's eye chillies, roughly chopped
1 tsp shrimp paste
1 tbsp palm sugar
1 tsp salt
3 tbsp vegetable oil
Juice of ½ lime

Put the peppercorns, nutmeg, nuts
and sesame seeds into a spice grinder
and grind to a fine powder. Tip into a
mini food processor, add all the other
ingredients and blend everything into
a very smooth paste.

Garam masala

*Many different types of garam masala
can be found all over India, Bangladesh
and Pakistan, depending on the region
and the personal taste of the cook. Common
ingredients include peppercorns, cumin,
cloves, cinnamon/cassia, cardamom seeds,
nutmeg, coriander and sometimes star
anise. Garam masala can be bought ready
made, but these mixtures usually contain
fewer of the expensive spices, and as with
all spices, the flavour begins to diminish
soon after grinding. Better to make your
own. This is my favourite combination.*

2 tsp cardamom seeds (from about
    40 green pods)
1 tsp cloves
2 × 6cm cinnamon stick, broken
    into smaller pieces
4 large pieces of blade mace
2 tbsp cumin seeds
2 tbsp coriander seeds
1 tbsp black peppercorns

Heat a dry, heavy-based frying pan over a very low heat. Add all the spices and shake them around for a few minutes until the aromatic oils are released, but don't let them colour. Then transfer to a spice grinder and grind to a fine powder. Store in a screw-top jar.

Roasted and unroasted Sri Lankan curry powder

One of the characteristics of Sri Lankan cuisine is their preference for freshly prepared curry powders rather than pastes. The unroasted curry powder, to which turmeric powder is often added to help with the colour of the finished dish, is mostly used in vegetable dishes, while the roasted curry powder is used in meat and seafood dishes as well as vegetable ones.

1 tbsp uncooked long-grain or basmati rice
50g coriander seeds
25g cumin seeds
25g fennel seeds
7.5cm cinnamon stick
1½ tsp fenugreek seeds
½ tsp cloves
½ tsp cardamom seeds (from about 10 green pods)
½ tsp black mustard seeds
1 tsp black peppercorns
3 dried red kashmiri chillies
1 tsp turmeric powder (for unroasted curry powder only)

For the unroasted or 'raw' curry powder, as it is sometimes known, heat a small, heavy-based frying pan over a medium heat. Add the uncooked rice and shake it around until it is lightly golden. Tip it into a small bowl and leave to cool. Then mix with the remaining spices, dried chillies and turmeric powder, and grind everything (in batches if necessary) into a fine powder.

For the roasted or 'black' curry powder, heat a dry, heavy-based frying pan over a medium heat. Add the rice and shake the grains around for about 3 minutes until medium-brown in colour, taking care not to let them get too brown or to burn. Tip the rice into a bowl and leave to cool while you do the same to the spices, and then to the dried chillies. Mix the rice, spices and chillies together and grind (in batches if necessary) to a powder. Store in a screw-top jar. Use within 3 months.

Panch phoran

This is my version of a special blend of five seed spices used in Bengali and Bangladeshi cooking. Unlike many other spice blends, the seeds are left whole rather than ground into a powder. Whole-seed spice mixes will keep in a screw-top jar somewhere cool, dry and dark for up to a year.

1 tbsp brown/black mustard seeds
1 tbsp nigella seeds (kalonji)
1 tbsp cumin seeds
1 tbsp fennel seeds
1 tbsp fenugreek seeds

Mix the seeds together and store in a screw-top jar.

ACCOMPANIMENTS

Cambodian sweet palm sugar and peanut sauce *Tuk pahem*

100g roasted peanuts
2 tbsp Chinese fermented black beans, crushed into a paste
2 tbsp dark palm sugar
1 tsp fish sauce
1 tsp lime juice

Put the ingredients into a mini food processor with 6 tablespoons cold water and blend into a coarse sauce.

Vietnamese dipping sauce *Nuoc cham*

2 tbsp lime juice
2 tbsp fish sauce
1 tbsp sugar
1 tsp very finely chopped fresh ginger
1 red bird's eye chilli, thinly sliced
1 garlic clove, very finely chopped

Mix the ingredients with 2 tablespoons water, then pour into dipping saucers to serve.

Vietnamese pineapple dipping sauce

2 slices fresh pineapple
2 tbsp palm sugar
3 tbsp fish sauce
10g garlic, crushed
1 red bird's eye chilli, finely chopped
1½ tbsp lime juice

Remove the core from the pineapple slices, put the flesh into a mini food processor and chop using the pulse button into a coarse pulp. Stir the sugar and fish sauce together in a bowl until the sugar has dissolved, then stir in the pineapple pulp, garlic, chilli and lime juice. It should be a little fishy, pungent and sweet. Divide between 4 dipping bowls and serve.

Thai chilli and dried shrimp sauce *Nam prik pao*

100g dried red kashmiri chillies
35g shrimp paste
125ml vegetable oil
50g dried shrimp
35g garlic, finely chopped
150g shallots, thinly sliced
60g seedless tamarind pulp
4 tbsp Thai fish sauce
60g palm sugar

Heat a wok or large, deep frying pan over a high heat. Add the dried chillies and toss them over a high heat until they darken slightly. This is a lot of chilli and the oils released might make you cough. Tip them into a spice grinder a handful at a time and reduce to a fine powder.

Wrap the shrimp paste in a small square of foil to make a flat parcel. Return the wok to a medium heat, add the foil parcel and roast the shrimp paste for 2–3 minutes, turning once. Remove, leave to cool, then unwrap.

Add the oil to the wok, then the dried shrimp and fry gently until they just begin to colour. Remove with a slotted spoon to a food processor. Add the garlic to the oil and fry until lightly golden. Remove with a slotted spoon and add to the shrimp in the food processor. Finally, add the shallots to the oil and fry, stirring frequently, until golden brown. Tip the shallots and all the oil into the food processor, add the roasted chilli powder and the cooled shrimp paste and grind together.

Transfer the mixture to a pan and add the tamarind pulp, fish sauce, sugar and 100ml water and stir over a low heat until the sugar has dissolved and the mixture is simmering, then continue to simmer for a few minutes until the mixture has thickened to a jam-like consistency. Remove from the heat and leave to cool. Spoon into a screw-top jar and store in the fridge. It will keep for at least 3 months.

Thai ginger and chilli dipping sauce

25g garlic
25g peeled fresh ginger, thinly sliced
1 medium-hot red chilli, thinly sliced
2 tbsp palm sugar
2 tbsp white wine vinegar
2 tbsp yellow bean sauce
2 tbsp dark soy sauce
1 tbsp white peppercorns, coarsely ground

Put the garlic, ginger and chilli into a mini food processor and blend to a smooth paste. Add the remaining ingredients, ½ teaspoon salt and the white pepper and blend once more into a sauce. Pour into dipping saucers to serve.

Southeast Asian dipping sauce

50ml white wine vinegar
100g caster sugar
2 tbsp fish sauce
50g cucumber, very finely diced
25g carrot, very finely diced
25g shallots, very finely chopped
2 red bird's eye chillies, thinly sliced

Gently heat the vinegar, sugar and 1½ tablespoons water in a small pan until the sugar has dissolved. Bring to the boil and boil for 1 minute. Remove from the heat and leave to cool. Then stir in the fish sauce, cucumber, carrot, shallots and chilli. Pour into dipping saucers to serve.

Thai chilli and tamarind sambal

50ml vegetable oil
30g garlic cloves, roughly chopped
60g shallots, roughly chopped
3 medium-hot dried red chillies, such as kashmiri, thinly sliced
2 red bird's eye chillies, thinly sliced
25g ginger, roughly chopped
½ tsp shrimp paste
30g palm sugar
Juice of 1 lime
30g piece of seedless tamarind pulp
2 tbsp fish sauce

Heat the oil in a small pan, add the garlic and shallots and fry for 3–4 minutes until golden brown. Add the chillies and fry for 30 seconds, then add the rest of the ingredients, 4 tablespoons water and ½ teaspoon salt, bring to the boil and simmer for 1 minute. Pour into a mini food processor and briefly blend.

Kecap manis and lime dipping sauce
Sambal kecap

3 tbsp kecap manis
2 tsp lime juice
2 red bird's eye chillies, very thinly sliced
15g shallots, very finely chopped

Mix all the ingredients together and pour into dipping saucers to serve.

Balinese peanut sauce
Bumbu kacang

2 dried red kashmiri chillies, soaked in hot water for 30 minutes then drained
1 tbsp vegetable oil
50g shallots, finely chopped
20g garlic, finely chopped
1 red bird's eye chilli, thinly sliced
40g tomato, skinned and chopped
½ tsp shrimp paste
1 tbsp palm sugar
125ml coconut milk
150g roasted peanuts
2 tsp kecap manis
2 tbsp lime juice

Roughly chop the drained chillies.
  Heat the oil in a small pan over a low heat. Add the shallots and garlic and fry gently until soft and golden. Add the chopped kashmiri chillies, fresh chilli, tomato and shrimp paste, and cook for a further 2 minutes. Stir in the sugar and coconut milk and leave to simmer for 2 minutes until it has reduced and thickened slightly.
  Meanwhile put the peanuts into a mini food processor and process until finely chopped. Stir the peanuts into the sauce with the kecap manis and lime juice and season to taste with a little salt. It should be sweet, sour, salty and spicy. Leave to cool to room temperature before using. Store in the fridge, covered, for up to 3 days.

Pickled carrot and mooli (daikon)

225g carrots, finely shredded
225g mooli (daikon), finely shredded
120ml rice vinegar
2 tbsp caster sugar

Put the carrot and mooli into a bowl with 2 tablespoons salt and toss together well. Put into a colander and set aside for 30 minutes. Meanwhile, put the vinegar and sugar in a pan with 120ml water and bring to the boil. Set aside and leave to cool. Rinse the vegetables in water, then squeeze out the excess and dry well on a clean tea towel. Transfer to a bowl, pour over the vinegar mixture and mix together well. Leave to stand for 1 hour before using. Lift out of the liquid to serve. This will keep for 2–3 days in the fridge.

Sweet green mango chutney with panch phoran

1.2kg green mango
4 tsp vegetable oil
7g dried red kashmiri chillies, sliced
1 tbsp *Panch phoran* (page 303)
700g jaggery or palm sugar
100ml coconut vinegar or white wine vinegar

Using a large sharp knife, cut the unpeeled green mango lengthways in half along either side of the stone, then slice the fruit across, skin included, into 6mm thick slices. Slice off any pieces of flesh still attached to the stone in small chunks and discard the stone.
  Heat the oil in a medium-sized pan over a medium heat. Add the dried chillies and panch phoran and leave it to sizzle for a few seconds. Add the sliced mango, sugar, vinegar and 600ml water and bring to a simmer. Leave to simmer very gently, uncovered, for about an hour, stirring now and then, until the mango is tender and the syrup is thick.
  Stir in 1½ teaspoons salt and leave to cool. Spoon into an airtight container and store in the fridge. It will keep for up to a year.

Malaysian crisp-fried anchovy, peanut and chilli sambal *Sambal ikan bilis*

Vegetable oil
25g dried anchovies
25g unroasted red-skinned peanuts
    (about 40g peanuts in the shell)
10g dried red kashmiri chillies, soaked in
    hot water for 30 minutes then drained
100g shallots, roughly chopped
10g garlic, roughly chopped
½ tsp shrimp paste
1½ tsp palm sugar
2 tbsp *Tamarind water* (page 299)

Heat a thin layer of oil in a small frying pan, add the dried anchovies and fry for a few seconds, stirring, until richly golden. Remove with a slotted spoon. Add the peanuts to the oil and fry until golden brown. Remove and pour away all but 2 tablespoons of the oil from the pan.

Put the drained chillies into a mini food processor with the shallots, garlic, shrimp paste and 1 tablespoon of fresh oil. Blend to a smooth paste. Heat the oil in the frying pan over a medium heat, add the paste and fry gently for 5 minutes, stirring now and then. Stir in the sugar, tamarind water and salt to taste, simmer for 1 minute then remove from the heat and leave to cool. Stir in the fried fish and the peanuts. The sambal is ready to serve.

Balinese lemongrass and shallot sambal *Sambal matah*

½ tsp shrimp paste
2 kaffir lime leaves, shredded
6 red bird's eye chillies, or to taste,
    thinly sliced
2 fat lemongrass stalks, core
    finely chopped
175g shallots, halved and very
    thinly sliced
2 garlic cloves, finely chopped
1 tbsp vegetable oil
1 tbsp lime juice
Freshly ground black pepper

Wrap the shrimp paste in a small square of foil to make a flat parcel. Heat a dry, heavy-based frying pan over a low heat, add the foil parcel and leave to roast gently for 2–3 minutes, turning it over once. Remove from the pan and leave to cool, then unwrap and crumble finely. Put the kaffir lime leaves, chillies, lemongrass, shallots, garlic and roasted shrimp paste into a bowl and mix together well. Stir in the oil and lime juice, and some freshly ground pepper and salt to taste, and serve straight away.

Sri Lankan mint and coconut sambol *Minchi sambol*

Traditionally this sambol would be made in a pestle and mortar, adding each ingredient one at a time and lightly pounding before the next one is added. Using a food processor is more convenient but you need to take care not to over-process it into a paste. It's a joy having a large mortar and pestle though. Sometimes a little turmeric is added to this sambol for extra colour.

25–30g fresh mint leaves
100g red onions, roughly chopped
15g garlic, roughly chopped
15g peeled ginger, roughly chopped
25g fresh coconut, grated
1 green cayenne chilli, roughly chopped
1½ tsp lime juice
½ tsp freshly ground black pepper

Put the mint, onions, garlic, ginger, coconut and chilli into a food processor and process using the pulse button until finely chopped. Tip into a bowl and stir in the lime juice, black pepper and ½ teaspoon salt.

Sri Lankan coconut and chilli sambol *Pol sambol*

If you want this sambol to be less hot yet still have the classic red colour, replace some of the chilli powder with mild paprika.

1 large dried red kashmiri chilli
100g red onions, roughly chopped
3 green cayenne chillies, roughly chopped
10g garlic, roughly chopped
1 tsp kashmiri chilli powder
10–12 curry leaves (about 1 sprig)
10g Maldive fish flakes or bonito flakes
50g fresh coconut, grated
1 tbsp lime juice
½ tsp freshly ground black pepper

Heat a dry, heavy-based frying pan over a medium heat. Add the dried chilli and shake it around for 2–3 minutes until it has darkened slightly.

Tip into a mortar, leave to cool and become brittle, then crush into flakes. Put the flakes into a mini food processor, add the onions, cayenne chillies, garlic, chilli powder, curry leaves, Maldive or bonito flakes and coconut, and process using the pulse button until finely chopped. Tip into a bowl and stir in the lime juice, black pepper and ½ teaspoon salt.

Sri Lankan sweet and spicy caramelized onion sambol *Seeni sambol*

Seeni sambol means 'sugar sambol' in Sinhalese, the sweetness coming from the caramelized onions and sugar, but it also contains spices, curry and pandan leaves, making it the most aromatic of sambols.

2 dried red kashmiri chillies
4 tbsp vegetable oil
10–12 curry leaves (about 1 sprig)
5 cardamom pods, lightly bruised
½ tsp mustard seeds
10cm piece cinnamon stick, broken
    into smaller pieces
5 cloves
10cm pandan leaf, cut into 4
450g red onions, thinly sliced
2 tbsp jaggery or palm sugar
2 tsp kashmiri chilli powder
20g Maldive fish flakes or bonito flakes
6 tbsp *Tamarind water* (page 299)

Heat a dry, heavy-based frying pan over a medium heat. Add the dried chillies and shake them around for 2–3 minutes until they have darkened slightly. Tip into a mortar, leave to cool and become brittle, then crush into flakes.

Heat the oil in a medium-sized pan over a medium heat. Add the curry leaves, cardamom pods, mustard seeds, cinnamon, cloves and pandan leaf and leave them to sizzle for a few seconds, then add the sliced red onions and sugar and leave to cook for 25 minutes, stirring frequently, until soft and caramelized.

Add the chilli flakes, chilli powder and Maldive fish flakes or bonito flakes, and fry for another 3 minutes. Add the tamarind water and 1 teaspoon salt. Serve warm or at room temperature.

SIDE SALADS

All over the Far East are local versions of what we call salads, though they're nothing like our lettuce-based ones dressed with oil and vinegar. The point of salads, whether in Bangladesh or Bali, is to create an acidic, crisp-textured, fresh vegetable dish to contrast with the rest of the meal.

Cambodian crunchy mixed salad

1 small head chicory (50g)
7.5cm piece cucumber
50g kohlrabi, green mango, green papaya, swede or mooli
50g green beans
50g bean sprouts
juice of 1 lime
1 tbsp fish sauce
1 tbsp sugar
½ bird's eye chilli, finely chopped

Thinly slice the chicory across. Halve the cucumber, remove the seeds with a teaspoon and shred lengthways. Finely shred the kohlrabi, green mango, green papaya, swede or mooli. Cut the green beans in half lengthways. Combine the lime juice, fish sauce, sugar and chilli. Mix everything together.

Kachumber salad

300g vine-ripened tomatoes, thinly sliced
½ cucumber, peeled and sliced
100g red onions, halved and thinly sliced
1 medium-hot green chilli, seeded and finely chopped
½ tsp freshly ground cumin seeds
¼ tsp kashmiri chilli powder
Large handful of fresh coriander leaves, roughly chopped
Freshly ground black pepper
1 tbsp freshly squeezed lime juice

Shortly before serving, layer the tomatoes, cucumber and onions in a shallow bowl with the chopped chilli, ground cumin, chilli powder, coriander, some black pepper and salt to taste. Sprinkle over the lime juice, check the seasoning, then serve.

Cucumber and mint raita

175g cucumber, seeded and finely diced
275g natural wholemilk yogurt
½ tsp caster sugar
3 tbsp chopped fresh mint
Freshly ground black pepper

Toss the cucumber with 1 teaspoon salt, tip into a sieve and leave to drain for 20–30 minutes. Then mix into the yogurt with the sugar, mint, a little extra salt and some pepper to taste.

BREAD AND RICE

Steamed rice
SERVES 4

I cook my rice for only 10 minutes as I like a very slight firmness to the grain. Simmer for 12-15 minutes if you like a softer texture.

350g long-grain or basmati rice

Put the rice into a 20cm heavy-based saucepan and add 600ml water. Quickly bring to the boil, stir once, cover with a tight-fitting lid, reduce the heat to low and cook for 10-15 minutes. Uncover, fluff up the grains with a fork, and serve.

Malaysian coconut rice
Nasi lemak
SERVES 4

This is also popular in Sri Lanka, where it is known as kiribath. It can be served warm, or smoothed out into a 5cm-high layer on a flat plate, left to cool to room temperature, then cut into diamond-shaped pieces.

350g short-grain pudding rice or long-grain rice
400ml coconut milk (page 299)
1 pandan leaf, tied into knot, or a few drops of pandan essence (optional)

Put the rice into a pan and add the coconut milk, 300ml water, pandan leaf or essence, if using, and ½ teaspoon salt. Bring to the boil, stir once then cover, lower the heat and leave to cook over a low heat for 10 minutes. Turn off the heat and leave to sit for a further 10 minutes before serving.

Sri Lankan ghee rice
SERVES 4

The pilau way of cooking is to briefly fry the flavouring elements in oil or ghee, stir the rice in and fry that too, then add water

or sometimes stock in an amount of slightly less than double by weight. With its use of ghee, sultanas and cashew nuts, this recipe is very much a festive rice dish.

4 tbsp ghee
10cm cinnamon stick, broken into smaller pieces
10 × 2.5cm pieces pandan leaf
10–12 curry leaves (about 1 sprig)
100g onions, finely chopped
350g basmati rice
6 black peppercorns
50g sultanas
50g unroasted cashew nuts

Melt 3 tablespoons of the ghee in a medium-sized pan. Add the cinnamon stick, pandan leaf and curry leaves and leave them to sizzle for about 30 seconds, then add the onions and fry until soft and lightly golden.

Add the rice and fry it for about 1 minute, stirring constantly, until all the rice is coated with the ghee. Add 600ml boiling water, the peppercorns and 1 teaspoon salt and bring to the boil. Stir once, cover with a tight-fitting lid, reduce the heat to low and leave to cook for 12 minutes.

Uncover the rice to allow the steam to escape, then re-cover and leave to stand for 5 minutes. Meanwhile, melt the remaining ghee in a small frying pan. Add the sultanas and cashew nuts and then fry gently for 2–3 minutes or until the nuts are golden brown. Uncover the rice, fluff up the grains with a fork, then fork in the sultanas and cashew nuts. Serve straight away.

Bangladeshi spiced pilau rice
SERVES 4

2 tbsp vegetable oil or ghee
6 green cardamom pods, lightly bruised
6 cloves
5cm cinnamon stick, halved
10–12 curry leaves (about 1 sprig)
350g basmati rice
⅛ teaspoon turmeric powder

Heat the oil or ghee in a medium-sized pan over a medium-high heat, add the cardamom pods, cloves, cinnamon stick and curry leaves and allow to sizzle for a few seconds. Add the rice to the pan and fry, stirring all the time, for 1 minute. Stir in the turmeric, 600ml boiling water and 1 teaspoon salt, bring to the boil, cover and reduce the heat to low. Cook for 10 minutes, then turn off the heat, uncover and allow the steam to escape. Re-cover and set aside for 5 minutes. Fluff up the grains with a fork and serve.

Sri Lankan gothamba rotis

MAKES 12

These are sometimes shaped using lots of oil before being cooked on the flat griddle, but I prefer them a bit drier.

300g plain flour
1 tsp ghee or vegetable oil, plus
    extra for cooking

Sift the flour and ¾ teaspoon salt into a bowl. Add the ghee or oil and about 250ml warm water. Mix until it comes together into a soft, pliable dough. Turn out onto a lightly floured work surface and knead for 5 minutes until smooth and elastic. Drop back into a clean, lightly oiled bowl, cover with clingfilm and leave to rest for at least 30 minutes and up to 1 hour.

Divide the dough into 12 evenly sized pieces (each should weigh about 50g). Working with one piece at a time, keeping the rest covered with clingfilm so they don't dry out, roll it out on a lightly floured surface into a thin 18cm disc.

Heat a flat griddle or heavy-based frying pan over a medium heat. Brush it with a little ghee or oil, add the roti and cook for about 2 minutes until slightly puffed up and marked here and there with brown spots. Turn over and cook for another minute, until crisp and golden brown on the outside and cooked through yet still soft in the centre. Lift onto a plate, cover with a tea towel and keep warm while you make the rest. Serve warm.

Indian leavened flat bread *Naan*

MAKES 8

200g plain flour
100g strong plain (bread) flour
1½ tsp caster sugar
1½ tsp easy-blend yeast
100ml milk
4 tbsp wholemilk natural yogurt
2 tbsp melted ghee or vegetable oil

Sift the flours, sugar, yeast and ½ teaspoon salt into a large mixing bowl. Warm the milk and 100ml water together in a small pan to blood temperature (38°C).

Add the yogurt, melted ghee or oil to the dry ingredients, followed by the warm milk and water mixture and gradually mix everything together, adding a little more warm water if necessary, to make a soft, pliable dough. Turn it out onto a lightly floured work surface and knead for 5 minutes until smooth. Return the dough to a clean bowl, cover with lightly oiled clingfilm and leave somewhere warm for up to 1 hour until it has doubled in size.

Place a heavy-duty baking sheet onto the middle shelf of the oven and preheat it to its highest temperature. Preheat the grill to high.

Turn the dough out onto a lightly floured surface and knead once more for about 5 minutes until smooth and elastic. Then divide into 6 evenly sized pieces. Set 5 pieces to one side and cover them with the clingfilm or a damp tea towel so they don't dry out.

Roll out the first piece of dough into a 13cm disc, then, using your fingers, stretch the disc into a teardrop shape. Remove the hot baking tray from the oven, quickly dust with a little flour, place the shaped bread on top and return to the oven for about 3 minutes. It will puff up immediately. Then remove the naan, still on the baking tray, from the oven and slide it under the grill, about 7.5–10cm away from the heat, and cook for about 30 seconds until it is coloured here and there with a few brown spots. Wrap in a clean tea towel, set aside somewhere warm, and continue to make the rest of the breads in the same way, making sure you reheat the baking tray each time before adding the next naan.

KEY INGREDIENTS

ASAFOETIDA (picture 1)
A pungent, resin-like spice, made from the sap of *Ferula assafoetida*. Can be bought in two forms: as pieces of rock-hard pure resin, which look a little like amber-coloured glass, or as a powder. The resin has a strong flavour and needs to be used sparingly; for home cooking, just scratch a little straight from the lump with a knife. The powder consists of 30 per cent ground asafoetida mixed with rice flour and gum Arabic, and is milder so can be used by the pinch. It smells awful in its raw state but once heated in oil or ghee along with other ingredients it adds a background taste reminiscent of fried onions and garlic. Acts as an anti-flatulent in lentil dishes. Keep in an airtight container because of its pervasive odour. Lasts indefinitely.

AUBERGINES
The aubergine (*Solanum melongena*) comes in many shapes and sizes. The small, pale-green-and-white-streaked aubergine that's often called the Thai aubergine or eggplant (picture 2) is about the same size and shape as a hen's egg, and native to tropical Asia. It has a more crunchy texture than most, which is why it is eaten raw as well as cooked. Other varieties of aubergine are long and slender, about the size of a small courgette, or round and up to the size of a tennis ball, but all have a slightly waxy, shiny skin, ranging in colour from deep purple to pale purple, pale green, white and bright yellow. All varieties are interchangeable; our Mediterranean-style aubergine is an adequate substitute for all of them. (*See also pea aubergines.*)

BAMBOO SHOOTS
Bamboo shoots have a crisp nutty flavour and are used across Southeast Asia, where they are, of course, available fresh. Here, they are most easily found sliced in cans, but you might come across vacuum packs of whole, unsliced shoots, which have a better flavour and texture. If they have a strong odour on opening, blanch briefly in boiling water.

BANANA LEAVES
The large, flexible leaves of the banana tree can be used to wrap food, both for cooking and serving. As well as helping to retain moisture, they add a delicate, unique fragrance. We can get them in the UK in Asian stores or by mail order.

BOK CHOI
Also known as pak choi, Chinese white cabbage or Chinese chard, this is a mildly flavoured leafy vegetable, popular in Asian cooking. Steam or stir-fry briefly before serving, so it retains some texture and its bright green colour. A possible substitute, should you find it, would be choi sum, also known as flowering cabbage.

CARDAMOM (picture 3)
From the same family as ginger and galangal come two plants that produce aromatic, oval seed pods, both important in the cooking of Asia. One produces the green cardamom, and the other the black cardamom. Green cardamom pods have a pale green papery shell inside which lies a cluster of intensely aromatic, small black seeds. These pods can be used whole, or cracked open to release the black seeds. If they are to be used whole in curries, rice dishes and dals, lightly bruise first so the outer casing cracks, allowing their fragrance and flavour to permeate the dish. They can be removed before serving but it won't harm you if you end up chewing on one. Black cardamom pods are quite unlike their green counterpart, being twice as large and different in flavour. They are aromatic, with a tinge of camphor, and a strong smoky flavour that comes from being dried over an open fire. Often used in Indian rice and dal dishes, with star anise in the making of Vietnamese pho, and for me indispensable in the making of Thai mussaman beef curry (page 101).

CASSIA BARK
This is a close relative of cinnamon (see below) but with a stronger, less delicate flavour and a woodier appearance. Much that is labelled cinnamon is in fact cassia, but cassia is easily recognized as it comes in shards rather than neatly rolled quills. It's sometimes referred to as 'bastard cinnamon'. Ground cassia is reddish brown, not the pale tan of cinnamon.

CHANA DAL
A chunky yellow dal, made from husked and split dried chickpeas; looks a little like yellow split peas. Also ground into flour.

CHILLIES, DRIED (picture 4)
I use the dried red chilli from India known as kashmiri in these recipes. It has an excellent flavour and a reasonable amount of heat, without being uncomfortably hot, and also gives a rich deep red colour to any curry paste. Use as they are, soak and whiz into a paste, or lightly toast in a dry frying pan then grind into a powder or crush into flakes. Eight dried chillies (10g in weight) will yield about 1 tablespoon powder. Making your own kashmiri powder is often a better option than using one of the highly variable commercial chilli powders.

CHILLIES, FRESH
I have used 3 types of fresh chilli in these recipes. First, the bird's eye chilli (picture 5), the hottest chilli in Thailand. It registers between 8 and 9 on a heat scale of 1 to 10, where 10 is the hottest. At 1–3cm long it's a bit small for seeding so in this book I have used them seeds and all, either whole, split open or chopped. The Bangladeshis prefer fresh green cayenne chillies (picture 6), which they call hari mirch. They are similar in shape to a large green bird's eye chilli, being long, thin and pointed, but they are larger and slightly less hot: 7–8 on the heat scale. They are available from Indian and Asian groceries, either fresh or frozen. The third chilli, which suits most other purposes in this book, is the Dutch or Lombok chilli (picture 7): 8–12cm long and either green or bright red. These are about 6 on the heat scale and large enough to seed easily if you want to reduce the heat even more. I refer to these simply as medium-hot red or green chillies.

CHINESE FERMENTED SALTED BLACK BEANS
These are soybeans that have been fermented and salted, becoming soft and black in the process. They have a sharp, pungent, spicy flavour, which is also salty and somehow faintly sweet. Found in Asian and Chinese food shops, in cellophane packets or cardboard tubs. They last almost indefinitely. Black bean sauce is not a substitute.

CHINESE RICE WINE
Traditional Chinese wine made from fermented glutinous (sticky) rice, yeast and water. Drunk as a beverage and also widely used in cooking, both in China and elsewhere that Chinese communities have settled, such as Malaysia. Shaoxing is, I think, one of the most flavoursome varieties. Dry or medium-dry sherry is a good substitute.

CINNAMON

Cinnamon, as with cassia (*see above*), is the bark of a laurel-like tree, peeled from the thinner branches and left to dry. Once dry, the curled-up pieces are packed one inside another and cut into short lengths to form the quills, or sticks as we call them. Cinnamon is more expensive than cassia, and the paler the colour, the finer the quality. Powdered cinnamon can be difficult to produce at home so it is best to buy it ready ground, but as with all ground spices, it loses its fragrance quickly.

CLOUD EAR MUSHROOMS, DRIED (picture 8)

Also known as wood ears or tree ears, these dried mushrooms are prized more for their gelatinously crunchy texture than their flavour. Reconstitute in hot water for 20 minutes. Dried shiitake mushrooms, although different in both flavour and texture, are a reasonable substitute.

COCONUT: FLESH AND MILK

Use either whole fresh coconuts or frozen coconut flesh. Desiccated coconut is not a good substitute. To prepare fresh coconuts, either for milk or for flesh, see Basic Recipes, page 299.

COCONUT OIL

The most heavily saturated of all oils, which in tropical countries remains liquid at room temperature, but in climates like ours solidifies and becomes opaque. Stand the bottle in a jug of hot water until it becomes liquid again. The oil remains stable at high temperatures and is a popular frying medium in southern India, Sri Lanka and parts of Southeast Asia. However, some people find it too rich. Any vegetable oil is a good substitute.

COCONUT VINEGAR

Also known as toddy vinegar, and used extensively in Southeast Asian cuisine. Produced from the sap of the coconut palm, it has low acidity and is milky-white rather than clear, with a mild, slightly fruity, almost yeasty flavour. Rice vinegar is a good substitute.

CURRY LEAVES (picture 9)

Large bunches of these small, slightly pointed, highly aromatic leaves are sold fresh, on the stem, in Asian groceries, and are much prized, especially in southern India and Sri Lanka, for their distinctive flavour. They deteriorate quite quickly so I remove the tiny leaves from the stem and store them in an airtight box in the freezer, along with my kaffir lime leaves. Don't bother with dried curry leaves – they are as much use as dried parsley.

DAIKON (SEE MOOLI)

DAL

This is the name used collectively for a wide variety of pulses, dried peas, beans and lentils that have been husked and split, as well as for the finished dish. (*See Chana, Masoor, Moong and Toor.*)

FENUGREEK

As well as the flat, oblong, mustard-coloured seeds that we are familiar with, fenugreek is also eaten fresh in India like a herb; it is related to the pea family. The seeds have a pungent, slightly bitter flavour and should be used sparingly.

FISH SAUCE

Known as *nam pla* in Thailand, *kecap ikan* in Indonesia, *tuk trey* in Cambodia and *nuoc mam* in Vietnam, this is a clear, amber-coloured liquid derived from salting and fermenting anchovies and other small fish. It adds the unmistakable flavour found in much Southeast Asian food, and is used for seasoning much as we would use salt. Buy one with a light, clear colour. If the liquid has become dark brown, it will be old and over-assertively fishy.

FISH, DRIED

Pla haeng in Thailand, *shukti* in Bangladesh, *ikan bilis* in Malaysia, *ikan teri* in Indonesia. Drying is one of the oldest forms of food preservation. All over the Far East, fish of all sizes are salted and left out on racks to dry in the sun, to be used either as a seasoning or as a snack. Very tiny dried fish (also often called silverfish), only 2–3cm in length, are often fried first to make them crisp and enrich their flavour, then used either whole or crumbled in sambals, salads and as an accompaniment to rice. Larger dried fish are used as a main ingredient in curries and added to vegetable dishes as a source of protein. (*See also Maldive fish.*)

GALANGAL (picture 10)

This rhizome is a member of the ginger family but is quite unlike it in taste. It has a pale, creamy-beige skin and spiky, bright pink shoots when young, is more woody in texture, and has a slightly resinous, citrus aroma. It can be either sliced then bruised, or pounded, usually with other ingredients, into a paste, before being added to a dish. Found fresh in Asian groceries and freezes well. Fresh ginger is the best substitute. Dried or powdered galangal is not worth bothering with.

GALANGAL, LESSER (picture 11)

Also known as *krachai*, *grachai* or wild ginger, this is another member of the ginger family. It looks like a small bunch of baby carrots, and can be used either raw or cooked. It is hard to find but if you do come across it, scrape off the pale brown skin and then shred or thinly slice. It will keep in a paper bag in the fridge for a few weeks, freezes well and can also be found ready-prepared in jars in brine.

GARLIC CHIVES

This herb is popular with the Chinese communities of Southeast Asia, which is why it is also known as Chinese chives. It grows in clusters of long flat leaves (hence another name, flat chives) and has a strong flavour, reminiscent of both garlic and spring onions. Used sparingly in its raw state, or lightly cooked and served as a vegetable. They're called *gau choi* in Chinese.

GHEE

This is the purest form of butter, clarified butter that has been long cooked so its natural sugars slightly caramelize, giving it a delicate nutty flavour. The process of clarifying butter gets rid of the milk solids and so prevents it from going rancid, important in tropical climates. It also makes it an excellent cooking medium, able to withstand high temperatures and constant reheating. Ordinary clarified butter is a good substitute.

JAGGERY (SEE PALM SUGAR)

KAFFIR LIME LEAVES AND KAFFIR LIMES

The distinctive double-lobed, waxy-looking leaves and thick, dark green knobbly skin of the almost juiceless citrus fruit are used extensively across Southeast Asia. Both the leaves and rind lend an indispensable flavour to soups, salads and curries. Kaffir lime leaves can be used whole in cooked dishes or finely shredded and eaten raw in salads. They are always bought frozen in the UK, and will keep in the freezer for up to a year. Dried leaves are a poor substitute.

KASHMIRI CHILLIES (SEE CHILLIES, DRIED)

KECAP MANIS

This is an Indonesian soy sauce, with a thick, almost treacle-like consistency and sweet flavour thanks to a generous addition of palm sugar. It is not interchangeable with ordinary or sweet soy sauce. Available now in some larger supermarkets and most Asian grocery stores.

KOHLRABI

A cultivar of the cabbage family, sometimes pale green in colour, sometimes purple, this vegetable is grown for its almost spherical heart rather than the leaves, which are chopped off before sale. It has a slightly sweet, mild flavour, and crisp and crunchy texture, rather like broccoli stem, and is used in many Southeast Asian dishes, such as soups, salads, stir-fries and vegetable curries.

LEMONGRASS

This is a tropical grass grown all over Southeast Asia, prized for its distinctive lemony fragrance. Whole stalks need to be bruised before using and can be removed from the dish before serving if you wish. For eating, whether raw in salads or cooked in stir-fries or curry pastes, peel away the outer 3 or 4 leaves until the pink ring surrounding the tender core is reached, then cut down to 7.5–10cm: the rest is too woody to eat. However, discarded pieces can be stored in the freezer (as can whole lemongrass) and used to flavour soups and stocks. Generally sold in bundles, lemongrass stalks should be pale green, unblemished and feel quite heavy. If they feel light, they are probably old and dry. Trimmed-down stalks make great skewers for satay and kebabs. One observation from my travels: lemongrass in the Far East is more fragrant than we get in the UK, so be generous with it over here.

MACE (SEE NUTMEG)

MALDIVE FISH, DRIED

Rather like bonito flakes from Japan (which are a good substitute), Maldive fish flakes (*umbalakada*) are an important ingredient in Sri Lankan cooking, used in much the same way as shrimp paste and fish sauce are elsewhere. Fish such as tuna and frigate mackerel are gutted, skinned, boned and filleted, then blanched, smoked and left to dry in the sun until rock-hard and wood-like, enabling it to be kept indefinitely without refrigeration. It is usually sold ready flaked, and is available from Asian grocers specializing in ingredients from southern India and Sri Lanka. If from a packet, transfer the flakes to a screw-top glass jar, as the aroma is quite pungent.

MANGO (GREEN)

Unripe yet mature mangoes are prized for their crisp texture and tart flavour and are popular all over Southeast Asia, frequently finely shredded and used in the classically hot, sweet and sour yam-style salads, but also used in curries, soups and pickles. Only available here from Asian food suppliers or online, but well worth seeking out. I've used a particularly unripe supermarket mango (which was being sold as fruit) to make a Thai salad on occasion.

MASOOR DAL

This is the most popular dal in Sri Lankan cuisine, known to us as red lentils. They have a rich orange hue when dried, do not need soaking and cook to a soft yellow purée.

MOOLI (*picture 12*)

Mooli is the Indian name, and daikon the Japanese name, for this large, white, mildly flavoured type of radish, which is used raw as a crunchy element in salads and sweet and sour vegetable pickles (page 304). Go for smaller ones, which have a less bitter flavour and finer texture.

MOONG DAL

There are two types of moong dal. Moong dal chilka is the whole, dried, green mung bean, which has been split, leaving the green husk still in place, and is mainly used in khichuri (page 287) and curries. Moong dal is the split and then husked bean. It produces a pale yellow pulse that can be soaked and boiled to produce the purée-like dish of the same name, used in soups or ground into a flour.

MORNING GLORY OR WATER SPINACH (*picture 13*)

This tall, semi-aquatic plant with long hollow stems and pointed green leaves is a popular leafy vegetable which grows all over Southeast Asia, flourishing alongside the waterways criss-crossing the land and needing little care and attention. The trick to successful cooking is to cut it into shorter lengths and briefly blanch in boiling water first, then refresh under cold water before braising or stir-frying, otherwise the stalks can be tough and stringy. It does not keep well so buy it no more than a day before use.

MUSTARD OIL

This pungent oil pressed from mustard seeds, is popular for cooking in northern India, particularly Bangladesh. It smells quite overpowering straight from the bottle, but mellows in use. It also has good preserving qualities, and so is popular in the making of chutneys and pickles.

MUSTARD SEED

Two main types of mustard seed are used in cooking: white (or yellow) and black (which is really brown). In Sri Lanka and India, and especially Bangladesh, black mustard seed is a popular and important spice, often added to the oil at the beginning of cooking, where it adds a nutty flavour and slight piquancy but without any heat. It is also one of the main ingredients of the Bangladeshi spice blend panch phoran (page 303), and commonly used in pickles and chutneys.

NAM PRIK PAO

This Thai chilli-based condiment comes in uncooked (*nam prik*) and cooked versions (*nam prik pao*). The cooked version combines the four important flavour elements of Asia: hot, sour, salty and sweet, from toasted dried red chillies blended with fried shallots and garlic, fish sauce, shrimp paste, palm sugar, and sometimes a little tamarind paste. Most often served as an accompaniment or added to dishes at the end of cooking. Available in bottles from good Asian supermarkets, and I have provided a recipe on page 303 if you want to make it yourself.

NIGELLA SEEDS

Also known as kalonji or onion seeds (a misnomer, as they are not), nigella seeds are used in Middle Eastern and Indian cuisine, particularly sprinkled over breads. Deep black in colour, with a slightly bitter flavour a little like mustard seeds, they turn nutty when lightly fried in oil. One of the five spices that make up the Bangladeshi spice blend panch phoran (page 303).

NOODLES: DRIED EGG

Both medium and fine dried egg noodles can be found in almost every supermarket today, alongside the rice and pasta, but quality varies. Those from good Asian supermarkets or suppliers often have a better flavour and texture. They need to retain some bite after cooking, like perfectly cooked, *al dente* pasta.

NOODLES: DRIED 'GLASS'

Made from mung bean starch, and known by several different names, such as cellophane noodles, bean thread noodles or jelly noodles. When cooked they become translucent. After cooking and draining, toss with a few drops of oil to help stop them sticking into clumps.

NOODLES: DRIED RICE

These noodles, commonly known as 'rice sticks' are usually flat rather than round, and are popular in Cambodia, Vietnam and Thailand, best known in the famous dish of pad thai (page 106). They come in a variety of widths but those of about the same width as tagliatelle are the most common. They are becoming more readily available in supermarkets, but are easily found in Asian groceries and online.

NOODLES: DRIED RICE VERMICELLI

Known as bahn hoi in Vietnamese, behoon in Malay and sen mee in Thailand, this type of noodle is popular all over Southeast Asia. Sometimes also labelled 'stir-fry noodles', they are fine and wiry, brittle and semi-transparent. If you find them in large bundles, cut them to size before using. After cooking and draining, toss with a little oil to stop them sticking into clumps.

NOODLES: FRESH EGG

These are popular all over Southeast Asia, and known as bahmi in Indonesia, ba mee in Thailand and Malaysia, and simply mi in Vietnam. They come in a variety of shapes and sizes, but it is the fine ones, thin and round, that you need for this book. Some supermarkets sell pouches of ready-to-use fine egg noodles from the chiller cabinets, but fine dried egg noodles are the perfect substitute if you can't get hold of fresh.

NOODLES: FRESH HOKKIEN

These are thick, egg-yellow noodles that originated in China, and the Hokkien Chinese in turn introduced them to Malaysia, where they are today a staple, served up at food stalls in dishes such as mee goreng (page 164) and hokkien mee (page 154). They are the thickest of all the fresh noodles and are sold fresh or vacuum-packed in the chiller cabinets of Asian supermarkets and some specialist food stores.

NOODLES: FRESH RICE

These medium-thick, opaque, round noodles are one of the most important noodles in Malaysia, where they are used in laksa, hence their other common name, laksa mee (mee being noodle). Also important in Vietnam, where they are known as bun. Fine rice noodles and dried rice noodles, more easily available here, make excellent substitutes.

NUTMEG AND MACE

These are the only two spices to come from the same tree. Nutmeg is the seed, found inside the nectarine-shaped (though not flavoured) fruit of the tree, and mace is the lacy reddish-coloured coating that covers the seed. Nutmeg should be moist with oil when cut in half with a knife; if it crumbles and is dry it is old and past its best.

OKRA

Also known as ladies' fingers. The trick is not to overcook it, so that it retains some of its crunchy texture and doesn't become the slimy vegetable so many people dislike. One day I was in an oriental supermarket and saw a girl snapping the pointed tips off each okra before selecting which ones to put into her bag. Intrigued, I asked her what she was doing. She said that if they gave a nice 'snap', they were fresh. If they bent over they were old and not worth buying.

ONIONS (SEE SHALLOTS)

PALM SUGAR AND JAGGERY

Palm sugar and its Indian equivalent jaggery are made from sap released by the flower-bearing stalks of certain species of palm tree, the most prized being the Palmyra and Kithul palms. The sap is boiled for hours until it thickens and eventually crystallizes, then it is left to set like fudge. Sold in clear packaging or plastic tubs, ranging in colour from pale amber to dark molasses brown, it is sometimes so hard it needs to be grated or pounded before use. The better the quality, however, the softer, darker and more fudge-like it will be. Store in a well-sealed container, somewhere cool and dry, or it will pick up moisture from its surroundings and become unusable. Light or dark muscovado sugar is a good substitute.

PANDAN LEAVES (picture 14)

Also known as fragrant screwpine or rampe, these are the long, blade-like leaves of a tropical tree, prized for their unique scent and flavour. They are often trimmed down to a more manageable size (usually about 60cm) for selling. They are used all over Southeast Asia, particularly in Sri Lanka, in both savoury and sweet dishes. In Southeast Asia many cooks tie a leaf into a knot and add it to the rice pot, where it imparts a beautifully subtle fragrance and flavour. Charmaine Solomon describes pandan as the vanilla bean of Asia, and there is truly nothing like it. Buy fresh or frozen from Asian groceries and keep in the freezer; pandan essence is excellent.

PANEER

Paneer is a very mild, fresh Indian cheese, made by curdling hot milk with lemon juice or diluted vinegar, then letting the whey drain off through a muslin-lined sieve. The remaining solids are lightly pressed until firm enough to hold their shape, after which the cheese can be cut into pieces for cooking. It is found in the chiller cabinets of most supermarkets.

PAPAYA (GREEN)

Although ripe papaya are eaten all over Asia, often with a squeeze of lime to balance their sweetness, it is the crisp white flesh of the under-ripe green papaya that is prized, especially in Thailand, where it is finely shredded and served in salads. Green mangoes (page 311) make a good substitute.

PEA AUBERGINES (picture 15)

These are tiny wild aubergines (Solanum torvum) about the size of hazelnuts, which grow in clusters. They have slightly tough skins and are quite bitter when raw but become nutty in flavour when cooked and are most often used in curries or soupy stews. Not regularly seen other than in Asian food shops.

PEANUTS

The peanuts commonly used in Asia are what we call monkey nuts, sometimes used straight from their shells, but also roasted. However, any type of roasted peanut, salted or unsalted, is adequate for the recipes in this book. If you buy monkey nuts in their shells, 50g will yield about 35g peanuts.

PEPPER

Peppercorns are the berries of a vine-like plant that grows in the tropical forests all over Southeast Asia. Strings of fresh green unripened peppercorns, like those I came across in Kampot in Cambodia, can be found here in food shops specializing in Indian and Asian foods. Loose green peppercorns preserved in brine are a good substitute. Black peppercorns are the mature berries left to dry in the sun, during which time the yellow flesh around the seed shrinks and darkens. White peppercorns are the dried seeds of mature berries whose flesh has been removed.

PICKLED CABBAGE (picture 16)
Another unusual Southeast Asian ingredient frequently added to soups and noodle dishes to give them a slight sweet and sour note and an additional bit of crunch. Buy it in rigid plastic pouches from Asian shops, or online.

PRAHOC
This moist paste made from fermented, salted, part-dried fish is a key ingredient in Cambodian food. Sometimes eaten as it is, but more commonly diluted in boiling water and then strained. The resulting liquid, known as *tuk prahoc* (page 299), is used in cooking, where it mellows in odour while adding depth of flavour. Can be found in specialist shops, where it might be labelled 'Gouramy fish sauce' or something similar. A little shrimp paste is a good substitute.

PRESERVED TURNIP OR RADISH
Made from salted and pickled mooli (daikon), this is one of the more unusual ingredients used in the authentic preparation of pad thai noodles (page 106), where it adds a tangy, sweet yet salty flavour to the finished dish. Sold in vacuum packs in Asian supermarkets. Two varieties: one salty, and one less salty and slightly sweetened – the slightly sweetened is the one you need to buy.

PUMPKINS AND SQUASHES
Pumpkins and squashes are members of the same family, which also includes melons, cucumbers, marrows and courgettes. Squashes come in two types, winter and summer, and it is the winter squash that is popular all over Southeast Asia and India, used in both sweet and savoury dishes. I find that pumpkins have a more delicate flavour and less densely textured flesh than squash. Some of the varieties of squash I like best are the kabocha, crown prince and butternut, but all are interchangeable in this book.

RICE PAPER (picture 17)
Vietnamese rice paper (*banh trang*) is made from rice flour, salt and water, rather as rice noodles are, but it is shaped into flat discs rather than strands. Left to dry in the sun on bamboo mats, which marks them with a distinctive criss-cross pattern. Sold in cellophane packets in Asian grocery shops, they come in varying sizes and two thicknesses, standard and extra thin. Soften briefly in cold water before using in fresh spring rolls (page 61) or crisp, deep-fried rolls (page 62).

RICE FLOUR
Flour milled from raw white rice. Because it does not form gluten, unlike wheat flour, it cooks very crisp and is ideal for making pancakes and fritters. The flour from Chinese and Asian food shops is better for these recipes than that from a supermarket or health food shop.

RICE VINEGAR
Made from fermented rice and popular all over Asia, this vinegar is milder and sweeter than our white wine vinegar. If you don't have any, just dilute 3 parts white wine vinegar to 1 part water and add a little caster sugar.

RICE: BASMATI
A variety of long grain from North India, with slightly longer grains than most other types of rice, which have the unusual property of becoming longer during cooking rather than fatter. Revered for its fragrance and delicate flavour, and the fact that it doesn't stick together during cooking. Instructions for this type of rice often call for it to be washed to get rid of the excess starch, then soaked in cold water before cooking. I prefer not to soak the rice so that the grains retain a firmer texture.

RICE: JASMINE
Another long-grain rice, also known as Thai fragrant rice. It has a nutty aroma and almost pandan-like flavour, but unlike basmati rice, the grains stick together slightly when cooked. However, it is not as sticky as some other Southeast Asian varieties. The perfect accompaniment to all Thai and Southeast Asian dishes. Incidentally, it doesn't contain jasmine.

RICE: SHORT-GRAIN
Various types of short-grain rice are used all over Asia; for this book, pudding rice is a perfect substitute.

RICE: WHITE GLUTINOUS OR STICKY
A short-grain rice, also known as 'sweet' rice, and very different to most other rices because it is quite chalky-looking in its raw state, benefits from soaking before cooking, and actually becomes more clear and glassy-looking as it cooks. It becomes very sticky, too, and is the preferred accompaniment to savoury dishes in the north of Thailand, Cambodia, Vietnam and Laos, where its stickiness enables it to be pinched together into clumps for eating with the fingers. Elsewhere in Asia it is more usually used for desserts.

ROSEWATER
Rosewater, a by-product in the making of rose oil, was one of the ingredients left behind by the former Arabic rulers of Asia. Its distinctive, perfumed flavour is used in desserts and drinks, such as rice pudding and sweet lassi, but also in moghul-style savoury dishes like biryani. Rosewaters differ in strength and I have found that some are too overpowering for the recipes in this book. I buy mine from Indian groceries – they are milder and better suited to Bangladeshi cuisine.

SAMBAL OELEK
The Dutch-Indonesian name given to a mixture of crushed fresh red chillies, vinegar and salt. If you can't find it under this name, you will easily find jars of minced red chilli paste, and it's essentially the same thing.

SESAME SEEDS
Unhulled sesame seeds come in black and golden brown varieties, and both the unhulled seeds and the pale hulled seeds are popular in Asian cooking. Black sesame seeds are worth seeking out from Asian or Japanese food stores to flavour and colour a particular Indian curry called a dohneiiong (page 269).

SHALLOTS (AND ONIONS)
Shallots, especially red shallots, are used widely across Southeast Asia and India, but onions are used too. For eating raw, for example in a salad, I prefer shallots for their sweeter flavour and because the 'rings' are thinner and more pleasing to eat. The thinness of the rings makes them ideal for frying, too, as they become crisper more quickly.

SHATKORA
This is a semi-wild citrus fruit (*Citrus macroptera*) that is found only in the Sylhet region of Bangladesh. About the size of a small grapefruit, it is green when unripe and yellow when ripe. It is seldom eaten raw as it is sour, quite bitter and does not produce very much juice, but its aromatic zest is cooked in curries and stews or made into pickle. It is available both frozen and fresh when in season from Indian grocers in the UK.

SHRIMP PASTE

A pungent paste made from salted and fermented prawns or shrimp: the smell is slightly offputting, but it is an essential ingredient in Far Eastern cooking. Sold in tubs or jars, good varieties, I have found, have a purple tinge. It keeps indefinitely in the fridge (in an airtight container). Can be used straight from the jar or dry-roasted first, which makes it more fragrant. To do this, wrap the required amount in a small square of foil and toast in a hot, dry, heavy-based frying pan for a minute or so.

SHRIMP, DRIED

Sun-dried peeled tiny shrimps are popular all over Southeast Asia and China, and used mainly as a flavouring ingredient. They are sold whole or shredded. Look for those that are salmon pink in colour and give slightly when squeezed. If they are rock hard, smell of ammonia or have gone brown, they are no longer any good. They keep for months in an airtight container.

SNAKE BEANS

These are very long beans – hence their other name, yard-long beans – which are found in Asian greengroceries, twisted into loops for selling. They are the fresh beans from which black-eyed peas come, and have a tender texture, with flavour a bit like asparagus. Dwarf or fine green beans are the perfect substitute.

SOY SAUCE

Fermented sauce made from soybeans, roasted grain, water and salt. Regional varieties exist all over the Far East, varying in taste, consistency, fragrance and saltiness, but those from China or Japan, readily available in our supermarkets, are ideal for this book. Light soy sauce, the thin, lighter brown sauce, is the one mainly used for seasoning and in dipping sauces, as it is more salty, adds flavour and doesn't greatly alter the colour of a dish. Chinese dark soy sauce has been aged for longer and contains added molasses for darker colour and sweeter flavour. I use it for slow-cooked dishes; its flavour develops on heating. Dark superior soy has been thickened with starch and sugar. Used more often as a dipping sauce than in cooking.

SPICES

Unless you use a lot of spices on a daily basis, buy them in small quantities and store them in well-sealed glass jars, in a cool, dry, dark place. If possible, buy seeds, such as coriander, cumin and cardamom, and grind them yourself.

SQUASHES (SEE PUMPKINS)

STAR ANISE

A star-shaped seed pod with an aniseed-like flavour, this comes from a small evergreen tree native to China but now grown all over the world. Widely used in Chinese, Malaysian and Indonesian cooking, an important flavouring in the making of Vietnamese pho, and one of the components of garam masala (page 302).

TAMARIND

The sticky pulp from inside the bean-like pod of the tamarind tree is used to add a slightly sweet tartness to many Southeast Asian and Indian dishes. Sold in two forms: rectangular blocks of raw pulp, which need to be mixed with warm water and strained to remove the hard black seeds, or in jars and tubs as a concentrated paste that might require diluting.

THAI BASIL

The most commonly used basil in Southeast Asia is Thai sweet basil (in Thai, *bai horapha*, picture 18), which has slim, pointed, medium-sized leaves and purple stems. Its aniseed-like flavour makes it different from the sweet basil common in Europe. Used raw in salads or added at the last minute to cooked dishes. The other Asian basil you might come across is Thai holy basil (in Thai, *bai grapao*, picture 19), which has more rounded, slightly serrated, lighter green leaves and pale green stems. Used in stronger-flavoured dishes, such as chilli-laden stir-fries.

THAI HOT CHILLI SAUCE

This is often referred to as Sriracha sauce, originally named after the seaside city of Si Racha in Thailand where it was produced for local seafood restaurants. Made from fresh chillies, vinegar, garlic, sugar and salt, and pungently hot. The traditional Thai version is thinner and more tangy than other variations, such as the well-known Vietnamese brand, Tuong ot Sriracha, which is more concentrated. Often served as a dipping sauce, particularly for seafood, but has become a popular condiment all over Southeast Asia, used much as we would use tomato ketchup.

TOFU

Tofu, or bean curd as it is sometimes called, is made by curdling soya milk, then pressing the curds into blocks. Firm tofu, not the much softer silken tofu, is what is needed for this book. It has a sufficiently firm texture to enable it to be cut into smaller pieces for cooking, and a very bland flavour, which allows it to take on other flavours very well, particularly spicy ones. If you don't use the whole block, keep it covered with fresh water in the fridge, where it will last for 2–3 days.

TOOR DAL

Also known as toovar dal, pigeon pea or red ram, this is a dark ochre-coloured split pea with a rich, earthy flavour.

TURMERIC (picture 20)

Another member of the ginger family, fresh turmeric comes in little-finger-sized pieces of root and has bright, carrot-orange flesh. Although powdered turmeric is an adequate substitute, it does not match the colour, fragrance and flavour of the fresh stuff. Found in most Asian groceries; keeps well in the freezer. Peel off the light brown skin and chop or pound into a paste.

VIETNAMESE MINT

A pungent herb, *Polygonum odoratum*, known as *rau ram* in Vietnamese and *daun laksa* (laksa leaf) in Malaysia but also known, rather confusingly, as Vietnamese coriander or Cambodian mint. Not related to the mint family but similar in appearance and odour. One of the classic flavours in Vietnamese fresh spring rolls, the Vietnamese chicken salad on page 82 and in Malaysian laksa (hence its other name). Not easy to come by outside Asia, but a combination of garden mint or spearmint and coriander can be used.

WATER SPINACH
(SEE MORNING GLORY)

WHITE POPPY SEEDS

These seeds are harvested from the opium poppy (though thankfully, they do not contain significant amounts of opiates). Mostly used in India and Bangladesh, they are ground into a paste called *posto*, and used to thicken curries and sauces. Available from Asian food suppliers. Blue poppy seeds are not a substitute.

YELLOW BEAN SAUCE

Fermented paste or sauce made from yellow soya beans, salt and water, which is not yellow but either dark brown or black in colour. Used in Thai soups and sauces.

YOGURT

A popular ingredient in Sri Lanka and India. Use one with a fat content of at least 4 per cent. Wholemilk yogurt is ideal and Greek yogurt is also good. Low-fat yogurt can curdle when used in cooking.

USEFUL EQUIPMENT

SPICE GRINDER
Spices are more aromatic if freshly ground, and quite a few recipes in this book also ask you to grind combinations of spices together. Doing this by hand, such as with pestle and mortar, can be hard – it's difficult to get them to a fine enough powder. So I recommend you buy an inexpensive electric coffee mill, which will do the job perfectly.

MINI FOOD PROCESSOR
If you are going to use a food processor instead of a mortar and pestle in this book for making the pastes and sambals in this book, it needs to be the right size. The quantities specified in most of the recipes in this book are too small for the normal bowl as the mixture just works its way up the side of the bowl and doesn't get near to the blades. You may be lucky enough to have a food processor with a smaller bowl for blending or chopping which is perfect but, if not, a mini food processor with a bowl of about 12cm across is the next best thing. Make sure you don't overload it as the motor sometimes can't cope with the full quantity of ingredients.

MANDOLIN
Finely shredded crispy vegetables are popular all over Southeast Asia, especially in salads and soups. Shredding vegetables with a knife can be tricky, and a traditional box grater does not produce the right shape or texture. Some food processors have shredding disc attachments, but these are not ideal for fruit, such as green mango, where the flesh needs to be shredded away from a central stone. A mandolin is the answer.

GREEN MANGO AND PAPAYA SHREDDER
During a trip to Thailand many years ago, Debbie, who works with me, came across a great little gadget for shredding green mangoes and papayas. Shaped like a potato peeler, it's now available from www.thai-food-online.co.uk – it's called the Kom Kom Miracle Knife.

WOK
An essential piece of equipment if you are going to cook lots of Chinese and Southeast Asian dishes. I have found that the best ones are those bought from Asian supermarkets. They are made of carbon steel and have one long wooden handle, which enables you to shake the wok around without getting too close to the intense heat needed for stir-frying. If your hob doesn't provide you with a stable-enough base on which to rest the wok, buy a wire or steel ring that sits over the heat source. The wire ones are best for use on gas hobs as they allow a free circulation of air.

STEAMERS
Some of the recipes in this book require you to use a steamer. A petal steamer placed in a large, deep pan is often sufficient, but in some cases you will need a stackable steamer that provides deep compartments with flat bases on which to place the food. Various options are available: stackable saucepan sets, electric tiered steamers, or bamboo or metal steamers that can be placed over an existing saucepan or wok.

MORTAR AND PESTLE
In Asia, most households have some sort of mortar and pestle for making curry paste but, realistically, a food processor takes considerably less time. For effective results you would need a mortar and pestle which is at least 10cm deep and 16cm wide (internally). They're quite cheap and look splendid in the kitchen but you may prefer just to buy a smaller one for crushing or bruising spices, lemongrass, chillies etc.

HEAT DIFFUSER
Indispensable for many curries and stews as they allow you to achieve a gentle simmer with the heat evenly distributed over the base of the pan, avoiding hot spots on which food can burn.

THERMAL PROBE
This is one of my most valued pieces of equipment. A quick-acting one is expensive, but a probe enables you to measure the temperature at the very centre of any piece of meat or fish, ensuring it is perfectly cooked every time. It's also great for checking the temperature of cooking oil, water, and so on. I like the ones called Thermapens, which you can buy online and from good cookware shops.

SCALES
Digital scales are cheap and I would say indispensable. They are accurate to 2g, 1g or even 0.5g. Especially useful are those that reset to zero so you can weigh each new ingredient as it goes in the bowl.

SUPPLIERS

For fresh ingredients such as lemongrass, galangal, lesser galangal, kaffir lime leaves, pandan leaves and curry leaves and even chillies, buy more than you need and keep the surplus, well sealed in plastic tubs, in the freezer, where they will keep for at least 3 months and probably come to no harm for up to 6. Store-cupboard ingredients such as bottled sauces, rice, noodles and dals all have a long shelf-life if well sealed and kept cool and dry. You can also buy frozen items, such as chillies, ready-grated coconut, fresh noodles and, if you live near a Bangladeshi community, shatkora.

www.thai-food-online.co.uk
For everything Thai, especially a nifty tool for shredding green mangoes and papayas called the Kom Kom Miracle Knife.

www.theasiancookshop.co.uk
For most Thai, Chinese and Indian cooking ingredients, including white poppy seeds and black cardamom pods, and sauces such as kecap manis, Sriracha and sambal oelek.

www.wingyipstore.com
For a wide range of Chinese and Southeast Asian ingredients, including dried anchovies (silver fish), yellow bean sauce, Shaoxing rice wine and cloud ear mushrooms (labelled as black fungus).

www.natco–online.com
For most things Indian: spices, oils, ghee, rice and rice flour, jaggery, tamarind pulp, rosewater, dals, pickles and chutneys.

www.spicesofindia.co.uk
For most Indian spices and ingredients, including the harder-to-find ones, such as aloo bokhara (listed under dried plums).

www.thespicespecialist.com
As you might imagine, good for spices.

www.seasonedpioneers.co.uk
For blends such as panch phoran and garam masala, and shrimp paste.

www.herbies.com.au
Very high quality spices from Australia but available in the UK. They sell kokam, a.k.a. fish tamarind, used in fish curries in Sri Lanka and Kerala.

www.enticefoods.com
For Thai, Chinese and Indian ingredients, including glutinous rice, pickled cabbage and preserved turnip.

ACKNOWLEDGEMENTS

I would like to thank Debbie Major for her leading role in putting the book together, testing recipes and cooking and styling the dishes for James Murphy's wonderfully lively and colourful photography. I would also like to thank James Murphy and Alex Smith for their epic photographic trip to most of the places I visited. A special mention to Alex for the delightful look of this book and to my commissioning editor, Shirley Patton, who has been the sort of quiet presence which all cookery book writers need, a real commitment to the book but no ultimatums for late copy, just a little insistent pressure.

Thanks too to the managing director of Ebury Publishing, Fiona Macintyre, for her good advice about keeping the authenticity of the recipes when I was tempted to make them a bit Westernized. And thanks to everyone else connected with producing the book, Mari Roberts the page editor – a really tough job which she does so well, Claire Scott my publicist, Penny Markham for the exquisite props for photography and Claire Heron-Maxwell for assisting on food photography.

I am grateful for the help of various others: my PA Viv Taylor, and Valli Little, food editor of *Delicious* magazine, for the loan of Asian books whilst writing and testing recipes in Sydney.

The book accompanies a rather atmospheric TV series of the same name and for that I would like to thank Director/Producer David Pritchard, my chum, and Assistant Producer Arezoo Farhazad, cameramen Chris Topliss and Steve Briers, sound recordist Peter Underwood and researcher Caroline Schwarz, and a handful of tripod carriers, my son Charles, Jay Miles, and Chris Denham who also owns the production company and who provided much morale boosting amusement for us in Bangladesh and Sri Lanka.

Finally a big thank you to Sarah Burns, my fiancée, for her unstinting support in this long journey.

BIBLIOGRAPHY

CAMBODIA:
Rivière, Joannès, *La Cuisine du Cambodge avec les Apprentis de Sala Baï* (Philippe Picquier)
Başan, Ghillie, *The Food & Cooking of Cambodia* (Anness Publishing Ltd 2007)

VIETNAM:
Trang, Corinne, *Authentic Vietnamese Cooking* (Simon & Schuster 1999)
Pham, Mai, *Pleasures of the Vietnamese Table* (Harper Collins 2001)
Başan, Ghillie, *Vietnamese, Fragrant and Exotic: a deliciously simple cuisine* (Aquamarine 2004)

THAILAND:
Thompson, David, *Thai Food* (Pavilion Books 2002)
Bhumichitr, Vatcharin, *Vatch's Thai Cookbook* (Pavilion Books 1994)
Crawford, William and Pootaraksa, Kamolmal, *Thai Home-Cooking from Kamolmal's Kitchen* (Plume Printing 1986)

MALAYSIA:
Ying, Pung Kim (Coordinating Editor), *Famous Street Food of Penang* (Star Publications Malaysia 2006)
Başan, Ghillie, *The Food & Cooking of Malaysia & Singapore* (Aquamarine 2006)
Tan, Terry and Tan, Christopher, *Shiok!: Exciting Tropical Asian Flavours* (Periplus Editions (HK) Ltd 2003)
Authentic Recipes from Malaysia (Periplus Editions (HK) Ltd 2005)

BALI:
De Neefe, Janet, *Fragrant Rice: My Continuing Love Affair with Bali* (Periplus Editions (HK) Ltd 2003)
Von Holzen, Heinz, *Feast of Flavours from the Balinese Kitchen* (Marshall Cavendish International (Asia) Pte Ltd)
Owen, Sri, *Indonesian Regional Cooking* (St Martin's Press 1994)
Başan, Ghillie, *The Food & Cooking of Indonesia & the Philippines* (Aquamarine 2007)

SRI LANKA:
Dassanayaka, Channa, *Sri Lankan Flavours* (Hardie Grant Books 2003)
Kuruvita, Peter, *Serendip: My Sri Lankan Kitchen* (Murdoch Books 2009)
Seneviratne, Suharshini, *Exotic Tastes of Sri Lanka* (Hippocrene Books 2003)
Ratnatunga, Manel, *Step by Step Sri Lankan Cookery* (Vijitha Yapa Publications 2002)

BANGLADESH:
Bhattacharya, Rinki, *Bengal Spices* (Rupa & Co 2004)
Banerjee, S, *Bangla Ranna: An Introduction to Bengali Cuisine* (Orient Longman 2006)
Banerji, Chitrita, *Bengali Cooking Seasons and Festivals* (Orient Longman 2006)
Kalra, J, and Singh, Gupta Prashad: *Cooking with Indian Masters* (Allied Publishers Pvt Ltd 1999)
Osman, Shawkat, *Bangladeshi Cuisine* (Mapin Publishing 2008)

GENERAL:
Trang, Corinne, *Essentials of Asian Cuisine* (Simon & Schuster 2003)
Alford, Jeffrey and Duguid, Naomi, *Hot Sour Salty Sweet: A Culinary Journey Through Southeast Asia* (Artisan Division of Workman Publishing 2000)
Alford, Jeffrey and Duguid, Naomi, *Mangoes and Curry Leaves: Culinary Travels through the Great Subcontinent* (Artisan Division of Workman Publishing 2005)
Jaffrey, Madhur, *Flavours of India* (BBC Books 1995)
Jaffrey, Madhur, *A Taste of the Far East* (BBC Books 1993)
Solomon, Charmaine, *Encyclopedia of Asian Food* (New Holland UK 1998)
Solomon, Charmaine, *The Complete Asian Cookbook* (Lansdowne Press 1976; Grub Street 1993)
Owen, Sri, *The Rice Book* (St Martin's Griffin, New York 1993)
Sahni, Julie, *Classic Indian Cooking* (Dorling Kindersley 1986)
Hutton, Wendy, *Green Mangoes and Lemon Grass* (Periplus Editions (HK) Ltd 2004)
Mowe, Rosalind (Editor), *Southeast Asian Specialities* (Tandem Verlag GmbH 2007)
Brissenden, Rosemary, *South East Asian Food* (Penguin Books Ltd 1970)

INDEX

Note: page numbers in **bold** refer to photographs.

COOK'S NOTES

All teaspoon and tablespoon measurements
are level unless otherwise stated, and are
based on measuring spoons:

1 teaspoon = 5ml
1 tablespoon = 15ml

People in Australia need to make a minor
adjustment as their tablespoon measure
is 20ml.

All cooking times are approximate. All
recipes have been tested in a conventional
oven. If you have a fan oven, adjust the dial
downwards by about 20ºC. So for 200ºC, set
the dial at about 180ºC. It's worth checking
the accuracy of your oven temperature
gauge with a thermometer occasionally.

Free-range chickens and eggs are
recommended.

I have given weights for garlic, ginger,
galangal, onions and shallots throughout
the book. In every case, the weight is of the
peeled, fresh ingredient. Here is a rough
conversion guide:

Garlic cloves:
7g = about 1 fat clove
10–15g = 2 fat cloves
20g = 3 fat cloves
25g = 4 fat cloves

Ginger and galangal:
25g = 5cm peeled piece

Onions:
100g = 1 small onion
175g = 1 medium onion
250g = 1 large onion

Shallots:
25g = 1 shallot
100g = 4 shallots (or 1 banana shallot)

I have described quantities of herbs as
handfuls throughout the book. Here are
rough weights:

small handful = 5g
handful = 10g
large handful = 20g